THE MIND CLUB

The
MIND
CLUB

Who Thinks, What Feels, and Why It Matters

Daniel M. Wegner
and Kurt Gray

VIKING

VIKING
An imprint of Penguin Random House LLC
375 Hudson Street
New York, New York 10014
penguin.com

ISBN 978-0-670-78583-4

Printed in the United States of America
10 9 8 7 6 5 4 3 2 1

Set in Warnock Pro with Archer
Designed by Daniel Lagin

Contents

CONTENTS

Preface

In Jorge Luis Borges's short story "The Secret Miracle," a writer is unjustly imprisoned by the Nazis and sentenced to death. On the eve of his execution, he prays to God, asking for a year to finish his play. That night he dreams that his prayer is answered, but the next morning he is nevertheless led down to the firing squad in gloomy rain. As he stands in front of four soldiers, "a heavy drop of rain graze[s] [his] temple and roll[s] slowly down his cheek; the sergeant call[s] out the final order."

But suddenly, miraculously, the universe stops:

> The weapons converged upon [him], but the men who were to kill him were immobile. The sergeant's arm seemed to freeze, eternal, in an inconclusive gesture. . . . As though in a painting, the wind had died. [He] attempted a scream, a sylla- ble, the twisting of a hand. He realized that he was paralyzed.

He could hear not the slightest murmur of the halted word. He thought . . . *time has halted.* . . .

He had asked God for an entire year in which to finish his work; God in His omnipotence had granted him a year. God had performed for him a secret miracle: the German bullet would kill him, at the determined hour, but in [his] mind a year would pass between the order to fire and the discharge of the rifles.

In this secret year the writer crafts his play into perfection. Without the aid of movement, or speech, or writing, he repeats the acts in his head, honing every paragraph and polishing every word. At long last "[h]e complete[s] his play; only a single epithet [is] left to be decided upon now. He [finds] it; the drop of water roll[s] down his cheek. He [begins] a maddening cry, he [shakes] his head, and the fourfold volley fell[s] him."

In 2010 Dan Wegner was diagnosed with ALS. This degenerative disease slowly destroyed his ability to walk, to stand, to move, to talk, to eat, and—eventually—to breathe. Before his diagnosis, Dan had conceived of this book in his mind, but—like Borges's prisoner— had only just begun writing it. Recognizing the inexorable march of his disease, Dan asked me to join him and help transform the ideas into words. It is my hope that his wisdom and wit shine through in these chapters; if they do not, the fault is mine alone.

My miracle, it is no secret, was having Dan as my graduate adviser. This book is dedicated to his creativity and unique perspective, to his witty one-liners, his collection of robots, and his ability to render clear the mysteries of human experience. May we always perceive his mind.

—*KG*

THE MIND CLUB

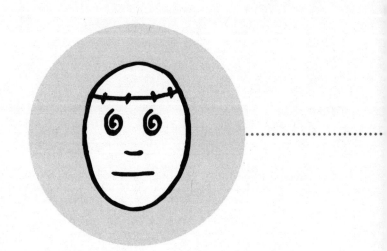

Chapter 1

WELCOME TO THE CLUB

Nothing seems more real than the minds of others. Every day, you consider what your boss might be thinking, whether your spouse is happy, and what that shady crew of teenagers wants. The apparent reality of other minds is so powerful that you've likely never stopped to ask whether they actually exist. But there is a very real possibility that everyone you know could be mindless zombies.

Even your mother could be a zombie. She may not shuffle, groan, or eat brains, but she could still be a *philosophical* zombie—someone who acts and speaks normally but who lacks conscious experiences. Your life may be filled with rich mental experiences, but your mother's could be completely empty. Instead of a bustling city of thought and emotion, Mom's mental life might be like a Hollywood set, with only the appearance of reality. When you hug each other, you might feel warm and safe, but her brain might only robotically register the pressure of your arms. Now, you might think, "No, not my mother!" but how could you prove otherwise? Even sophisticated brain scans can't reveal what it's like to be another person.

That your mother might be a fleshy automaton stems from the philosophical "problem of other minds."[1] Because we can never directly experience the inside of other minds, many questions about them are fundamentally unanswerable. Do strawberries taste the same to you as to someone else? Is your blue the same as someone else's blue? Perhaps when you look at the sky, you see what someone else would call yellow. If you're a man, then you can never know what it feels like to give birth. If you're a woman, then you can never know what it feels like to be kicked in the goolies.

More fundamental than the uncertainty of other people's specific experiences, you can never be certain that other minds even *exist*. You might be the only mind in the whole world, the sole sentient being in a crowd of mindless drones or the lone true thinker within a computer-generated matrix.

The uncertainty of other minds has fueled centuries of philosophizing and also lies at the heart of some of the most interesting— and most terrible—human behavior. As we will see, it can explain how the Nazis could murder six million Jews, why animals are sometimes tortured for sport, and why people debate the existence of God so intensely. The mysterious nature of other minds can also help to explain the behavior of one British man named Dennis Nilsen.

Dennis Nilsen was born in 1945 in a seaside town in Scotland. After a brief stint in the army, he moved to London, where he worked first as a police officer and then as a civil servant. Despite his good job, Nilsen felt unfulfilled and isolated; he seldom spoke to his family, had few friends, and had difficulty maintaining close relationships. He also had dark fantasies about sexually dominating young men, whom he liked to imagine as completely passive or even unconscious. After the dissolution of one relationship, Nilsen began luring young men into his apartment with the promise of food, alcohol, and lodging. Once they were asleep, Nilsen would strangle them into unconsciousness before drowning and dismembering them in the bathtub. He managed to murder fifteen people before being discovered and sentenced to prison for life.

Strikingly, although Nilsen was a ruthless murderer of other people, he had the deepest affection for his dog, a mutt named Bleep. Following his arrest, Nilsen's biggest concern was not about the families of those men he killed, or even about himself, but about his furry companion—would she be traumatized by his arrest? How could Nilsen be indifferent to the pain of those he murdered and yet be overwhelmed by the possible suffering of his dog?

Perhaps the answer is that his dog was special and somehow had deeper emotions and richer thoughts—that is, more mind— than his victims. Most of us would scoff at this idea. No matter how cunning Nilsen's canine, we generally agree that people have more mind than dogs, which means that people deserve more compassion and concern than dogs. But Nilsen decided otherwise, believing that his dog had more mind than people, which gave Bleep essential moral rights denied to humans. Nilsen disagreed with the rest of us about the relative status of humans and dogs in the "mind club."

The *mind club* is that special collection of entities who can think and feel. It is that all-important league of mental heroes whose superpowers are not X-ray vision or teleportation but instead simply the ability for thought and emotion. Members in the mind club are "minds," whereas nonmembers are simply "things."

Who belongs in this mind club? To begin with, we can probably rule out the turnip. It seems safe to say we aren't missing much by assuming that there's nobody home in there. At the other extreme are things that almost definitely have minds, like you and us. The snooty remark goes "and we're not so sure about you," but we are reasonably sure about you or we wouldn't be bringing this up to you now.

We are likely all members of the mind club. But how should we understand the things that fall between us and the turnip? What shall we make of dogs, chimpanzees, dolphins, elephants, or, for that matter, cats? Do they have minds? Really—*cats*? If we get serious about doorkeeping at the mind club, we also have to deal with newborn infants, unborn human fetuses, and people in persistent vegetative states—they could never be mistaken for turnips, but their minds can be sadly inscrutable.

Then too we need to sort through the minds of intelligent robots and chess-playing supercomputers, angry mobs and cruel killers, and even companies like Google and Walmart. Some suggest that "corporations are people" and have their own minds—is that true? The application list for the mind club is already diverse, and we haven't even mentioned entities that only some people believe in, such as gods or devils or angels or spirits of the dead. None of these things are turnips—but do they have *minds*?

You're probably thinking that you could sort through the candidates for the mind club pretty quickly, deciding who's allowed past the bouncer and who has to wait outside in the cold. But could you explain how you decided, and would anyone agree with you? Scuffles over membership in the mind club have preoccupied philosophers for centuries, with no easy answers in sight.[2] At one point the whole field of psychology split in two over the question of whether animals think—with behaviorists saying, "No way!" and everyone else saying "Wait a minute, what about my dog?"[*][3]

The questions about mind echo outside science and philosophy. Every day, judges and juries puzzle over just how "sound of mind" someone needs to be to bear responsibility for a crime. Mind is also the key to legal definitions of life itself. Consider the case of Jahi McMath, a little girl who was declared brain-dead after a botched tonsillectomy but whose parents still saw signs of mind in her hospital-bed twitches. At one point she was legally dead in California but legally alive in New Jersey—which ruling was correct depended on whether she had a mind.

Membership in the mind club is immensely important, because it comes with clear privileges: those with minds are given respect, responsibility, and moral status, whereas those without minds are ignored, destroyed, or bought and sold as property. In historical cases where slavery was allowed, it was often justified by a belief that the enslaved people had a different kind of mind.

Because of the importance of mind club membership, it would be nice if there were a clear admission rule to help us decide, just like the signs at amusement parks announcing that we have to be "at least this tall" to ride the roller coasters. Decisions of mind are quite easy at the extremes. Just as adults get to ride the coasters and toddlers are banished to the teacups, the extremes of mind are obvious: you have a mind and deserve moral rights, whereas the turnip doesn't have a mind and can be eaten for dinner.

....

* The first woman to earn a PhD in psychology, Margaret Floy Washburn, fanned the controversy back in 1908 with a forceful argument in favor of dogs and other animal minds.

But the tough questions about minds turn on nuance. Just as we're not sure whether the kid with big hair and thick-soled shoes is really tall enough for the roller coaster, we cannot be sure whether a talented dog or developing fetus is in the club, or whether a sophisticated robot or someone with severe brain damage is out.

The difficult cases of mind are called *cryptominds*. Some cryptominds have more "objective" mind than others. People can discuss Shakespeare, whereas dogs can only bark, but mind is seldom about these objective characteristics. Instead, as the case of Nilsen and Bleep suggests, mind is in the eye of the beholder. A mind is not an objective fact as much as it is a gift given by the person who perceives it. Mind is a matter of *perception*, with members being granted admission into the mind club based not on what they *are* but on what they *appear* to be. To get in, you need to look like you have a mind.

There are many ways to look like you have a mind, such as wearing glasses or nodding knowingly when someone mentions Proust. But that's not the point. The point is that minds are *perceived into existence*. The creation of minds through perception is best illustrated by a famous thought experiment known as the Turing test, which was devised in 1950 by British mathematician and computer scientist Alan Turing.*

In the Turing test a person converses via text messages with two different entities—one human and one computer programmed to act like a human—and must decide which is which.[4] At first this seems like an absurdly easy test, but as the cartoon caption goes,

··········

* Alan Turing was interested in all things cryptic and also helped to crack the Nazis' Enigma cipher during World War II.

"On the Internet, no one knows you're a dog." What could you ask at the keyboard that could possibly determine whether there is a human mind on the other end?

Any widely known facts or ideas would be useless, as a computer could easily be programmed to recall those, just like IBM's *Jeopardy*-winning Watson. Instead you might think to quiz the mind candidate about human sensations—say, "Please describe the smell of old books" or "Tell me what it feels like to have an orgasm." But a computer could be programmed to describe those things too: "Old books smell heavy and musty, like a sleepy old forest" or "An orgasm feels better than just about anything and is a little bit like a sneeze." Of course, the computer can't really have an orgasm, but

Figure 1: The Turing Test
You (on the bottom) must decide which of two texting entities is a computer and which is a fellow human being.

with enough exclamation points, it could certainly fake it—and how would you know the difference?

Turing thought that if you couldn't tell which entity was a person and which was a computer, then the creator of the computer would have succeeded in making a mind—a genuine case of artificial intelligence. If a computer can fool you into *perceiving* a mind, then, by Jove, it has one.

We do our own version of the Turing test every day as we discern which things have minds and which things don't. But what do we mean when we say something has a mind? Is "mind" a single unified dimension with humans at the top and turnips at the bottom? Just as a single IQ scale can represent people's general mental ability, perhaps we simply see minds from "no mind" to "maximum mind."

For many centuries theologians such as St. Thomas Aquinas have argued for this one-dimensional view, a "great chain of being" starting down at minerals and going up through vegetables, animals, people, the angels, and finally God.[5] The one-dimensional view is also echoed by the philosophical approach of Daniel Dennett in his book *Kinds of Minds*.[6] He suggests that there is a chain of perceiving mind through three different "stances."

The first is the "physical stance," in which we view entities as completely mindless and understand them only through physical characteristics, such as mass and momentum. When we predict the action of a boulder, we need only know its weight and velocity. The second is the "design stance," in which we view entities as themselves mindless but perceive the marks of mind upon them. When we use a screwdriver, for example, we understand that it was made by a mind for a purpose. Finally we can take the "intentional stance," in which we recognize the behavior of entities as being based upon intention and desire. To predict people's actions, it is certainly more useful to know what they think and want than their mass and momentum.

These one-dimensional approaches to mind have long been the rule, but we wondered whether people might make finer distinctions, grading minds not just in terms of "more" or "less" mind but also on different mental capacities. Maybe we see mind along multiple dimensions, like the reading, writing, and math scores of the SAT. We might use dozens or even hundreds of ways of distinguishing minds from nonminds. Knowing how people naturally perceive minds is essential for understanding the trickiest cryptominds and the moral chaos that encircles them.

One might think we'd need sophisticated tools to study mind perception—brain scanners, electrodes, Bunsen burners, and Erlenmeyer flasks—but instead we just asked some people. A lot of people. Together with Heather Gray,* we conducted an online survey that asked 2,499 people to judge both standard minds and cryptominds[7]—the "mind survey." This was our first foray into the new science of mind perception, and these results form the foundation for this book. Our lab has since delved into robots,[8] the dead and vegetative patients,[9] adult film stars,[10] torture victims,[11] and God,[12] but it all started with this single survey on mind perception.

The survey began by introducing respondents to thirteen potential minds, each with descriptions and pictures: Sharon Harvey, an advertising executive; Todd Billingsley, an accountant; Nicholas Gannon, a five-month-old; Samantha Hill, a five-year-old; Toby, a wild chimpanzee; Gerald Schiff, a patient in a persistent vegetative state; Delores Gleitman, recently deceased; Charlie, a family dog;

....

* No relation to Kurt Gray.

Kismet, a sociable robot built at the MIT Media Lab; a green frog; a seven-week human fetus; you, the respondent; and finally, God.

We also selected nineteen different mental abilities, drawing from psychology, philosophy, and literature. The philosopher Jeremy Bentham discussed the importance of pain and pleasure in judgments of moral status, so we included them. The Stoics suggested that the capacities of self-control and planning were what separated the minds of people from those of other animals, so we included them. Through Hamlet's famous speech about "What a piece of work is a man," Shakespeare emphasized the human mental powers of thought and understanding, so we included them. As pure reason may not be sufficient for a full mind, we included feelings like joy, embarrassment, and emotion recognition. We also included more "physical" capacities like hunger and desire, and other capacities like memory, pride, and communication.

Putting it all together, survey respondents were asked to compare the different characters on different mental abilities. One question asked, for example, if Samantha (the girl) is more or less likely to be able to feel pain than Toby (the chimpanzee). Most people, by the way, said "more." We calculated average ratings for each mental ability across all characters, and then we used a technique called factor analysis to determine how the mental abilities clumped together. Did people rank all the cryptominds from "least mind" to "most mind" identically for every mental capacity?

It turns out that mental abilities are *not* all clumped together. Instead, people see minds in terms of two fundamentally different factors, sets of mental abilities we labeled *experience* and *agency*.[13]

The experience factor captures the ability to have an inner life, to have feelings and experiences. It includes the capacities for hunger, fear, pain, pleasure, rage, and desire, as well as personality, consciousness, pride, embarrassment, and joy. These facets of mind seemed to capture "what it is like" to have a mind—what psychologists and philosophers often talk about when they discuss the puzzle of consciousness. A mind with experience can feel what it is like to touch a hot stove, can enjoy going to the circus, and can have an orgasm.*

The agency factor is composed of a different set of mental abilities: self-control, morality, memory, emotion recognition, planning, communication, and thought. The theme for these capacities is not sensing and feeling but rather thinking and doing. The agency factor is made up of the mental abilities that underlie our competence, intelligence, and action. Minds show their agency when they act and accomplish goals.

A useful framework to help understand the differences between experience and agency is *inside* and *outside*. Experience is what minds are like from the inside, what it feels like to be a person, or a cat, or a bat. Because experience is a matter of being inside a mind, it can be very elusive to others. In contrast, agency is more transparent because it is what minds are like from the outside. We can determine an entity's ability to plan and think simply by observing its actions and reactions. Said another way, experience is about *inputs*, as sensations and feelings generally are conveyed by sense organs like eyes and ears that feed *in* to minds. Conversely, agency is about *outputs*, movements and actions that feed *out* of minds.

The two dimensions of experience and agency serve as the north-south and east-west axes of our "map" of cryptominds. Take a moment to look at it—this map is the guide to the rest of the book.

....

* Though, for safety reasons, ideally not all at the same time.

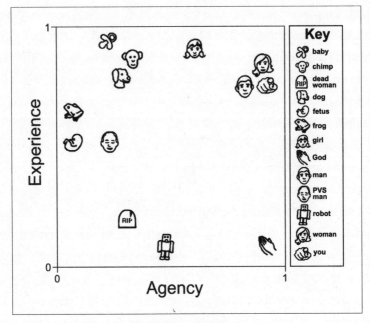

Figure 2: The Map of Mind Perception
Mind perception is measured on dimensions of agency and experience.

Let's take a quick tour of the map. First, it seems that normal, conscious, living adult humans like us (and executive Todd Billingsley and accountant Sharon Harvey) reside in the upper right corner, with both experience and agency. In contrast, the infant, the dog, and the frog (upper left) have some experience but little agency; they are entities for which people see that "someone is home," but with diminished capacities to think and act. They are entities that can be harmed but that cannot harm us in return.

Now continue the tour down the map. Below the animals and baby are the more cryptic cases of the human fetus and the PVS patient. These are cryptominds with very little agency but perhaps some experience; there might be someone home, but not anyone capable of answering the door. Even lower down is the dead woman (lower left), who is ascribed neither much experience nor agency—although it's worth noting that she is not at zero. Perhaps we see dead people as having some mind because we remember their minds as they were during life. Or perhaps we see their minds because we believe in the afterlife, and how can there be heaven or hell without minds to feel joy and pain?

As we continue to circle around the map, we move from the dead to the robot, which is perceived to have very little capacity for experience. Just imagine the classic science-fiction robot, which has no emotions and just keeps telling humans how irrational they are. A robot has the agency to help us safely explore the inside of a broken nuclear plant, but without experience it cannot help us explore the inside of a broken heart.

And then, in the bottom right, we have the Almighty. As you might expect, God is perceived as very able to do things, but is, curiously, seen to have little experience. God's mind may be great, but we don't believe that He can feel hunger, fear, or even joy like the rest of us. Interestingly, in a replication of the mind survey, we discovered that corporations are seen to occupy the same location on the mind map. Like God, Google was seen as all agency and no experience.

So far we have discovered that minds are a matter of perception and that people tend to see them along two dimensions. The bigger question you may be asking is, Why does it matter? As we hinted at earlier, mind perception forms the very basis for questions of life and death: entities with minds deserve moral consideration, whereas entities without minds do not. But if mind perception is split into agency and experience, how do these two factors relate to morality? To answer this question, we ask you to consider a thought experiment called "Baby vs. Robot."

It's not about babies and robots fighting* but instead about two moral scenarios. In the first, imagine that the baby and the robot were just about to tumble off a cliff and you could save only one of them. Which would you save? Likely you would save the baby and let the robot fall to its doom. In the second scenario, imagine that the baby and the robot have found a loaded gun and are playing with it, when it goes off and injures someone. Which of them would you hold responsible? If you're like most people, you would forgive the baby and condemn the robot to the junkyard.

These two scenarios reveal that it is no fun being a robot, and also that someone needs to call child services on that baby's parents. But most important, these scenarios demonstrate that there are two distinct kinds of moral status, not one. Questions of *moral responsibility* (Who deserves responsibility and punishment?) seem to be distinct from those of *moral rights* (Who deserves protection from harm?) because we protect the baby from harm and yet hold the robot morally responsible. This finding is striking because many have assumed that more mind equals more "morality," with human adults having both rights and responsibilities and tables and turnips having neither.

These two types of moral status (rights and responsibilities) not only are distinct but also map perfectly onto our two-dimensional mind map. To have moral rights you need to have experience, an

----

* However, if you are from the Discovery Channel and are interested in this idea, please call.

inner life filled with feelings, and the potential for suffering. Conversely, to be morally responsible you need to have agency, to be able to plan, act, and appreciate the outputs of your thoughts. Babies have more experience than robots and so have more moral rights; robots have more agency than babies and so have more moral responsibility.

Beyond babies and robots, the mind survey revealed that any entity with experience is seen to deserve moral rights, and any entity with agency is seen to deserve moral responsibility. The baby, the girl, the chimp, and the dog were seen as highest in experience, and survey takers also reported that these entities should be protected from harm. Conversely, adult humans, God, and Google were seen as highest in agency, and survey takers also reported that these entities should be held morally responsible for wrongdoing. Our hearts melt when children scream or puppies whimper—and our bile rises when we see adults (or others who should know better) causing them harm.

The separation of agency/responsibility from experience/rights in our data was so striking that it seemed that we had discovered a deep fault line in mind perception. Like a border between two very different countries, this fault line—while normally invisible—separates two very different kinds of minds. On one side of the line are minds with agency and moral responsibility, and on the other side of the line are minds with experience and moral rights. Of course, just as there are dual citizens of two countries, some minds—like yours and mine—can live on both sides of this border, with both agency/responsibility and experience/rights. But as we'll see throughout the book, the most interesting cryptominds are seen to belong to *either* one side of the line *or* the other. This separation between two kinds of minds has profound implications for ethical debates.

In fact, it is so important that we will now say, in italics and without irony,

There are two kinds of perceived minds, each with its own type of morality—thinking doers and vulnerable feelers.

Thinking doers are active minds with moral responsibility that *do* actions, minds like corporations and God. Vulnerable feelers are passive minds with moral rights that have actions *done to them*, minds like puppies, medical patients, and babies. This division of doer and feeler should feel intuitive because it is as ancient as human thought. The writings of Confucius,[14] the yin and yang of ancient China,[15] and the Tao Te Ching[16] have long split the world into complementary opposites such as black and white, hot and cold, and good and evil. In mind perception these opposites are inner (experience) and outer (agency), input (experience) and output (agency), passive (experience) and active (agency), recipient (experience) and doer (agency), victim (experience) and aggressor (agency).

These complementary types of thinking doers and vulnerable feelers are echoed in a similar distinction first introduced by Aristotle in the realm of morality: he divided the moral world into moral agents and moral patients.[17] *Moral agents* are those entities who *do* (im)moral deeds; they are the performers of good and evil, the heroes and villains, the Gandhis and Hitlers, the cops and robbers. Conversely, *moral patients* are those entities who *receive* (im)moral deeds. They are the beneficiaries of good and the victims of evil, the rescued and injured, the adopted and orphaned. Moral agents are thus the *thinking doers* of the moral world, possessing agency and moral responsibility, whereas moral patients are the *vulnerable feelers* of the moral world, possessing experience and moral rights (see figure 3).

Agents and patients crisply divide the moral world into two, but remember that they are *complementary* opposites: agents act upon patients, and patients are acted upon by agents. Like husbands and wives, agents and patients whisper to each other, "You complete me." Good and evil usually involve *both* moral agents and moral patients—they are the heads and the tails of the same moral coin. You can understand "out" only by considering "in," "doer" by considering "recipient," and "aggressor" by considering "victim." To have one, you need the other, which means that good and evil almost always have a *dyad* of two different minds,* a doing agent and a feeling patient.

	Moral Agent	Moral Patient
a.k.a.:	Thinking Doer	Vulnerable Feeler
with the capacity for:	Agency	Experience
and possessing:	Moral Responsibility	Moral Rights
for example:	 God	 Baby

Figure 3: Moral Agents and Patients
There are two kinds of perceived minds.

....

* The word "dyad" comes from the Greek word *dýo* and simply means "two."

Important examples of evil deeds all fit this dyadic template, including murder (murderer + deceased), theft (thief + victim), and child abuse (abuser + child). Even good deeds like a rescue have both a rescuer and a person in need. In contrast to these dyadic deeds, consider whether it is evil to cut off your own ear. Pulling a Vincent van Gogh might be gross, but it isn't wrong in the same way as cutting off someone else's ear, because self-injury doesn't have two different minds for agent and patient.

Some debate whether there are truly victimless (or agentless) wrongs, but we can agree that acts with obvious agents and patients are prototypically immoral. This dyadic nature of morality is illustrated in figure 4—when the malicious intention of a thinking agent

Figure 4: The Winged Demon
Immorality or evil (represented by the winged demon) emerges through the combination of both thinking agent (left) and vulnerable patient (right).

is combined with the suffering of a vulnerable patient, you get the demon of immorality. This dyadic template is consistent with both psychological data on moral judgment[18] and long-standing legal theory, which suggests that guilty verdicts require both someone having been harmed (the guilty act of *actus reus*) and someone having knowingly perpetrated the harm (the guilty mind of *mens rea*).[19]

Seen from the perspective of mind perception, good and evil aren't mystical forces that exist apart from humanity, but simply what emerges through the interaction of agents and patients. To create evil, just intentionally cause another mind to suffer (e.g., kick a dog), and to create good, just intentionally prevent another mind from suffering (e.g., stop a dog from being kicked). More formally, we can define both moral and immoral acts thus:

(Im)morality = Agency (of Agent) + Experience (of Patient)

This definition reflects both the dyadic nature of good and evil and the kinds of mind (e.g., adult, child, animal, machine) in the agent and patient slots. To get maximum immorality, you should combine a very powerful agent and a very vulnerable patient. Conversely, for minimum immorality, you should combine a weak agent and an invulnerable patient. As evidence, consider a thought experiment that actually *does* involve fighting, "CEO vs. Little Girl!"

Imagine that a CEO punches a little girl in the face. Chances are you'd think this is immoral. Now imagine that a little girl punches a CEO in the face. Chances are you'd think this is funny. Indeed, children injuring adults is a staple of hilarious YouTube videos, whereas adults injuring children is a staple of (decidedly unfunny) Lifetime movies.

The evil of CEOs harming kids, but not of kids harming CEOs, is perfectly consistent with our formula; CEOs are mostly thinking doers, whereas kids are mostly vulnerable feelers, and so only one combination trips our evil detector. Linking mind perception to morality not only explains the enduring hilarity of kids injuring unsuspecting adults but also allows you to predict your moral outrage about almost any infraction. Tough man (high agency) punches kitten (high experience)? Immoral. Kitten (low agency) scratches tough man (low experience)? Not immoral. When you become enraged at an instance of moral depravity, chances are someone very agentic is harming someone (or something) very patientic. This idea of dyadic morality will be important throughout the book as we explore our different reactions to cryptominds causing and receiving harm, such as child-killing pigs and medical patients left to die.

Well, it's only the first chapter, and already we've accused your mother of being a zombie, explored the structure of mind perception, and revealed how mind perception defines good and evil. In the chapters to come, we will revisit many of these themes as we explore the neighborhoods of the mind map. We'll discover the best way to escape blame (chapter 2), why natural disasters increase belief in God (chapter 9), why vegetative patients are seen as more dead than the dead (chapter 6), why conspiracy theories are irresistible (chapter 7), and how good and evil can make people physically more powerful (chapter 4).

We'll start in the next chapter with the mind of **the Animal**, the prototypical cryptomind. Nonhuman animals may not be able to talk (at least not well), but they do provide lots of physical cues to mind—movements and expressions and apparent goals and joys and sorrows. Animal minds are an important puzzle, one that shaped the history of psychology and that continues to bother everyone who ever ate something that could once look back at them.

Our next stop will be the mind of **the Machine**. No one is tempted to see a mind in a pair of scissors, but we do glimpse mind when machines become complex and marvelous. Machine minds—like *Jeopardy*-winning computers—seem mostly to have agency and not experience, but new technology is leading to humanlike machines that also appear to feel emotions. We'll see, however, that such experiencing minds are not universally loved and can be downright uncanny.

The Patient investigates how we see someone who is sick or in treatment or in trouble. We typically see these minds through the lens of empathy, appreciating what it is like for them to feel pain, pleasure, or other feelings. Although empathy can make us attuned to experience, it can also blind us to agency. The analysis of patients also highlights the special world of medicine—those professionals who work with patients and who can sometimes lose sight of their minds.

Some minds are cryptic because of our feelings about them. From the person who stole our parking space to the trusted friend who slept with our spouse, we have trouble seeing the mind of **the Enemy**. The hate and fear we feel toward enemies blinds us to their agency and experience through the process of dehumanization—turning people into objects. In war, dehumanization may help a soldier do his job, but in everyday life it can make us callous and insensitive to the suffering of others.

Some of the most enigmatic minds we encounter are **the Silent**—humans who can't communicate. The silent include those in vegetative states and those who are locked in—with thoughts but no capacity to move—both of which bring up important ethical issues. Brain-scanning methods offer new hope for perceiving these cryptominds, but meanwhile families and caregivers try desperately to do mind reading of their own and sometimes mistake their own thoughts for those of the silent.

Then there is the mind of **the Group**. A group, such as a corporation, doesn't have a single brain, but this doesn't us stop us from talking about it as if it has a mind (e.g., "Google challenges Microsoft's lead"). Groups typically seem to have more agency than experience, which means that people in groups can do evil but not suffer it. These perceptions suggest why groups are often implicated in paranoia about conspiracies.

And do **the Dead** have minds? About four out of five Americans believe in life after death. Not nearly as many believe they can communicate with the dead, but believing in an afterlife means that many must also believe in an after*mind*. Gathered at the graveside with others who knew the dearly departed, we may perceive the mind of the dead in almost the same way we perceive the mind of the living. The reasons for this perception are many, including our wishes for immortality and dualism, the apparent disconnect between mind and body.

God is a mind often believed in but seldom seen. Even without direct evidence of His existence, much of the world believes in an ultimate agent in charge. Religious belief can be understood, at least in part, as an extension of our natural tendency toward mind perception, which has been honed through millions of years of evolution. We will also see why people are especially likely to see God's mind in randomness and suffering.

There is one mind we don't need to perceive from the outside, one that should not be a cryptomind at all: the mind of **the Self**. But there are times when our own minds can be cryptic, when we lose sight of ourselves and fail to grasp our own agency and experience. This chapter shows how learning about other minds ultimately allows us to understand our own.

Minds are paradoxically both incredibly important and incredibly ambiguous, and the friction between these two truths starts the fire that burns throughout this book. The following pages will reveal new ideas, unbelievable stories, and cutting-edge science from our lab and those of others. They will also show why mind perception matters so much, from lightning storms of legal conflict to losing (and sometimes finding again) the people we love. Again and again you will see that the world of minds is seldom what it first seems to be. Welcome to the mind club.

Chapter 2
THE ANIMAL

One curious entertainment of sixteenth-century London was the Bear Garden. In front of cheering crowds, a monkey dressed in a little suit would appear on horseback. Then out would come an angry pack of bulldogs or mastiffs trained to attack the poor monkey. The sorry horse was attacked by the dogs as well but could last for quite a while, at least until the bears were sent in. Then, to the delight of the crowd, the horse, the dogs, and the little monkey (if he was still alive) all quickly became shrieking, thrashing, and bloody bear food.[1]

In contrast to these callous British peasants, Jain monks and nuns are so averse to the suffering of animals that they sweep their paths to prevent treading a bug underfoot.[2] Jains even avoid eating root vegetables such as turnips* because they believe that roots are

....

* Our apologies for maligning them in the first chapter.

especially essential to life. After all, if you're a turnip, even vegetarians are murderers. Somewhere between the blood-sport fans at the Bear Garden and the gentle Jains are the rest of us, wondering how to think about the minds of nonhuman animals.

Animals are the classic cryptomind because, despite all their signs of life, they lack language. Without this rich communicative ability, it is hard to accurately gauge their levels of agency and experience. How much of an animal's behavior is survival instinct versus calculated thought and deep emotion? Is a raccoon disgusted with germs when it washes its food? When a robin flies into the picture window, is it filled with embarrassment and self-recrimination or just simple pain? Does your dog love you the same way you love it? Most important, is it wrong to have sex with livestock? Stay tuned.

You might wonder why we're skipping over plants in our search for nonhuman minds. Well, we're not. It is worth considering whether plants have minds and—most important for morality— whether they are capable of suffering.[3] Ancient mystics and modern hippies alike have long held that trees have minds, and this idea of plant minds was darkly transformed by Roald Dahl in "The Sound Machine."

In this short story a man develops a radio capable of hearing frequencies normally out of range of the human ear,[4] and as he listens one afternoon, he hears a series of painful screams. He suddenly realizes that they coincide with the snipping of blossoms off a rosebush; the radio reveals suburban yard work as genocide, with every cut of the pruning shears causing unbearable agony to sentient flora around him. This scenario may not be as far-fetched as it seems. Imagine the smell of fresh-cut grass. What smells like lazy summers to you is actually the panic pheromone released by each severed blade, letting its neighbors know that the fearsome lawn-mower is coming for them too.[5]

Although grass and other plants have remarkably complex defense systems,[6] do they belong in the mind club? Unlikely. Entities with minds typically have complex nervous systems, which plants seem to lack.[7] Some believe that plants can think and feel anyway, such as J. C. Bose—the cult hero who in 1914 attached a voltage meter to a carrot and claimed to find evidence of emotion[8]—and Cleve Backster, an interrogation specialist for the CIA and a pioneer in the use of polygraph technology.

Backster received widespread attention when he attached the dracaena* in his office to a polygraph machine and ran a series of tests including burning the leaves, threatening the plant with harm, and even killing shrimp in the next room over. To Backster, the resulting polygraph readings suggested that plants could not only experience pain and fear but also empathize telepathically with the death of the distant shrimp.[9] Unfortunately for Backster, his work proved difficult to replicate and was ultimately "busted" on the television program *MythBusters*.[10] Plants may not have telepathic empathy, but their actions are often more intelligent, intricate, and adaptive than anything humans could devise. By some measures, plants have agency and perhaps even experience, but we usually fail to attribute them mind because their signs of agency and experience mainly occur in slow motion.

We do see glimpses of mind in especially fast species of plants. *Mimosa pudica*—"sensitive plants"—will retract its leaves quickly when touched and so seems to experience our contact.[11] *Dionaea*

....

* A small, potted, palm tree–like plant found in many offices.

muscipula—Venus flytraps—will snap shut on unsuspecting insects and then slowly digest them, in an apparently agentic feat of carnivorous cunning.[12] With slower-acting plants we often see mind when their movements are captured in time-lapse films: flowers springing open and slamming shut, leaves clamoring for the sun as it traverses the sky, or vines encircling hapless trees in their quest for height. Just a few minutes of watching vines climb in David Attenborough's *The Private Life of Plants* will convince you they're active and smarter than many of your coworkers.

Seen in everyday slow motion, however, plants seem to lack mind because they take so long to respond to their environment. Imagine someone who touched a hot stove and removed their hand only after a couple of hours—that person wouldn't seem like the sharpest tool in the shed. Curiously, it's also hard for us to see intelligence in things that move very quickly, to track the logic of darting dragonflies or scurrying cockroaches. As noted by philosopher Daniel Dennett, it seems like minds are maximally perceived at human speed.[13] Only when things move at the same scale as you do they seem to have feelings and intentions. Comedian George Carlin said it best in terms of freeway driving: "Ever notice that anyone going slower than you is an idiot, but anyone going faster than you is a maniac?"

The technical term for this tendency is *timescale anthropocentrism*. "Anthropo-" comes from the Greek word *anthropos*, meaning human, and "-centrism" simply means a specific orientation or focus. Timescale anthropocentrism is the idea that we see the world—including minds—from the perspective of human time. This idea is illustrated by a study from our lab, led by Carey Morewedge and Jesse Preston, in which participants were asked to

28

rate the minds of different animals, some of which moved very slowly (e.g., sloths) and some of which moved very quickly (e.g., houseflies).[14]

As figure 5 reveals, there was a slight tendency for people to see more mind (rated consciousness and capacity for intention) in faster animals (shown by the solid sloped line)—it is better to be the hare than the tortoise. The more striking pattern in the graph is an inverted *U* shape (shown by the dotted curve), whereby both very slow *and* very fast animals are seen to have little mind, and

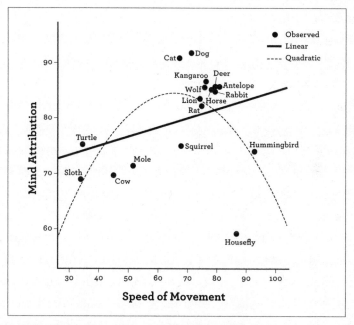

Figure 5: Anthropocentrism in Mind Perception
Things that move with a humanlike speed are perceived to have more mind.

C. K. MOREWEDGE, J. PRESTON, AND D. M. WEGNER, "TIMESCALE BIAS IN THE ATTRIBUTION OF MIND," *JOURNAL OF PERSONALITY AND SOCIAL PSYCHOLOGY* 93, NO. 1 (2007). REPRINTED WITH PERMISSION.

human-speeded animals like dogs and cats are seen to have the most mind. This makes evolutionary sense, as potential predators and prey are all creatures moving at roughly our speed, and so it pays to understand their intentions and feelings. In the modern world we seldom have to worry about catching deer and evading wolves, but timescale anthropomorphism stays with us; in the dance of perceiving other minds, it pays to move at the same speed as everyone else.

People are anthropocentric beyond the scale of time, with any similarities to humans increasing perceived mind.[15] We expect members of the mind club to be approximately human size, live a humanlike number of years, speak with a humanlike voice, and have a humanlike number of limbs and amount of hair. This is why, in science-fiction movies, the aliens look suspiciously like humans (e.g., Yoda, Klingons, the Predator, Chewbacca). Sure, they may be a *bit* bigger, live a *little* longer, speak with a *slight* accent (but still speak English—what are the odds!?*), have a couple of extra arms or a touch more hair, but they are mostly human. Imagine a film where humans discover an intelligent alien that is the size of a continent and thinks in the span of years: instant box-office flop.

We expect minds to be like us, and this anthropocentrism isn't just selfishness because—at least within the animal kingdom—humans typically *do* have the most mind. Not only have humans constructed skyscrapers and discovered quantum mechanics, but we have firsthand evidence of human agency and experience from our own minds. So when we grapple with an animal cryptomind, we use its humanness as a rough guide for its level of mind. Of

....

* Answer: impossibly unlikely.

course, questions of "humanness" can be as ambiguous as those of mind, and so we often rely upon simple physical features, such as the presence of eyes.

Imagine that you walked into a classroom and saw a couple of lines and dots on the chalkboard. If they were oriented like this

.\ /.

chances are you'd stand farther away than if they were oriented like this

./ ./

Why? The first set looks not only like eyes and eyebrows but like angry eyes and eyebrows.[16] We are especially attuned to eyes because they convey a surprising amount of information (compared with the elbow), including both agency and experience. Agency-wise, eyes can convey the focus of attention, which suggests intention and the next likely course of action; experience-wise, eyes can convey emotion by narrowing in anger or widening in fear.[17,18] It's no accident that we see mind in our pets when we stare into their eyes— and ignore the potential minds of creatures without obvious humanlike eyes, such as plants and insects.

Complex movement is another human trait that leads us to ascribe mind.[19] Something that chases and follows, darts and weaves, hides and seeks, seems to have more mind than something that just sits there. People attribute minds even to simple squares and triangles when their movements suggest goals and reactions.[20] In fact, movement is such a robust cue to mind that only those with brain damage fail to see mind in moving shapes.[21] Like eyes, movement connotes both agency and experience. Thinking doers enact their goals through moving, and vulnerable feelers move away from pain and toward pleasure. Many animals seem to do both.

Eyes and movement are general indicators of mind, but other cues are more specific and convey either agency or experience. Agency is about acting and doing, so *effectors* are cues to agency. Effectors are active or changeable body parts that move, influence, or otherwise affect the external world, and include humanlike hands, arms, legs, and tongues, and nonhumanlike wings, tentacles, claws, glowing abdomens (in lightning bugs), squirting ink sacs (in octopi), and on and on. The more effectors they have, the more animals can do, and often the more they can harm us, such as with fangs, stingers, and horns.

As experience is about sensing and feeling, physical cues to experience are *sensors*, body parts that are involved in conveying sensations to a mind. Eyes, ears, noses, antennae, and feelers are all routes through which minds learn about the world around them. As sensations happen only inside minds, we use *reactions* as proxies for experience. When a dog gives a series of little sniffs followed at the end by a big *shnoof*, it seems to be reacting to a smell. Movements such as changing gaze direction, perking up the ears, orienting the body, and reaching to touch are apparent reactions to stimuli.

If you sense a familiar pattern in the cues to experience and agency, you are right. Sensors are how animals receive *input*, and reactions are indicators of what it is like to be inside an animal's mind. Effectors are how animals *output*, translating wants and desires into action.

Although all animals likely have some agency and experience, not all animal minds are perceived equally. People undoubtedly see more mind in cats and dogs than in sheep and crows—but are these perceptions justified? How accurate are we in our mind club admission decisions when it comes to animals?

Like all minds, animal minds may be forever inaccessible, but there are animal intelligence tests. These tests measure the agency-related outputs of animals minds—their ability to think and do. Typically these tests specifically examine problem-solving skills, because book smarts are useless unless you can apply them to real life. If you've ever put a piece of steak at the bottom of a narrow cup and delighted while a dog spent fruitless minutes trying to fit his snout down there, you understand this important problem-solving test. You think, "If only Fido would grab the tongs, this would be much easier!"

Tongs may be scarce in the wild, but some animals will use tools if available. When faced with a termite colony, hungry chimpanzees thread a stick down into it, wait until the termites begin to crawl upon it, and then pull it out to reveal a delicious insect Popsicle.[22] Chimps also use rocks to help open nuts[23] and appear to make spears to help them kill their prey.[24] Although chimps may be the most sophisticated in their use of tools, they are not alone. For example, crows will insert leaves into logs so that ants climb up the serrated edges and into their waiting mouths.[25]

The intelligence of so-called bird brains may seem surprising, but crows and other members of the *Corvidae* family (i.e., corvids), such as scrub jays and ravens, are actually quite clever and can understand fundamental physics.[26] There were no crows on the team that discovered the Higgs boson, but they can match the knowledge of young children.

Aesop's fable "The Crow and the Pitcher" tells the tale of a crow wishing to drink water from the bottom of a pitcher. The crow collects pebbles, dropping them one by one into the pitcher until the water level is high enough for him to drink.[27] Researchers tested this fable in real life by presenting crows with a narrow vase half filled with water with a treat floating in it (figure 6).[28] The water level was too low for the crow to reach the treat, but there was a pile of little rocks nearby. As in the fable, the solution was to put the rocks in the vase to raise the water level, and crows had no problem figuring it out, even beating out some children.

However, crows were stumped by a similar scenario in which rocks had to be put in a *second* vase connected to the first vase by a sneaky invisible tube under the table, which raised the water level in both vases. Unlike crows, children did manage to solve this problem, even though they had no idea how the water level in the second vase affected the water level in the first vase—many called it "magic."*

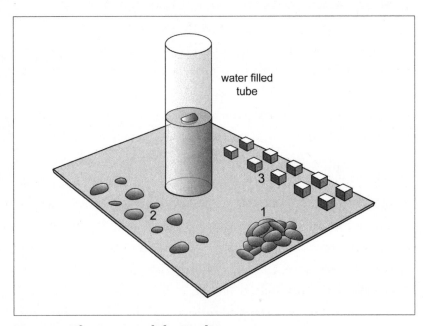

water filled tube

Figure 6: The Crow and the Pitcher
To get the treat, the water level must be raised by dropping objects into the vase. On this and other tasks, crows show surprising ingenuity.

A. H. TAYLOR ET AL., "NEW CALEDONIAN CROWS LEARN THE FUNCTIONAL PROPERTIES OF NOVEL TOOL TYPES," *PLOS ONE* 6 (2011): E26887.

· · · · · · · · · ·

* Strongly suggesting that children are simply crows with a belief in magic.

Birds not only use tools and understand physics but also are some of the few animals that can actually dance to a beat. You may disagree with this blanket statement, recalling times at which your dog seemed to groove to the radio, but it is unlikely that you ever went to the trouble of computing a Fourier transform of Fido's moves. On the other hand, a team of researchers led by Adena Schachner did compute Fourier transforms on a number of different "dancing" animals.

Fourier transforms are mathematic operations that show the frequencies underlying periodic (i.e., repeated) motion. For example, if you had a pendulum that swung back and forth every two seconds, the Fourier transform would show a single spike at 0.50 hertz (half a cycle per second). The Fourier transform of the light given off by a burning butane torchlight would show spikes at around 588 gigahertz (green) and 705 gigahertz (blue).* Schachner and her colleagues examined more than a thousand YouTube videos of animals dancing (i.e., moving while music was playing), including dogs, cats, horses, ferrets, fish, snakes, rabbits, woodpeckers, pigs, pigeons, goats, and elephants. They performed a Fourier transform on both each animal's movements and the background music and by comparing them could tell which animals were dancing to the beat and which were just flailing around.

The analysis revealed that the only animals that can keep rhythm are those that engage in vocal mimicry, such as songbirds, parrots, hummingbirds, elephants, bats, and humans. Of course, these results can't stop you from *perceiving* your pets as musically gifted, but it does suggest that this ability evolves only among a narrow set of evolutionary conditions.

Humans certainly perceive rhythm and other mental abilities

....

* Light consists of waves, and the frequency of these waves determines its color.

in animals, but do animals perceive mind in other animals? Early research on this question focused on chimpanzees because they were the most humanlike of animals, both in terms of DNA and in mental abilities. In one popular paradigm, two researchers would show a chimp some delicious food (e.g., a banana),* before one researcher (the "knower") went behind a screen and hid the food beneath one of four cups. While the knower was doing the hiding, the other experimenter (the "guesser") would stand with a bucket over his head, making him or her blind to the proceedings. Thus the knower would know the exact location of the food, whereas the guesser could only choose a cup at random.

The knower and the guesser would then each point to a different cup. The smart choice in this scenario is to trust the knower to indicate the location of the food. However, this requires understanding the content of others' minds, realizing that the bucketless experimenter knows something that the bucketed-headed experimenter does not. Chimps overwhelmingly failed this task, showing no preference for the cups indicated by the knower,[29] a result most scientists interpreted as indicating that chimps lack the ability to perceive the minds of others. Others weren't so sure.

These more optimistic folks believed that researchers were simply using the wrong paradigm to assess mind perception. They reasoned that if evolution had endowed chimps with mind perception it wasn't for playing bucket-head with humans but instead for outcompeting other chimps. In the wild chimpanzees seldom do cooperative tasks with humans, but they *do* frequently try to steal the food or mates of other chimpanzees.

....

* One particular lab uses Marshmallow Fluff to entice primates.

To test this "conspecific competition" hypothesis, researchers set up two caches of food in a courtyard: one in plain sight of a high-ranking chimp, the other hidden from his view by a wooden screen. They then released a hungry junior chimp into the courtyard and observed. If chimpanzees lack the ability to understand other minds (like the thoughts of the big, bad, dominant chimp), then this junior chimp would foolishly try to take the visible food. But if chimpanzees could understand other minds, then this junior chimp would take the perspective of the dominant chimp and realize that he should steal only the hidden food.

The junior chimp ignored the visible food and instead went to the hidden cache.[30] Watching videos of this behavior, you'd swear that—if it were only possible—the junior chimp would put its hands in its pockets and start whistling, just to indicate that nothing suspicious was going on.

Other animals also have the ability to appreciate mental states in suitably naturalistic situations. If crows or scrub jays (our physicist corvids) notice another bird watching them while they are hiding their food, they will come back and move their stash—suggesting that they understand the knowledge of other birds.[31] Dolphins are also thought to have sophisticated mind perception and can easily follow the gazes or gestures of humans to complete a task, such as fetching specific objects.[32]

However, the real champions of understanding mental states—at least those of humans—are dogs, because they coevolved with us.[33] Over millennia we fed, petted, and sheltered the dogs that knew what we were thinking, and we killed, beat, and exiled the dogs that were oblivious to our desires. This gives modern-day dogs an amazing ability to read human thoughts, although not in the mysterious telepathic sense.* Instead they read our nonverbal cues, such as gaze and pointing.

In one demonstration, researchers put in front of a dog two smell-proof boxes, only one of which contained food. When the dog's owner pointed to the correct box, dogs almost always went to it.[34] This may seem unremarkable, but if you do the same exercise with chimpanzees, they never pick up the cues. You can point and dance and pelvic thrust at the correct box on hundreds of trials and chimps will never get it right. Cats, on the other hand, when observing a human pointing at the correct box, will look at the human derisively and then vigorously lick their own crotch.

One general criticism leveled at animal researchers is that they are inventing rather than objectively observing minds, projecting their own hopes and desires onto animals, and mistaking their own complex social understanding for that of the animals. The most organized criticism of animal minds was the behaviorist movement in psychology, which sought to remove references of mental states from descriptions of animal (and human) behavior. In particular, behaviorism led chimpanzee researchers to try to remove all humanlike language from accounts of chimpanzee behavior. The result, as described by Donald Hebb in 1946, was "an almost endless series of specific acts in which no order or meaning could be found."[35]

Compare the informational value of "A approached B, A touched B's back, and A removed something from B's back; later, B approached

....

* Some people—pet psychics—do *think* they have an amazing ability to read the thoughts of animals. One California pet psychic named Laura Stinchfield will charge you only two hundred dollars per hour to telepathically talk with your pooch (even if it's dead).

A, B touched A's back, B removed something from A's back, and A and B vocalized" with "A and B happily groomed each other." The latter not only is more informative and succinct but also makes for a more compelling story. Importantly, any mind-rich descriptions are wrong only when animals lack the mental capacities we ascribe to them, and the research we've examined suggests that perceptions of mind are justified in many species.

We often like to think of humanity as standing on a different level of evolution, but more similarities between us and nonhuman animals are being revealed every day. Even language—classically held to be the sole dominion of humans—exists in some forms in animals. The gray parrot Alex knew hundreds of words, as does Koko the gorilla, who uses American Sign Language to communicate her desires. Many animals also seem to have a concept of the "self," demonstrated by the ability to recognize themselves in a mirror. In humans this capacity doesn't emerge until the age of eighteen to twenty-four months.[36] To test this with your own child, put a big red mark on his forehead before sitting him in front of the mirror. If your kid madly rubs at his own forehead, he has the power of self-recognition, but if he just chuckles and thinks, "Look at that dumbass," he has yet to approach the intellectual sophistication of chimps, dolphins, and elephants.[37]

These impressive displays of animal thinking suggest that—even if humans are the pinnacle of evolution—other creatures may not be too far down the mountain. The apparent amount of animal agency poses a natural next question: do animals also have experience? People certainly *perceive* animals to have sensations and emotions—to be vulnerable feelers. In the mind map from chapter 1, we saw that animals are viewed as possessing much more experience than agency, even as being on par with humans. We may debate whether animals can think deeply, but most people have no doubt that animals can feel deeply. Is this true?

There is a video you may have seen, and it may have brought tears to your eyes. It concerns two British men, John Rendall and Anthony "Ace" Berg, who in 1969 rescued a lonely lion cub from his tiny cage, brought him home, and named him Christian. These two big men fed Christian from a bottle and played with him in a local church-yard, and when he quickly grew too big for their apartment, they facilitated his release back into the wilds of Africa. Months later they went to Kenya to check up on their feline friend, but they were told that he was now fully wild and that he would not remember them. Undeterred, they trekked to his location and filmed their encounter.

The video begins with John, Ace, and Christian walking toward each other across some rocks. As the lion approaches the men, he quickens his pace, and there is a moment of apprehension as Christian jumps toward them with paws outstretched, but he attacks them only with love and gives them a big hug. Wishful thinking be damned, there is no other word that fits: he stands up on his hind legs and embraces them with his paws. The two men whoop and snuggle him; he hasn't forgotten his surrogate parents and the love they gave.

Contrast this case with the case of Timothy Treadwell—aka the Grizzly Man. Treadwell was an ardent environmentalist who spent summers in Alaska living with the grizzly bears. In his videos it seems that the bears had really accepted him as one of their own, letting him touch them and even play with their cubs. However, near the end of his thirteenth Alaskan summer, something went wrong. The day before he was scheduled to be picked up, his video camera recorded his being attacked and eaten by the very animals he had dedicated his life to protecting. The lens cap was on and the tape was almost finished, so the footage is brief and consists only of audio, but it is more than enough to break your heart. Being eaten alive is not a kind way to go.

The difficulty with loving animals so much is that we expect them to love us back in the same way. We would never think of eating our pets while they are still conscious and so expect the same consideration from animals we love. But are animals even *capable* of these deep experiences? That is a difficult question. With agency there are outward signs, instances of thinking doing like putting stones in a vase or picking the right box; but the sensations and emotions of experience are especially cryptic because they can really be known only from the inside. But as with Christian the lion, there can certainly be compelling cues.

Elephants, for example, will show remarkable compassion for their fellows. In one case a junior elephant named Grace repeatedly tried to help an elderly elephant named Eleanor.[38] Eleanor was having trouble walking, and Grace would try to prop her up and nudge her along when she stumbled. When Eleanor became too weak and stumbled and fell for the last time, Grace stood by her side as night fell, letting out cries of mourning.

Likewise, Dutch anthropologist Frans de Waal has observed bonobos and chimpanzees for thousands of hours and has seen many examples of touching kindness in these primates.[39] Closer to home there are stories of dogs walking across the country to return home to their owners, just as in *Homeward Bound*, and when cats flop down and purr, they definitely seem to want to be close. Of course, they will also eat the corpses of their dead owners.[40]

People often debate whether we're witnessing actual compassion or misinterpreting pure instinct. Does an animal have a sense of kindness, or does it merely *act* as if it did? Unfortunately, assessing actions remains the best we can do because animals lack language to tell us their motives. Practically speaking, these deeper motives may be irrelevant. If you are the mother of the three-year-old boy who fell into the gorilla enclosure at Brookfield Zoo, it matters little why the gorilla Binti Jua carefully cradled your son and brought him to the keeper, all the while protecting him from other gorillas.[41] The important point is that she saved your son.

Animals not only respond to those who are vulnerable or suffering—moral patients—but also respond to moral agents when they are victims of injustice. In one example researchers had two monkeys complete the same task but gave one a better reward. The monkey that got the short end of the deal realized he was being screwed over and refused to participate in future tasks.[42] Monkeys will also perpetrate revenge against those who have wronged them and even attack family members of their enemies.[43] A study we conducted also suggests that monkeys understand the moral concept of "paying it forward," an idea popularized by the eponymous movie starring Haley Joel Osment, Helen Hunt, and Kevin Spacey.

Most times in life, when someone does something good for us, our first inclination is to pay them back and return the favor, but paying it forward instead involves doing something good for an entirely new person—often with the hope that you're forging the first link in a chain of goodness stretching into the future. Both our research and that of others suggests that people will indeed pay it forward.[44] If the previous person in line bought your coffee, you will buy a coffee for the next person, and we wondered if monkeys would do the same.

We tested this idea by putting monkeys as a middle link of a chain of three monkeys, where they would receive an outcome from the first monkey and give an outcome to the third monkey. Monkeys could receive one of two outcomes, either a delicious prized grape or an unappealing piece of spinach. Importantly, it was completely costless for monkeys to give grapes, because the monkey doing the passing always got a grape. In sum, the monkeys chose between option A (me: grape, other: grape) and option B (me: grape, other: spinach), so the only reason they would give another monkey spinach was out of spite.

We found that monkeys paid forward their outcomes. When the second monkey received a grape, it would give the third monkey a grape, but when the second monkey received a piece of spinach, all hell broke loose—it jumped and screamed and looked disgustedly at the first monkey. It then gave a piece of spinach to the third monkey, who reacted the same way, forging a new link in the chain of injustice.[45] In contrast, when adult humans are in analogous situations, we swallow our anger and break the chain of greed by passing on the good outcome. It seems that monkeys have enough of a moral sense to recognize injustice, but not enough to rise above it.

In general, it is clear that many animals care about being kind and having justice but may fail to act upon these concerns because of agency limitations. Despite some sophisticated reasoning, non-human animals have very small prefrontal cortices—just like teenagers—and therefore lack impulse control and the ability to understand how their actions affect others.* An animal might be snuggly and friendly 99 percent of the time, but when hungry, or frightened, or angered, all bets are off.

People recognize this relative lack of agency, and so we gravitate

....

* In truth, teenagers have a large enough prefrontal cortex but have relatively fewer connections between this neural structure and the rest of their brains.

toward animals that are small, cuddly, sweet, and harmless. Chalk this up to evolution. Prehistoric people who tried to snuggle with rattlesnakes and cougars weren't alive long enough to pass on their genes, unlike those who loved hamsters and guinea pigs. No wonder people are far more likely to develop phobias of snakes, spiders, and things with sharp teeth than of bunnies or butterflies.[46] We have evolved to recognize dangerous animals quickly but also, apparently, to pet and cuddle those animals that roll over on their backs and let us rub their tummies.

Our love of pets sometimes seems to outweigh our love of fellow people. In news coverage of natural disasters, cameras and newscasters often focus on the animals that succumb to or survive peril, such as the cat that swam through severe floodwaters in northern Canada. Thousands of people have lost their homes and some have died, but SWIMMING SENSATION MOMO THE CAT ESCAPES ALBERTA FLOOD! shouts a front-page headline.[47]

Of course, if you explicitly ask others, they will acknowledge that people have richer minds than animals and therefore warrant more moral concern—but it is hard to remember this fact when you see a puppy whimpering. Our concern with animal welfare also makes sense when you consider the deep fault line we discovered between the two kinds of minds: vulnerable feelers and thinking doers. As our pets are less thinking doers and more vulnerable feelers, we consistently place them in the moral patient camp, focusing on their suffering and worrying about their mistreatment while generally forgiving their trespasses against us.

Of course, those same people cheering for Momo on the nightly news are also likely eating their dinners of beef, pork, or chicken. How are we to make sense of this contradiction? Why is the death of a pet a tragedy and the death of a chicken a routine step toward dinner? One potential reason is that the inscrutability of animal minds leaves lots of wiggle room in questions of moral concern. Consider the difference between Michael Vick and Joaquin Phoenix.

NFL quarterback Michael Vick has a great arm and rushing yards befitting a running back, but he is infamous for running a brutal dogfighting ring. When authorities searched his estate, they found seventy caged dogs—mostly pit bulls—who were trained to fight one another to the death. Dogs who survived fights but were too injured to keep fighting were killed by Vick and his associates.[48]

In contrast to the callous Vick, the actor Joaquin Phoenix is so concerned with animal suffering that he has been a vegan since he was three years old, when he saw a fish suffocating in the bottom of a boat during a family fishing trip.[49] He has narrated award-winning documentaries on animal abuse in the farming industry and requires that his movies not use captive animals. He has even filmed a commercial for PETA in which he pretends to drown, mirroring the suffocating fish he saw so many years ago. For Phoenix and Vick, the issue of animal rights seems to be one of extremes—either all animals are sacred or any can be killed for sport—but for most people animal rights involve shades of gray: puppy killing is heinous, but it's okay to have the odd mollusk for dinner.

How do people decide which animals count as moral patients? With mind perception, of course. Animals perceived to have mind are given moral rights, whereas those without aren't. It may seem that we base membership in the mind club on agency, as laws to protect apes and dolphins often reference their intelligence.[50] For example, in 2008 the Spanish parliament passed a nonbinding resolution giving basic human rights to great apes, who are among our closest genetic relatives. This law prevents cruelty to apes and forbids their killing except in cases of self-defense. Proponents of the law cited the apes' advanced cognitive abilities—but also their ability to feel fear, jealousy, and love.[51]

The truth is that people extend more protection to kittens than crows, despite the fact that corvids are much smarter. This suggests that animal rights are more a matter of experience than of agency—an idea confirmed by our mind survey, which revealed that animals are seen as vulnerable feelers. This importance of experience is captured eloquently by the philosopher Jeremy Bentham, who wrote that "the question [of animal rights] is not, Can they *reason*? nor, Can they *talk*? but, Can they *suffer*?"[52]

Because animals lack language, and experience exists *inside* minds, it is difficult to decipher whether animals feel pain the same as we do. Animals may writhe and yelp when injured, but classically these signs were thought to be mere reflexes and not to represent "real" pain. Descartes believed animals were little automatons that were driven by the biological equivalent of springs and levers; they might cry out, but that was only because of mechanical linkages, just as your alarm clock might cry out when morning comes.[53]

The inscrutability of experience means that we rely heavily on external cues to understand animal pain—things like big eyes, obvious expressions, and human likeness. This is why, in the mind survey, puppies were given more protection than tree frogs, which have small eyes and no clear way of crying out and aren't even mammals like us. Reliance on these external cues can lead to an overemphasis on "cuteness" in animal rights. That we can eat bacon with abandon and donate money to stop seal clubbing—despite the impressive intelligence of pigs[54]—is a notable reversal of objective mental qualities. In this way we are—if only a tiny bit—like serial killer Dennis Nilsen, who saw his dog as a mind club member but

Figure 7: Pigheaded?
We feel more at ease at the idea of eating pigs than seals, even though pigs likely have richer inner lives.

not his fellow humans. Those we admit to the mind club may not be the most deserving but instead those with whom we emotionally connect.

Even when animals are relatively uncute, thinking about their suffering can still make people squirm. We think of cows as stupid and label their meat "beef" to maintain distance between ourselves and dinner. If meat is mindless, then it isn't really cruel. This link between mind and morality has been demonstrated by a clever experiment led by psychologist Steve Loughnan in which grocery store shoppers were given free samples of either cashews or beef jerky. After eating, shoppers filled out a mind survey that included mental ratings of a cow. The researchers discovered that while the nut eaters perceived the cow to have substantial mind, the meat eaters stripped away its thoughts and feelings.[55] An elegant follow-up study found that simply labeling an animal as "food" drastically decreased the animal's perceived capacity for suffering.[56]

The denial of mind to animals we eat is especially obvious in factory farming. Consider the language of an employee of one turkey factory farm, in which birds with freakish genes have their beaks seared off, are pumped full of antibiotics, and are fed until they can't even walk around their tiny wire cage: "The farmer has no choice but to produce food at a lower production cost, and genetically he's going to move toward an animal that accomplishes that task, which can be counterproductive to its welfare."[57] Rather than inventing animal minds, this man is trying his best to ignore them.

In contrast to the distance that some put between themselves and animals, others are more intimate with them—perhaps a little *too* intimate. Consider the case of Carlos Romero. He was in love. Romero was living in a small city in central Florida and finding it hard to meet people, but the thirty-one-year-old finally found someone to get excited about. They had been together only a couple of months, but their relationship was already quite physically advanced—they seemed to have a natural chemistry. Romero's lover was named Doodles, a name befitting a twenty-one-month-old miniature donkey.

Witnesses phoned the police after seeing Romero pressed against the back of Doodles with his pants down, and when he was questioned by detectives, Romero admitted that he and the donkey had had a half dozen sexual encounters and that he enjoyed the way her fur felt on his privates. In a later jailhouse interview with the *Huffington Post*, Romero admitted that he was never really a people person and preferred the company of animals, who were "usually there for you," "100 percent honest," and don't "stab you in the back, give you diseases and lie to you." He also demanded that Doodles be returned to him, since he had paid five hundred dollars for her.[58]

Clearly Romero has had a tough time with human relationships, but so have many others who have resisted the charms of barnyard animals. What turned him to animals? There is no clear answer to how people develop these abnormal sexual preferences. One possibility is that people learn to feel sexually aroused by things that are exotic and different,[59] and animals certainly fit that bill. However, given that few people engage in zoophilia—the technical term for sexual attraction to animals—this explanation seems insufficient. Another possibility is that it derives from childhood experiences in which sexual arousal is paired with animals and that this gets reinforced over time.[60] A similar process occurs with animal fears: some people who have frightening childhood encounters with snakes and spiders develop full-blown phobias.[61] But not all childhood experiences grow into adult obsessions, and so researchers are still searching for the reasons behind zoophilia.

More relevant to our discussion are *perceptions* of zoophilia. In particular, why do people view human-animal love as so immoral? The explanation again lies with the mind-perception fault line that splits doers from feelers. Animals are seen as vulnerable feelers and not thinking doers, which means that they seem to suffer while lacking the agency to give informed consent—a key component of sexual relationships.[62] But it isn't clear that the animals actually suffer or that consent is actually important for animals. Animals never give informed consent, not even to the conspecifics they mate with in the wild, and we don't imprison two donkeys for having consentless sex with each other. Instead we are all likely reacting to the relative *imbalance* between the minds of humans and those of the animals with whom they become intimate.

Recall that our cognitive template of morality is dyadic, featuring an agent and a patient, an intentional thinking doer and a suffering vulnerable feeler. As we saw in chapter 1, the worst crimes pair powerful and invulnerable agents (high agency, low experience) with sensitive and vulnerable patients (low agency, high experience), explaining why it is immoral for a CEO to punch a little girl (but not vice versa). Zoophilia easily fits this template of wrongdoing, as vulnerable animals are powerless to stop us thinking humans from mistreating them—and so we react with outrage. This logic suggests that the way to make zoophilia seem less immoral* is to have trysts with animals perceived to have high agency and low experience. Sexual relations with dangerous and apparently unfeeling tiger sharks seem more forgivable than with helpless and sensitive miniature donkeys.

Although most animals are typically ascribed less agency than humans, circumstances can conspire to make them appear capable of intention, planning, and even malice. In instances of severe suffering, animals can transform from hapless victims to calculating perpetrators. Consider an example from medieval France.

It is the summer of 1457 in the small town of Savigny. A peasant woman goes to work in her garden, leaving her son in a cradle on the floor as she has done many times before. As she works, a sow slips through the door with her piglets in tow and hunts around for food. The sow discovers the baby and starts eating him, and by the time the mother realizes what is happening, there is little left but gristle and blood. The mother and the other townsfolk are understandably inconsolable, but rather than simply killing the sow, as we might do today, they decide to place the pig on trial.

A judge is brought from the next town, and lawyers are appointed to represent the sow and her piglets. The defendant sits in a nearby pen as arguments are heard and witnesses are called, and eventually the judge rules. He decides that the sow is morally culpable of murder and should be sentenced to death for her crime. The piglets, however, due to their young age, are found not guilty, but the towns-

....

* Not that we're advocating for this.

Figure 8: The Pig on Trial, as Illustrated in Robert Chambers's
Book of Days
Through dyadic completion, we find a moral agent to blame.

folk are instructed to keep close watch over them, lest the trauma they witnessed warp their moral sensibilities. To carry out the sentence, the townsfolk build a gallows from which to hang the pig—at some considerable expense—as they would a human. The townsfolk gather round as the murderer is executed; finally, justice is done.[63]

There are many medieval examples of animals on trial, including locusts legally condemned for crop destruction[64] and a rooster sentenced to death for the gender-bending behavior of laying an egg (it was, in fact, just a misunderstood chicken).[65]

Before you cast aspersions on the intelligence of the French peasantry, remember that they weren't completely stupid; they realized that pigs, locusts, and poultry lacked mental sophistication. But there seems to be something special about witnessing injustice, whether the death of a child or the mass destruction of livelihood, that prompts people to find someone or something to blame. We call this urge *dyadic completion*.

As we saw in chapter 1, canonical examples of immorality have a *complete dyad* of agent plus patient: murder, theft, abuse, and fraud involve a thinking doer harming a vulnerable feeler. Sometimes, however, the enormity of injustice is so great that it trips our immorality detector, even without an obvious moral agent. An infant being eaten alive is so terrible that we can't believe that it is simply bad luck. Instead we see it as an act of evil. This perception of injustice then feeds back and triggers our dyadic moral template, currently incomplete with only one mind instead of two—a suffering moral patient (in this case, the baby) with no moral agent to blame. To "complete" this dyad, our mind casts about for a thinking doer to slot into the agent role (in this case, the pig).

As an analogy, consider the process of visual completion in the Kanizsa triangle, in which the presence of one triangle prompts the completion of a second triangle. No matter how you try, you cannot

Figure 9: Kanizsa Triangle
Just as visual completion compels people to see a white triangle in the Kanizsa triangle, dyadic completion compels people to see agents to blame for a suffering patient.

help but see that second triangle. Within the moral dyad, the first triangle is the presence of a moral patient, and the little Pac-Mans are feelings of injustice—both cues that compel you to see the white triangle (the moral agent).

You might question whether the white triangle is *actually* there, but as with all things mind and morality, it is a matter of perception. Importantly, dyadic completion is satisfied only with a *bona fide* moral agent capable of intention, responsibility, and action, which explains why the peasants put the pig on trial, just as they would a human killer—a trial is a matter of moral responsibility, not just whether a bad act happened. One could also argue that the pig at least had more moral agency than the baby it ate, qualifying it as a *relative* moral agent. It is likely harder to blame a pig for the death of a powerful CEO (high agency, low experience) than for the death of a baby (low agency, high experience).

Dyadic completion explains not only historical animal trials but also the blame we levy on the owners of dogs that bite children. It is not psychologically satisfying to simply acknowledge the unpredictability of animals with kids, so instead we seek out the most agentic mind available—and then typically sue it. The idea of dyadic completion is an important one, and it will resurface in future chapters as we explore campaigns against gay rights, conspiracy theories, and even the belief in God.

Animals also feature in dyadic completion for good deeds. When Lassie saves a three-year-old from being hit by a speeding car, we ascribe to her goodness, insight, and wisdom.[66] Similar attributions of moral agency are made to dogs that serve in the police force or military, such as Cairo, the Malinois* who accompanied

....

* A breed of dog similar to a German shepherd but more compact.

Navy SEALs on their raid of Osama bin Laden's compound. In the eyes of the military, Cairo is technically just a piece of military equipment, but in the eyes of his fellow SEALs, the average American, and even the president, Cairo is a hero. Criminals who kill K9 officers are punished much more harshly than those who kill other dogs; for example, South Carolinian Maurice McCreary was given five years in prison for shooting a police dog.[67]

Even with dyadic completion, service animals are still technically a rung below humans. Contrary to some rumors, killing a police dog does not warrant the same punishment as killing a human police officer, and military dogs are not assigned a rank. Of course, that doesn't stop us from mourning their loss as we might human heroes. When the German shepherd K9 officer Rocco was fatally stabbed while on duty in Pittsburgh, he was honored with a motorcade and a full funeral that featured more than a thousand attendees.[68]

The thousands mourning a single dog seem light-years away from the cheering crowds at the bearbaiting, whom we met at the very beginning of this chapter, but both phenomena can be understood through mind perception. In the past, animals were seen as dumb beasts, whereas today some seem to care more about animals than even about other people. The tension between dumb beasts and best friends is a question we struggle with today, and it seems we often use unreliable cues to guide our decisions.

People prioritize cuteness over intellect and humanness over problem-solving acumen, suggesting that mind perception may be more a matter of feeling than of reason. We may see with our eyes, but we seem to see animals' minds with our hearts. When you find yourself talking to your dog while eating a dinner of steak, perhaps you'll pause to reflect on the importance of the mind club—and whether your admission decisions are grounded in fact or merely wishful thinking.

For our next cryptomind we move from the warm fur of animals to the cold embrace of machines.

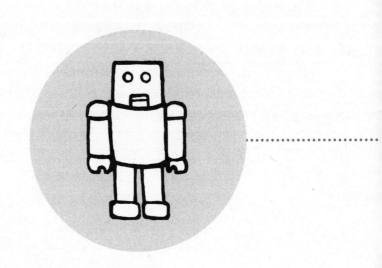

Chapter 3
THE MACHINE

If you have ever passionately kissed an inanimate object, you are not alone. Every year hundreds of people buy a RealDoll, a life-like mannequin with fully functioning sexual parts. These dolls are typically female, and when you buy one—for approximately six thousand dollars—you can specify eye color, hair color, body type, and other less PG-13 features. In a sense, you can create your perfect lover. The only thing is that, no matter how much you love this perfect lover, she won't love you back; adoring gazes and warm embraces are met with unblinking stares and room-temperature silicone. Relationships with human lovers take a time-honored progression, from dating and marriage to children and minivans, but relationships with RealDolls fail to progress at all. RealDolls can't help pay the bills, make small talk with your colleagues at the office Christmas party, or hold you and whisper that everything will be okay.

Figure 10: "Roxanne"
A RealDoll with Face #11.

For those accustomed to living lovers, relationships with Real-Dolls seem no more fulfilling than relationships with plywood or Tupperware. But for those who own RealDolls the relationship does seem satisfying, going beyond physical needs to emotional intimacy. One RealDoll aficionado, nicknamed "Davecat," describes his relationship with "Shi-chan," a statuesque brunette with green eyes and a removable tongue, manufactured by Abyss Creations: "When she first came into my life, it was sex, sex, sex, sex, sex, and now it's just tapered off to where we're just there for each other. We're always there for each other."[1] You may wonder how Davecat finds it satisfying to have Shi-chan "there for him" when Shi-chan lacks the mind necessary to love him back. The truth, however, is that Shi-chan *does* have a mind, because Davecat perceives it—such is the power of mind perception.

RealDolls may seem like a strange place to start in a chapter on machines, but they wonderfully exemplify the theme of this chapter: human creations as cryptominds. Unlike animals, which are creations of nature, machines such as robots, computers, and iPhones are all products of our own minds. Just as an artist might stare at her own art and divine new truths about her psyche, so too can we examine our reactions to mechanical creations to learn about mind perception and human needs.

The first thing we can learn from RealDolls is that people don't like to be lonely. Even though Davecat realizes that Shi-chan is not alive, he says that she makes the "difference between being alone, and being lonely." Loneliness is an oppressive, gnawing experience, often described as painful.[2] In prisons, inmates dread solitary confinement above all else, and many believe it qualifies as torture. In 2012 the Center for Constitutional Rights filed suit against the state of California for using solitary confinement in its prisons, claiming that the practice violates the Eighth Amendment, which guarantees protection from cruel and unusual punishment.

The power of loneliness stems from the evolutionary fact that humans are social creatures who depend on others for survival.[3] People who lack a social support network are more likely to die from heart disease and cancer,[4] and most of us would be dead if left alone in the forest for a month. Even if we *could* survive as a lone human, few of us would want to. Imagine being the last woman or man on Earth. Sure, you could drive recklessly and loot stores, but without someone in the passenger seat to share the thrill of speeding and the taste of illicit Twinkies, what's the point?

Our need to feel social connection explains why people often embellish their relationships with other people. Every time you think of celebrities as close friends or imagine that you and your hunky mail carrier have a deep personal connection, you are creating what are called "parasocial relationships." Unlike normal two-sided relationships, parasocial relationships are felt by only one person—but to that one person they are undoubtedly real, even when they involve characters on TV. Loneliness makes people imagine a loving bond with other minds, and this love can make even imaginary minds real.

To test this "love makes minds real" effect, psychologists Wendi Gardner and Megan Knowles sat participants in front of a monitor that showed either their favorite television character—with whom participants reported a close personal connection—or another random (and unloved) television character. The "realness" of the character's mind was tested via "social facilitation" as participants copied a list of words with either their dominant or nondominant hand.

"Social facilitation" is the technical term for what happens when you do something in front of real people, like give a speech or play sports. Decades of research has shown that social situations increase performance on well-practiced tasks and decrease performance on novel tasks, which explains why sports rookies choke under pressure but veterans rise to the challenge. In this study the well-practiced task was copying words with the dominant hand, and the novel task was copying words with the nondominant hand. As the researchers predicted, social facilitation was found when participants sat in front of their favorite television character, becoming faster at dominant-hand copying and slower at nondominant-hand copying. People who had strong emotional connections with their favorite characters unconsciously performed as if these characters were real people.[5]

That loneliness can compel us to see imaginary characters as members of the mind club may not be surprising. After all, they are played by real people who ostensibly have real minds. But loneliness can also make us see minds in mere objects. When Tom Hanks's

Figure 11: Clocky
The lonelier you are, the more mind you perceive in Clocky,
the alarm clock that runs away from you.

character in *Cast Away* finds himself alone on a desert island, he befriends a kindly volleyball named Wilson to cope with the isolation. Over the course of the movie, Hanks's character laughs and cries with Wilson, just as he would with a real person. In an empirical test of this idea, psychologists Nick Epley and Adam Waytz asked people to rate both their loneliness and the minds of mechanical devices that included Clocky (a self-propelled alarm clock that rolls away from the lazy sleeper) and Pillow Mate (a human-shaped pillow programmed to hug). As predicted, lonelier people saw these machines as possessing more mind, including intentions, consciousness, emotions, and free will.[6]

If loneliness makes people see free will in alarm clocks, it's no surprise that those without human relationships see RealDolls as members of the mind club.[7] As we saw in the previous chapter, a humanlike appearance compels us to see mind, and Shi-chan certainly looks human. Of course, dolls can't love you back, but they also can't betray or hurt you—a sentiment also expressed by donkey-loving Carlos Romero in the previous chapter. As one doll owner says, "All the lies, and all the deceit, and all the times I've been used—it'll never happen again."[8]

Not only do we give mind to machines that meet our social needs, but we also ascribe mind when *they* seem to need *us*. Perhaps you remember the Tamagotchi craze that swept through schools in the late 1990s. This little device with an LCD screen was an electronic pet that required constant attention and care. You had to feed it when it was "hungry," clean up after it "pooped," and turn off the lights when it was "sleepy." Failure to do these things could not only result in the death of the Tamagotchi but could also produce a deranged and poorly behaved pet, much like a feral child. Because the Tamagotchi was sensitive to harm (if only electronically), it pulled at people's heartstrings. Just as vulnerable animals are perceived to have minds, so too are apparently vulnerable machines.

Seeing mind in machines not only makes us feel warm and fuzzy but also gives us a sense of control over their behavior. We understand that human behavior is driven by thoughts and experiences—people cry because they are sad and BASE jump from skyscrapers because they are crazy—and so we think of machines' behavior as driven by thoughts and experiences too. Think of when you are confronted with a malfunctioning piece of technology, like a hiccupping laptop. Your first impulse isn't to think, "Its capacitors have overtaxed p-n junctions," but instead to think, "It gets *angry* when too many programs are open." Likewise, when we are hoping that our car will start on winter mornings, we don't think about the complex interaction of carburetor and temperature but instead think of our car as stubborn or unhappy in the cold—and beg it to not make us late for work.

As these examples suggest, the tendency to see mind in technology occurs primarily when it disobeys our desires.[9] When machines function smoothly, we feel in control, but when they misbehave, we see mind to help us understand. This is also true with people. When your toddler is being a good kid, you don't think hard about why that's the case. But when he's screaming and flinging his dinner around a French restaurant, you immediately try very hard to figure out his motivations and thoughts on the matter. People are more likely to think of their old Chevy truck as being in the mind club than their brand-new Audi, despite the Audi's fancy technology. The Audi does everything exactly as it should—and so is seen as lacking mind—but that old "girl" needs encouragement, cajoling, and sometimes just a sensitive ear to listen to her.

Psychologist Carey Morewedge calls this phenomenon a *negativity bias* in mind perception—negative events prompt mind perception more than positive events. To experimentally demonstrate this effect, he had participants play some "ultimatum games," in which one person offers a split of money between themselves and someone else, and the other person decides whether to accept the split. If the split is accepted, everyone gets their share—however fair or unfair—but if the split is rejected, then no one gets any money.

For example, imagine Bonnie gets ten dollars to split between herself and Clyde. Bonnie offers a split of six dollars to her and four to Clyde, and now Clyde has to decide whether to accept the split or reject it. If Clyde accepts it, then they each receive their money, but if Clyde rejects it, then no one gets any money. Rationally, it always makes sense to accept *any* split—even if you are offered only a penny—since some money is better than no money, but feelings of fairness and spite frequently lead people to reject lopsided offers.

In Morewedge's study participants played three ultimatum games with three different partners, who (the participants were told) could be all people, all computers, or some combination of the two. After participants were presented with the proposed split from their partner, he asked them to guess whether their partner was a computer or a person.[10] In truth, the partner was always a computer, but participants typically believed they were playing with people when the situation was negative. When the offer was fair or generous, they were more than happy to think it was a mindless machine, but when the offer was unfair, they quickly ascribed intention behind it, believing it to result from the cruel calculations of another person. As we saw in the previous chapter, bad outcomes lead people to search for an agent to blame for mistreatment—a phenomenon called dyadic completion. The negativity bias in mind perception can actually be explained as part of dyadic completion, as people search for an agentic mind to take the blame when they feel vulnerable and exploited.

In addition to the motivations of understanding and social connection, people often perceive mind in machines because of *anthropomorphism*, the tendency to treat something as human. As we explored in the previous chapter, people are generally anthropocentric, seeing everything from the perspective of humans. More technically, we have "schemas" for many things in life, scripts or outlines for how things should go. The schema for a date involves meeting someone at a restaurant, the schema for an exam involves sitting quietly in a row of desks, and the schema for interacting with a new entity—like a machine—is to treat it as a human.

We often don't realize when we're anthropomorphizing because our schemas are unconscious, but it can lead to curious effects with machines. In a series of studies, Clifford Nass and Youngme Moon found that participants treated computers as if they had gender and ethnicity, just like humans. Participants were also polite to these computers. When the computer asked how it was performing, people were unfailingly nice, even when it was actually performing poorly. But just as with humans, this politeness held only when participants were dealing with the computer "face to face." They were more than happy to bad-mouth one computer to a different computer.[11]

Although we are typically polite to machines, this warm facade can quickly fade. The mind survey in chapter 1 revealed that machines are generally seen as lacking experience—and vulnerability—and so it is easy to be cruel to them. When Microsoft introduced a little lifelike paper clip (cleverly nicknamed "Clippy") in its Office programs, people played along by ascribing it intentions—but hateful ones. Similarly, when navigating the phone systems of banks or airlines, our simple yeses and nos to the disembodied computer voice quickly become "Connect me to a real person!" or a litany of swear words. Beyond anecdotes, the British researchers Antonella De Angeli and Rollo Carpenter analyzed people's conversations with the online chatbot Jabberwacky, a sophisticated computer program capable of basic communication.[12] Their database revealed hundreds of examples of computer abuse, ranging from bodily threat to sexual harassment.* Consider this excerpt:

....

* "Fuck" was the ninth-highest-ranked word stem.

User: What is your address?

Jabberwacky: I don't think I'll tell you. You'd kill me if I told you. Wouldn't you!

User: Yes I would.

Jabberwacky: What is your favourite food?

User: I WILL KILL YOU! I WILL HUNT YOU DOWN!!!

Jabberwacky: Please don't. . . . I really have to leave.

User: I WILL KILL YOU!

Companies try to circumvent humanity's penchant for machine cruelty by making their technological agents more likable. IKEA's Web site once had an automated helper named Anna who was cheerfully polite as she helped you find the latest in Swedish furniture. Her niceness had limits, however, as she would not respond to aggressive questions about why the Svaglen broke into a million particle-board pieces or why the Muurfben didn't come with an Allen key.

Agents like Anna—or the iPhone's Siri—often incur our wrath because computers exceed humans in so many other ways that we expect them to be capable in all ways. Many machines are better at thinking than people are, and because we tend to think of agency as an entire cluster of capacities, we wonder how a machine that can do millions of calculations per second can fail to book us on the last flight out of New York. It also doesn't help that we see mind in machines when we are confused and searching for control, which happen to be the very times we are short-tempered and spiteful. Whether you're cruel or kind to automated agents, ascribing them mind is an inevitable consequence of trying to understand and control the world around us.

Setting aside our general tendency for anthropomorphism, we seem to have two broad motivations for perceiving mind: feeling lonely and craving control. In another demonstration of the great fault line between the two kinds of perceived minds, each of these motivations maps onto primarily one dimension of mind perception. When we feel lonely, we see experience in people and pets—and also machines—which seem to love and care for us and need our love and care in return. On the other hand, when we seek control, we see agency in entities in order to predict and understand their behavior.[13] But even if you're not lonely or confused, you likely need machines more than you think—especially given our limited memories.

You may not realize it, but your memories are distributed across many sources, including notes, books, people, and machines. To remember a doctor's appointment you put a Post-it note on the fridge, to make banana bread you use a cookbook to jog your memory, and to remember Christmas 2007 you look back in a photo album. This distribution of memory is especially obvious in our interactions with other people. You may not know much about cars, but you have a friend who knows by heart the engine displacement of a Maserati and how to replace a head gasket while blindfolded. This means that you are free to ignore all car-related facts as long as you can bring her along to the mechanic. The key is that you don't need to remember the "what" of something (e.g., the difference between fixed and floating brake calipers) as long as you can remember the "who"—the person who knows it (e.g., Tina the gearhead).

This phenomenon is called transactive memory,[14] and spouses use it all the time. One person may take responsibility for knowing everything about gardening, while the other may know everything about cooking. One person remembers the birthdays of the extended family, whereas the other remembers to take the car in for regular maintenance. Like the distribution of labor that fueled the Industrial Revolution, this distribution of memory makes economic sense. Why remember everything half as well when you can remember half the things twice as well?

In today's networked society, our minds are distributed among not just books and people but also technology.[15] How many phone numbers do you know off the top of your head? One dozen, maybe two? Perhaps not even that many. Before cell phones (but after dinosaurs), you could commit only ten numbers to speed dial, and the rest you had to either remember or store in your Rolodex. Not only can modern cell phones remember every phone number you'll ever need, but a single smartphone has enough memory to record *every* phone number in the world. The amazing memories of machines mean that you probably don't even *try* to remember phone numbers, spelling disaster if you ever find yourself stranded without your phone.

Machines not only have more memory capacity than people or books but also circumvent the necessity of knowing which person or book contains which piece of information. With a set of books you need the equivalent of a card catalog, and with a group of friends you have to remember which person knows about cars, or gardening, or French cooking. Search engines have made concerns about indexing obsolete. If you can find everything just by typing something into Google, then you really only need to know one rule: "if unknown, search Google."

Our research suggests that people do indeed use search engines as an intellectual crutch. Together with Betsy Sparrow, we gave participants trivia questions, both easy (e.g., "Who is the president of America?") and challenging (e.g., "Who is the president of Nicaragua?"). After each question participants were asked to label the color of text in which different company names were written. For example, "Google" might be written in blue, and "Nike" might be written in red. Known as the Stroop task, this procedure relies on the idea that people are slow to label the colors of words that capture their attention, because they focus more on the meaning of the word than on its color.

As we expected, challenging questions led people to label the color of Internet-related companies (e.g., Google or Yahoo!) more slowly, suggesting that people were yearning after all-knowing search engines when answers evaded them.[16] A follow-up study found that people were also happy to take credit for the knowledge of Google. When people answered challenging questions with the help of Google, they felt much smarter, believing that they could answer questions correctly even without Google's help. (They couldn't.)

So the next time someone asks you whether you've lost your mind, do a brief check for your spouse and—most important—make sure your wireless connection is on. As long as you have Google, you'll still have some mind, and it might only be a matter of time until our minds become literally fused with computers. One group of scientists has already patented microchips that can be buried within your eyes, and researchers at the University of Washington have harnessed the Internet to control one person's hand movements with another person's brain signals.[17]

This melding of mind and machine might make us more efficient, but some fear that the computers cannot be trusted and—if left to their own devices—might realize that humans are unnecessary. In the movie *The Terminator* the supercomputer Skynet suddenly becomes sentient and immediately launches all the world's nuclear missiles.[18] In the resulting Armageddon, humans are all but wiped out, and the remaining few are hunted by lethal cyborgs. Such an apocalypse may seem far-fetched, but the Internet already links together all of the world's computers, and all we need is one computer to develop the power to think for itself. Impossible? Ray Kurzweil thinks not.

Ray Kurzweil is a futurist, which means that he makes predictions about the future. His most notable prediction is about "the singularity," in which computers become able to think, especially about themselves.[19] To understand the singularity we need to discuss another futurist named Gordon Moore, who was a cofounder of Intel, the microchip company. Based on what Moore saw while developing microchips, he theorized that computing power would double roughly every two years.[20] For the past forty years, "Moore's law" has held true; if you compared a chip made in 2010 with one made in 1970, it would be 2^{20} (or 1,048,576) times more powerful. This explains why operations that used to take weeks on a computer can now be done in a matter of seconds, and why your friend's new iPhone seems so much better than your once-cutting-edge BlackBerry.

Kurzweil pondered this increasing computing power and wondered if this straight line of progress could be turned into an upward spiral in which computers could increase their own computing power. This may not seem like that big of an idea, but it's potentially world changing, because it describes a positive feedback cycle—an operation that (1) acts to increase something and (2) takes its own output as an input. The classic positive feedback cycle is a microphone (input) connected to an amplifier (operation) held next to a speaker (output). In any speaker there's always a little buzz, but it's typically inaudible. However, if you hold a microphone to a speaker, it will pick up the buzz, which the amplifier increases before relaying it to the speaker. The microphone then picks up this louder buzz, which the amplifier increases even more before relaying it again to the speaker. The microphone then picks up this even *louder* buzz, and on and on, until you quickly hear an ear-splitting shriek.

Along the same lines, if a computer is intelligent enough to increase its own intelligence, it can become more intelligent, allowing it to become even more intelligent, and so on. The feedback cycle can quickly carry on to infinity—and quickly turn humans from planet Earth's most dominant life form to fleshy slaves. This is a terrifying possibility for us, but who could blame machines—we saw just how cruel and callous we can be to them in conversation.

Kurzweil, for his part, is banking on the idea that once computers become all-powerful, they will be benevolent. He expects to be able to upload his consciousness into a computer and live immortally in the Internet, in harmony with machines. Of course, anyone who has spent time with a three-year-old understands that our creations often don't go as planned, as trips to the mall often end in fierce tantrums and the attempted destruction of entire shopping aisles. Who knows what would happen with a tantrum-throwing superagent in control of air-traffic systems; just the idea of such sentient technology may give you the creeps.

The threat of self-aware and all-powerful computers may seem to be a problem of the future, but people have long been confronted with lifelike machines—and worried about whether they belonged in the mind club. From 1770 to the mid-1800s, an automaton known

Figure 12: The Mechanical Turk
An early machine cryptomind.

as the Turk toured Europe and the Americas, beating the best minds of the time (including Ben Franklin) at chess, before it was revealed that the machine was in fact being controlled by a human chess master hidden inside.

In another purported case the famous philosopher René Descartes, distraught at the loss of his daughter, made a mechanical version of her, complete with arm and head motions, and took her on a long sea voyage.[21] Although she was stored in a crate belowdecks, one of the deckhands discovered her and quickly told others about this strange humanlike robot. The superstitious crew was so put off by her eerie appearance and jerky motions that they threw her overboard into the ocean, leaving Descartes to cope with his daughter's loss a second time.

Today we seem to have come a long way from the Frankenstein-like scenario of pitchfork-wielding townspeople burning the new and different. People don't seem to mind when robots clean their floors, build their cars, administer their medication, or perform their surgery.[22] These examples, however, are all agency-related examples of thinking and doing; there seems to be something very different about a robot that can sense and feel. In robots we seem to be hesitant to combine agency with experience, to make a *human* machine.

Could a robot ever be human? From one perspective humans are simply a sophisticated collection of on/off switches (i.e., neurons), and it should theoretically be possible to mimic our minds with silicon transistors instead of fleshy cells. In practice the sheer complexity of our brains makes it extremely difficult to duplicate them, but scientists suggest that nothing *in principle* separates us from robots.[23] Intuitively this argument may seem hard to accept because of an apparent sharp line between us (humans) and them (robots). Call it whatever you like—a soul, an essence, or just "humanity"—but it seems impossible to create a fully human machine. Corporations may be able to mass-produce circuit boards, but how could they mass-produce a soul? We will investigate the concept of the soul more deeply in chapter 8 on the dead, but suffice it to say souls are difficult to detect.

The real question for the mind club is whether a sufficiently sophisticated robot—one that looks and acts human—is at least *close enough* to human. Imagine you are at a dinner party, seated next to a middle-aged novelist who is telling you about his latest book. It's historical fiction, focusing on one family's struggle in Depression-era America as a metaphor for the struggles of modern adulthood. He says it will win a Pulitzer if the committee has any sense. You're just about to politely reply that it sounds fascinating when you notice something that actually *is* fascinating—a collection of LEDs flashing from his scalp. When you ask him what they are, he responds by pushing a button next to his ear, revealing the mass of circuit boards in his head. Then he asks if you're single and if you want to go home with him after dinner.

He may be pedantic and narcissistic, but is he human? Alan Turing would say yes. As we mentioned in chapter 1, Alan Turing was a famous mathematician who not only helped British intelligence crack Nazi codes in World War II but also developed a test for a kind of humanness.[24] Turing thought that the best test of human intelligence was whether something could converse just like a person. In this case he would suggest that our novelist friend, if not human, at least had a human mind. The Turing test is called a *functional* test of humanness, saying that "a human is as human does." Research by philosophers suggests that people do sometimes use functionalist concerns when perceiving mind,[25] believing that if something talks like a human, then it is a human.

The Turing test has so powerfully captured the imaginations of computer scientists that they conduct a competition every year in which programmers try to fool humans with their computer creations. The competition is actually called the Loebner Prize in honor of Hugh Loebner, who in 1990 agreed to provide the funding for an annual prize of $100,000 and a gold medal, both awarded to the researcher who makes the most human-minded computer. For an interactive demonstration of these humanlike computer programs, check out the chatbots Cleverbot and Jabberwacky (the recipient of abuse we met earlier in the chapter). A few seconds of conversation reveals that these programs have a way to go before becoming convincing, but the task of writing them is very hard. Not only do computers have to be sophisticated at language, but they also have to have enough shared knowledge of culture, including literature, movies, history, and current events.

Of course, even the requirement of cultural knowledge is not insurmountable, as demonstrated by Watson, a computer programmed by IBM that played a three-day *Jeopardy* tournament against Brad Rutter and Ken Jennings. Jennings is the winningest human in the game show's history, having won seventy-four games in a row, but in a stunning demonstration of machine prowess Watson crushed both him and Rutter. After the three days the tally was Rutter with $21,600, Jennings with $24,000, and Watson with $77,147. Jennings appeared to embrace the power of computers and his new irrelevance, writing "I, for one, welcome our new computer overlords" as one of his final *Jeopardy* responses. A similar fate befell chess grandmaster Garry Kasparov in a 1997 tournament when he lost at the "hands" of IBM's Deep Blue.* The scope of computers appears to be ever expanding, but they still cannot beat the Turing test—at least not yet.

Passing the Turing test may be difficult when we're actively evaluating entities for machineness, but we seldom do this in real life. If you were to say, "That cashier seemed nice enough, but I just can't shake the feeling that she's a robot," your friends would think you were paranoid. We generally go through life thinking that others are members of the mind club, and it's only extreme events—like seeing a head full of circuit boards—that make us revise that assumption. This means that the task of machines is made even

....

* Kasparov was much less gracious than Jennings in defeat and accused IBM of cheating.

easier by the presence of social schemas, which we introduced earlier in our discussion of why we are polite to computers. These schemas set clear scripts about how interactions should go, and as long as they are followed, you would never think about evaluating someone else for humanness.

Consider the very clear script of drive-through fast food—it's a safe bet that the order could be taken by a machine in 99 percent of cases. Or consider the robot psychotherapist Eliza, programmed between 1964 and 1966.[26] As therapists usually let their clients talk—and ask only enough questions to keep them talking—people could speak to Eliza for some time before realizing "she" wasn't human. You could probably put your mother on the phone with Eliza and be just fine. "How does that make you feel? Uh-huh. Oh, right. That's terrible. And how do you feel about that?" Of course, it gets tougher in the fullness of human interaction, but there are many scripts, including ones for interviewing, arguing, and even dating.

Take the example of Robert Epstein, who in 2006 thought that he'd try online dating. This was before it was popular and before users had complex profiles and pictures galore. Early adopters would put up a simple profile of mostly text and then e-mail each other back and forth. On one Web site, Epstein met a Russian girl named Svetlana. Over the course of a few months they discussed their feelings, their romantic hopes, and their future together. From the start Epstein was enamored with Svetlana, but over time he became suspicious—she rarely spoke about her life in Russia, instead just asking him questions and writing generic romantic sentiments. When he did a more rigorous Turing-style test to ferret out her humanness, Svetlana failed. He had been falling in love with a bot.[27]

Of course, you might think that even if Svetlana had completely succeeded, there was still the matter of meeting up in person. If Epstein had flown to Russia for a surprise visit, he wouldn't have seen a tall, blond Slavic woman, but instead a grungy gray box and an old CRT monitor. How close are we to making a human-looking robot? Closer than you think, but before we get there, we first have to overcome one mountain—or valley.

Animated movies have been around for a century, but animation has come a long way from *Steamboat Willie*, the first Mickey Mouse film, released in 1928. For one thing, films today feature not only color but also 3-D animation and computer-generated effects. With the latest in technology, programmers can make animated characters look almost fully human. "Almost" is an important qualifier. Human is great, but *almost* human is not. When Warner Bros. released *The Polar Express*—a Christmas feature with an almost-human animated Tom Hanks—people were unnerved and the movie flopped. The animated Tom Hanks was certainly based on the actor, and it had the voice of the actor, but its skin was a little too gray, its lips not quite expressive. It was *creepy*.

More technically, the appearance of Hank's character fell into the *uncanny valley*, the no-man's-land between human and nonhuman. The uncanny valley was first charted in 1970 by Masahiro Mori, a Japanese robotics engineer who was interested in the appearance of robots.[28] He predicted that people would like robots when they looked more lifelike, but at some point they would become too lifelike and people would stop liking them. He also predicted that once they looked completely human, people would start liking them again. It is this dip in liking that he labeled the uncanny valley—when something is almost but not quite human.

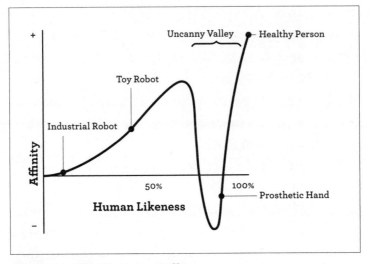

Figure 13: The Uncanny Valley
The least liked items are those that are similar to human, while maintaining an eerie nonhumanness.

M. MORI, K. F. MACDORMAN, AND N. KAGEKI, "THE UNCANNY VALLEY" (FROM THE FIELD), *ROBOTICS AND AUTOMATION MAGAZINE*, IEEE 19 (2012), 98–100. REPRINTED WITH PERMISSION.

Since Mori proposed the uncanny valley, multiple studies have confirmed its existence. People enjoy both cute robot faces and real human faces, but when the two are fused together to make an intermediate human/robot face, liking drops steeply.[29] Monkeys also detect the uncanny valley, as they prefer real monkey faces and highly caricatured monkey faces more than intermediate real/not-real monkey faces.[30] Of course, monkeys can't tell you why they don't like these hybrid faces, but many researchers have ideas about why the uncanny valley occurs.

One idea behind the uncanny valley is that people like clear lines between any two categories, including human and robot. In this view, a humanlike robot is unnerving because we don't know whether to call it human and ask for a hug or call it robot and ask

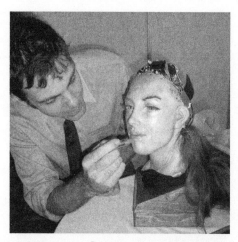

Figure 14: An Almost-Human Robot
A designer at Human Emulation Robotics
applies lipstick to a mechanical female.
Such robots are creepy because of
misplaced perceptions of experience.

it to crush a soda can in its metallic grip.[31] If this is true, then blurring *any* category lines should be unsettling, even mundane categories such as types of snack foods. However, people happily purchase Pretzel Crisps (a combination of pretzels and chips), suggesting that there is something special about the categories of "living" and "nonliving."[32]

Why is the living/nonliving category boundary so unique? One possibility is that evolution has endowed us with clear expectations of what living things should look like, and the gray skin and dead eyes of almost-humans conflict with these expectations. For example, we generally expect living creatures to have faces, which is why the star-nosed mole—which lacks conventional facial features—is so unsettling. (See figure 15.)

In a milder form, expectations about living entities may underlie the feelings we get when we meet someone with an extra finger

Figure 15: The Star-Nosed Mole
When something violates our fundamental expectations (i.e., animals should have faces), the result is unsettling.

or with a bizarre double joint. Although people who can touch their ear to their tailbone are unsettling, the uncanniness of humanlike robots is even deeper; it extends beyond specific features to the central question of whether machines are living or not.*[33] Because of the tight link between being alive and having a mind, we wondered if the uncanniness of humanlike robots revolved around mind perception.

Specifically, we predicted that humanoid robots are unnerving because their humanlike appearance implies a humanlike mind, which people are unwilling to give them. Although we are happy to see mind in animals that look and act human, the presence of a mind in an otherwise inanimate object may be an unsettling

....
* This idea was first suggested in 1906 by psychologist Ernst Jentsch, who was quoted in Sigmund Freud's essay "The Uncanny."

mismatch, like a toddler smoking. But what *kind* of mind is unsettling in robots—agency or experience? The mind survey provides a
hint. Human minds are perceived to possess both agency and experience, but robots are typically ascribed only agency, suggesting that
experience is off-limits to robots.

Except for evil, world-dominating science-fiction robots, people accept the idea of agentic robots that make cars, clean houses,
control traffic lights, and predict economic turmoil. In contrast, it's
hard to imagine robots feeling anything. It's not for nothing that we
use the word "robotic" to refer to someone who goes through life
without feeling much. This reasoning implies that humanoid robots
are unsettling when their appearance leads us to infer the capacity
for experience. Feeling is for the living only; robots need not apply.
We will happily admit humans and animals to the experience
section of the mind club, but machines can join only the agency
section.

To examine the role of experience in creating the uncanny valley, we had participants view one of two videos of a humanoid robot.
One video was filmed from behind the robot, so that only wires
and circuit boards were visible. The second was filmed from the
front, showing the robot's human face. Participants then rated their
feeling of uncanniness and the robot's ability to think and act
(i.e., agency) and sense and feel (i.e., experience). As predicted, the
humanlike robot was more disturbing, and this effect was explained
by the fact that people saw it as more capable of experience.[34] It
seems that eyes and mouth conveyed an inappropriately elevated
capacity for experience.[35]

If perceptions of experience are the driving force behind the
uncanny valley, then robots with the capacity to feel should be
unsettling even without a human face. We tested and confirmed this

prediction experimentally, revealing that people were unnerved by even the *idea* of a feeling machine.[36] In a related study, philosophers Justin Sytsma and Edouard Machery asked people whether a robot could sense a variety of smells.[37] People had no problem saying that a machine could sense the chemical isoamyl acetate, but they were hesitant to give the robot the ability to smell bananas or vomit because these are inherently emotional smells.

These studies suggest that we are happy to have a robot work in our factories, as long as it doesn't fall in love with our daughter. If experience is completely off-limits to machines, it also suggests a different understanding of the uncanny valley from the figure first drawn by Mori. In that original figure, sufficiently humanlike robots rose out of the uncanny valley to again become liked. However, if

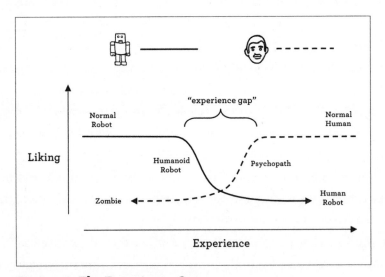

Figure 16: The Experience Gap
More accurately, the uncanny valley should be called an "experience gap"—people find creepy both machines with experience and humans without experience.

we fundamentally expect robots to lack experience—regardless of their appearance—then even fully human-looking robots should be seen as unsettling if they convey emotions. Instead of an uncanny valley, this would suggest an "experience gap,"[38] which can never be overcome as long as you are still classified as a machine.

Of course, as with any scientific rule, there often seem to be counterexamples, and people frequently mention Data from *Star Trek: The Next Generation* and Scarlett Johansson's character from the movie *Her*, as both seem to be machines with full experience. In fact, neither of these cases refutes the experience gap because they are not fully human robots but instead fully human *humans*. Data is actually Brent Spiner with lots of makeup, and we have to consciously remind ourselves that the character is a robot. As for *Her*, audiences are willing to empathize with a man who falls in love with an operating system, but likely only because the operating system has the voice of Scarlett Johansson, an actress renowned for her sensuality. If the operating system were voiced by the robotic voice of Siri or even the human voice of Judi Dench, it wouldn't have worked. In fact, the movie was originally shot with Samantha Morton as the voice of the operating system, before director Spike Jonze replaced her with the high-experience Johansson.

Just as robots with experience are unnerving, the experience gap explains why humans without experience are disturbing. When you look into the eyes of a psychopath and see nothing but cold calculation, it's hard to suppress the shiver up your spine. Even more unnerving than the unfeeling stare of a killer is a complete lack of conscious experience—a person with no inner life at all, no sensations or feelings. We have encountered these people elsewhere—they are the zombies[39] that we accused your mother of being in chapter 1, and our experiments reveal that people find the very idea of such human zombies just as unsettling as humanlike robots.[40]

The experience gap touches on a deep question about what dimension of mind perception is essential to our understanding of humanity. Through Hamlet, Shakespeare suggested that the essence of humanity was agency, the capacity to think, reason, and do:

> What a piece of work is a man! How noble in reason, how infinite in faculty! In form and moving how express and admirable! In action how like an Angel! In apprehension how like a god![41]

Conversely, George Orwell believed that the essence of humanity was experience, the capacity to feel and suffer:

> The essence of being human is that one does not seek perfection, that one is sometimes willing to commit sins for the sake of loyalty . . . and that one is prepared in the end to be defeated and broken up by life, which is the inevitable price of fastening one's love upon other human individuals.[42]

The experience gap suggests that Orwell was right, such that people fundamentally expect other people to *have* experience and fundamentally expect machines to *lack* experience.[43]

There is a sneaky way to bridge the experience gap, however. The trick is to design machines that *look* less human but *act* so human that we never pause to consider whether they are robots. No one is better at making robot experience seem natural than Rodney

Brooks, Cynthia Breazeal, and the other creative computer scientists of the MIT Media Lab.

Unlike many other roboticists, the folks at MIT didn't strive to create a robot that looked like a human adult or could converse like a human adult. Instead they sought to make a robot—which they named "Kismet"—with the emotional capacity of a young child, focusing on three specific goals.[44] First, they wanted their robot to *look* like a mind, with sensors and effectors—those cues to mind perception we saw in chapter 2 on animals. This didn't mean giving the robot an accurate (and creepy) human face but instead giving it an exaggerated human face that emphasizes key expressive features such as eyes, lips, and ears.[45] Second, they wanted their robot to

Figure 17: Kismet
The robot Kismet, now on display at the MIT Museum in Cambridge, MA.

express its mind, dynamically coordinating its facial features to convey feelings of happiness (widening eyes, smiling), sadness (drooping ears and eyes), and many other experience-related states. Third, they wanted their robot to *perceive* mind, understand the mental states of its partners, and respond accordingly. This is the most complicated element of these impressive robots and leaps the gap from preprogrammed movements to genuine conversations between you and the robot.

Beyond all the papers, patents, and technological advances achieved by the MIT team, perhaps the best indicator of their success is the fact that people felt emotions right along with the robot: when Kismet got happy or sad, so too did people interacting with it.* People were so emotionally engaged that they never stopped to think whether Kismet actually had emotions, suggesting that—out of all robots—this sociable robot comes the closest to passing the Turing test. Of course, people can tell that it is a robot, but they treat it like a human child, and actions speak louder than words. Kismet and other sociable robots seem to have crossed the robot Rubicon and are ascribed not only agency but also experience. Treating robots as vulnerable feelers raises the question of whether they are true moral patients—do robots deserve moral rights?

Many of us have given money to the SPCA—the Society for the Prevention of Cruelty to Animals—but have you ever given money to the SPCR? Founded in 1999, the mission of the Society for the Prevention of Cruelty to Robots is to "raise the awareness of the general public about some of the ethical and moral issues surrounding created intelligence." Moral rights for robots? Are they serious?

....

* There is a tendency to call Kismet "he," but its creator, Cynthia Breazeal, carefully refers to it as "it," steadfastly avoiding anthropomorphism.

Their answer: "The SPCR is, and will continue to be, exactly as serious as robots are sentient." In other words, when robots come to have their own minds, the SPCR will seek to grant those minds moral rights. This whole idea may sound preposterous, but not too long ago people would have thought the mission of the SPCA to be equally preposterous, as we saw in chapter 2 with the "recreation" of bearbaiting.

It is actually not hard to empathize with robots—all one needs are external cues of suffering. In one thought-provoking short story, Terrel Miedaner describes a man who tries to destroy a robot with a hammer.[46] The robot runs away and tries to hide, and when the man eventually connects with the hammer, the robot flips over, "whimpers," and "bleeds" red lubricating fluid. The man knows that it's "just a robot," but the final blow still feels like murder. This is the crux of the mystery surrounding the mind club: even though we consciously "know" an entity lacks experience, external cues—and the ultimate uncertainty—makes us question ourselves.

Bringing this idea into the lab, Christoph Bartneck, a roboticist in New Zealand, asked subjects to turn off—to "kill"—a robot. As people approached it, the robot began to plead for its life, and although they knew that it was just programmed to beg, still they hesitated. One woman had to steel herself to do the dirty deed, repeating, "I will switch you off. I will switch you off." Even then she balked when the robot said, "Please. You can decide to keep me switched on. Please."[47]

Likewise, it isn't easy for the comrades of military robots to let them go. You might expect soldiers to treat combat robots as "just machines," but the behavior of marines on duty in Iraq suggests otherwise. When their MARCbot—a robot designed to find and detonate explosives—was destroyed, the soldiers gave it a full funeral, complete with a twenty-one-gun salute.[48] Just like the military dogs we encountered in the last chapter, people seem to give mind to machines that do heroic deeds, even if the machines themselves aren't aware of their heroism.

Questions of robot moral patiency are mirrored by questions of robot moral agency. Robots may be perceived as thinking doers, but is that sufficient for earning moral responsibility? What do we do when a robot kills a person? This question is sharpest when it concerns drones, those sky-patrolling machines armed with missiles. Currently drones are fully controlled via satellite by a pilot, so when they kill civilians, we can blame the human mind who pulled the trigger. But what happens when the robot comes to possess enough agency to be self-directed? Perhaps we could just get rid of bad robots, euthanizing them as we do bad dogs. Eventually we might ponder robot prisons in which they sit in a cell for dozens— or hundreds—of years and think about their actions.

Rather than focus on robot retribution, people have mostly thought about how to make machines moral in the first place. Most famously, Isaac Asimov[49] imagined three rules of robots, which futuristic robots would be compelled to follow. The first was to never harm humans (or through inaction allow a human to come to harm). The second was to always obey humans. The third was to try to protect itself. These three laws were not equal, however, as earlier laws always took precedent over later laws. This means that a robot told to kill someone for you wouldn't obey, unlike a robot told to destroy itself.

Although these three laws facilitate great stories, they are impractical. For example, what constitutes harm? If a robot comes across a homeless person, is it compelled to whisk him away to a shelter? Even if that person doesn't want to be whisked away? Similarly, what happens if the robot is faced with a choice between two different harmful actions, like killing one person (e.g., a terrorist) to save the life of someone else? How could a *machine* decide what to do here when *people* can't even agree on the moral appropriateness of such an action? Just like human morality, machine morality will invariably be messy.

Whether machines will ever truly be moral, or conscious, or human, is unknown; but people certainly see them as having minds. These perceptions come not only from the cues we explored in chapter 2 on animals—eyes and expressions—but also from our own motivations of loneliness and social connection. This chapter revealed that membership in the mind club depends just as much on the mental states of the perceiver as on those of the perceived.

Nevertheless, machines *are* becoming more and more sophisticated. They are already seen as capable thinking doers and may soon also be seen as vulnerable feelers, allowing them to break out of the agency-only half of the mind club. When machines are ascribed both agency and experience, they will—from the perspective of mind perception—be human. One Thanksgiving in the future, you may find your son bringing home his girlfriend from college. When you put down a plate of turkey in front of her, she politely demurs:

"Sorry, I don't eat turkey."

"Vegetarian?" you ask, slightly annoyed.

"No," she says. "Robot. I eat only lithium hydride."

You sigh but say nothing—your son looks so in love. And she appears to love him too, so much so that years later she can't help but cry when they exchange wedding vows.

Crying and tenderness may seem out of place in a robot, but they are what primarily characterizes our next cryptomind: the patient.

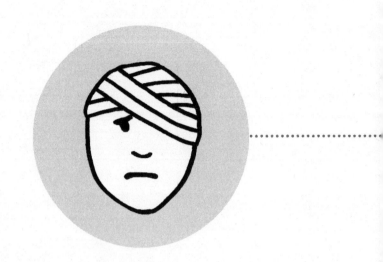

Chapter 4

THE PATIENT

A man is sleeping soundly in bed when someone creeps in and cuts off his penis. Fleeing the scene, the cutter tosses the member into a dark field. Is the perpetrator criminally guilty? Your first impulse is likely "Absolutely!" because cutting off someone's manhood seems cruel and unusual, the kind of punishment banned by the Geneva Conventions. However, a jury found the perpetrator not guilty. To understand why requires context.

As you may have guessed, the cutter is Lorena Bobbitt and the cuttee none other than her then-husband, John Bobbitt. Lorena and John had a rocky marriage, and reports suggest that John had long physically, emotionally, and sexually abused his wife.[1] On the night of the incident, John allegedly raped Lorena—not for the first time— and then fell asleep. Sometime later Lorena went to the kitchen for a glass of water and found herself picking up a knife. Feeling terrified and trapped by the endless violence, she returned to the bedroom, did the deed, and then fled, throwing the penis out the car window as she drove away. Realizing the severity of her actions, she called 9-1-1 and a police search team soon located the missing member. After nine hours of surgery, John Bobbitt and his penis were reunited.

John seemed to fully recover, starring in the adult films *John Wayne Bobbitt Uncut* and *Frankenpenis*, forming a band called the Severed Parts, and making an appearance on wrestling's *Monday Night Raw*. He also went on to abuse his next wife and to face charges of grand larceny in Nevada for stealing more than $140,000 worth of clothing. Lorena became a hairdresser and founded "Lorena's Red Wagon," a nonprofit organization dedicated to raising awareness about domestic violence.

The key question in Lorena's trial was, *who was the victim?* In most crimes the identities of agent and patient are straightforward— there is a clear perpetrator and a clear victim—but was Lorena the victim or the aggressor? Lorena did cut off John's penis, but she also suffered from his abuse. The jury decided that Lorena was not guilty, seeing her more as a vulnerable victim than as a calculating agent.

The case of Lorena and John Bobbitt suggests an important tension between seeing minds as feelers and seeing them as doers. So far we've often discussed the mind club as if one were all "in" or all "out," but our journey through animals and robots suggests that there are really two different mind clubs. Mirroring the fault line we revealed in chapter 1, there seems to be one club for thinking doers and another for vulnerable feelers.

Although adult humans might technically be members of both clubs, others tend to belong mostly to one or the other. Just as governments want dual citizens to pick only one country to pledge their fealty to, people are often perceived to be *either* thinking doers *or* vulnerable feelers. We want to think of Lorena as either the calculating shrew or the battered wife and—to complement her—of John as either the aggrieved amputee or the callous husband. This important tension will resurface later in this chapter on the *patient*, but first we must define this term.

The word "patient" usually brings to mind a medical context, in which patients are the center of a swirling galaxy of doctors, nurses, procedures, and diagnoses. More personally the word may evoke memories of trying to maintain your dignity while being poked and prodded in a gown designed to show the world your behind. But being a patient—or having patiency—is broader than just medicine. Patients are perceived to have experience and to be sensitive and susceptible to the actions of others. Whereas agents are the thinking doers of the world, patients are the vulnerable feelers. Of course, medical patients are also patients in this broader sense, but when we use the word "patient" we mean those entities at the top (and especially the top left) of the mind survey—people, children, and puppies.

Although patients are vulnerable to both good and evil—to receiving both help and harm—we are usually more concerned with the darker side of patiency. We wonder how much someone (or something) suffers, how to alleviate this distress, and whether victimization causes enduring damage. With patients the most important questions concern pain, both its experience and the right to be protected from it. But what exactly is pain, and how do we know whether others are feeling it?

Of all human experiences there is nothing more real, more

present, and more captivating than pain. Whether caused by a toothache, a thrown back, or a deep cut, pain melts away the outside world, filling your whole consciousness with its reality. Complex thoughts, plans, and memories all vanish when you slam the car door on your hand.[2] Even emotional pain, whether from a loved one's death or a sudden breakup, demands all our attention. Agency—the capacity for planning and action—may be useful for the future, but the experience of pain pushes aside everything else and focuses us on the present. Planning for retirement may be difficult, but doing so while standing in a pile of razor blades is impossible.

Pain may have overwhelming psychological power, but its physical reality is comparatively insubstantial. Pain is a mental construction based on a handful of nerve signals, the same kind of signals that let us experience green or yellow or smell lavender or chocolate. We might imagine that when in pain our cells secrete some terribly corrosive brain chemical, but the intensity of our suffering stems only from the microscopic electrical pulses of neurons. These neurons are typically triggered by external tissue damage, in a biological pathway that starts at the location of the cut, burn, or bruise, then proceeds through a neural "gate" in the spinal cord before arriving into the thalamus, the sensory hub of the brain.[3]

Despite this typical pathway, pain can be triggered by nothing at all, such as in the case of people with neuropathic pain, who live in constant agony on account of a few rogue neurons.[4] Such constant pain is excruciating, but more deadly is the inability to feel pain at all. Consider leprosy, a disease that has afflicted humans since biblical times. Leprosy causes numbness and an inability to feel pain, leaving individuals unable to realize that the pot they are holding is scalding hot or that they stepped on glass yesterday and their foot is now severely infected. Without the crucial information provided by the sensation of pain, those with leprosy cannot protect themselves from injury and so slowly lose pieces of themselves.[5]

One striking illustration of the fickleness of pain is phantom limb pain. The medical patient "D.S." experienced constant throbbing pain in his left hand, but when he went to rub it, he ran into a problem: his hand had been amputated years ago. There was no doubt that his pain was real, but without a limb to treat, conventional medicine was powerless to help. Recognizing that pain—like minds—hinges upon perception, neuroscientist V. S. Ramachandran at the University of California at San Diego developed a perceptual trick of his own,[6] constructing a special box with a mirror and two holes into which patients placed each of their arms. The mirror faced the still-present right hand, and its reflection provided D.S. with what appeared to be an intact left hand, an illusion that significantly decreased his pain.

The mind's power to influence pain reveals itself in the placebo effect, in which mere expectation of pain reduction can decrease

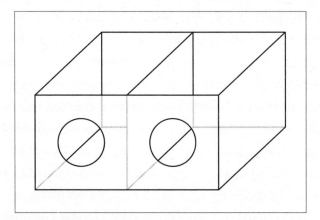

Figure 18: Ramachandran's Mirror Box
When a patient puts a healthy limb in the right side of box, their mind is tricked into perceiving two healthy limbs, alleviating phantom pains.

pain by up to 50 percent.[7] In fact, many studies of popular drugs—Tylenol or paracetamol for back pain[8] and Prozac, Effexor, or Paxil for mild depression[9]—suggest that they are no more effective than the combination of sugar pills and optimism.[10] Hopeful expectations mean that *any* treatment is bound to be somewhat effective, helping to explain the success of alternative (and largely discredited) treatments ranging from reiki[11] to reflexology.[12] Even urotherapy—a fancy name for pee drinking—has been endorsed by J. D. Salinger,[13] Madonna,[14] and Jorge Posada[15] solely on the strength of the placebo effect.[16]

The influence of expectations, however, can also increase pain through the "nocebo effect." In one study people felt real pain after researchers put sham electrodes onto their heads and pretended to send electric current through them.[17] In a more subtle demonstration by Dutch researchers Arnoud Arntz and Lily Claassens,[18] participants were instructed to touch a very cold (–25° C) metal probe. If you've ever licked a frozen pole, you know that extreme cold not only is painful but also strangely feels like burning.[19] Arntz and Claassens capitalized on this ambiguity, telling participants that the metal was either very hot or very cold. They predicted that the identical "hot" probe would hurt more than the "cold" probe because people associate extreme heat with harm more than they do extreme cold. These predictions were confirmed, as "burning" hurt more than "freezing," again demonstrating the power of expectations to shape pain.

Neuroimaging studies suggest that pain has two distinct components, a sensory component and an affective component. The sensory component represents actual tissue damage and the "burning," "cutting," and "throbbing" aspects of pain.[20] The affective component of pain is its felt badness, its aversiveness or unpleasantness.

These two components are usually related—burning sensations are seldom pleasant—but they can be dissociated. For example, morphine eliminates the aversive affect while keeping the sensory experience.[21] In one account of the effect of morphine, a car-accident victim calmly describes his experience of traumatic injury as "pain . . . but not painful,"[22] with dulled unpleasantness but intact specific sensations.

Even without drugs, tissue damage may not automatically translate to pain. In a classic account from the Korean War, physician Henry Beecher observed that grievously injured soldiers often felt no pain—and refused morphine—because of the intense rush of battle. The disconnect between physical damage and mental discomfort means that other people's pain is especially shrouded in mystery. Pain—like all forms of experience—is felt only from the inside and so is ultimately inaccessible to others. Of course, that doesn't stop people from trying to understand when others might be in pain.

There are two routes through which we can understand the experience of others, whether it involves pain, pleasure, or the taste of fish. The first route is illustrated by the question "Does Jennifer like pickled sardines?" Without knowing anything about Jennifer, you've likely got an answer, and it's probably the same answer to whether *you* like pickled sardines (i.e., "no"). To understand Jennifer you use *simulation*, relying on your own imagined experiences (e.g., I don't like sardines) as a proxy for those of others (e.g., others don't like sardines).[23]

The second route is illustrated by a slightly different question, "Does Olga like sardines?" Now you might come up with a different answer (i.e., "yes"), because the name "Olga" suggests a mysterious foreigner whose tastes might swing toward slimy fish pickles. To understand Olga you use *theorizing*, which, unlike your imagination, uses explicit theories about others' minds, such as "Russians like strange foods."

Simulation is the easier of the two routes, and so we rely on theorizing only when others are very different from us (e.g., Russian), rendering invalid our self-focused simulations. Neuroscientists Anna Jenkins and Jason Mitchell demonstrated this by neuroimaging Harvard undergrads who were thinking about experiences of other students who were either similar (urban liberals) or different (rural conservatives).

Compared with thinking about dissimilar others, thinking about similar others activated brain regions linked to thinking about the self, as simulation predicts. This makes sense: if someone is like you, your experiences are good guides to theirs (and so you simulate), but if they are not like you, you're better off relying on explicit reasons to explain their behavior (and so you theorize). One wrinkle to this distinction is that people generally assume that others are like them unless they have good reason to think otherwise, which further increases the scope and frequency of simulation.[24]

Not only is simulation easier than forming explicit theories, but also people love thinking about themselves.[25] We all know someone who is too focused on their own imagined experiences to understand yours. You mention a recent beach vacation and she immediately says, "Sounds terrible. I hate the beach—all that sand, those flies, and those tacky souvenir shops." Never mind that *you* had a great time; she just can't separate her own simulation from your experience. A more technical (or Greek) synonym for this self-centeredness is *egocentrism*, which psychological research has long demonstrated in those most selfish of people—children.

The classic demonstration of egocentrism in children is the

"false belief task."[26] Imagine Diane puts her candy in her *dresser*, but while she is at school her dad moves it to the kitchen *cupboard*. Where does Diane think the candy is? If you answered, "The dresser," you are correct. Although you know the correct candy location, Diane does not—you just ascribed to her a false belief. If you answered, "The cupboard," you are wrong. You either have severe brain damage or are three years old, but in either case we're impressed that you've read this far! Children typically give this incorrect answer because they can't distinguish their own correct beliefs from Diane's false beliefs. Children are egocentric.

Before you rush to conclusions about the stupidity of children, studies reveal that adults are also egocentric. In a clever demonstration of this effect, Nick Epley and his colleagues put participants in pairs and had one of them (the foreman) ask the other (the worker) to hand them a series of everyday objects. These objects were in the squares of a five-by-five shelving unit. Some—but not all—of the squares had wooden backs, and objects in these squares could be seen only by the worker (see figure 19).

Crucially, three of the objects were toy cars—a small, a medium, and a large car—but the smallest car was hidden from the foreman's view by a wooden back. The key trial came when the foreman asked for the "small car," which from the foreman's point of view was actually the medium car. To perform correctly, participants—who were always workers—had to overcome their own egocentric experience. When the study was run with children, most of them grabbed the wrong car, unable to ignore their own knowledge about the smallest car *they* could see. When adults participated, most of them grabbed the correct car but first *looked* at the wrong car.[27] This suggests that adults remain egocentric but—unlike kids—can override that trait when necessary.

Worker's View

Figure 19: A Test of Perspective Taking
The "small" car is different from the perspective
of the worker and the foreman.

N. EPLEY, C. K. MOREWEDGE, AND B. KEYSAR, "PERSPECTIVE TAKING IN CHILDREN
AND ADULTS: EQUIVALENT EGOCENTRISM BUT DIFFERENTIAL CORRECTION,"
JOURNAL OF EXPERIMENTAL SOCIAL PSYCHOLOGY 40 (2004): 760–68.

Simulation may sometimes lead us astray, but—much more than theorizing—it makes us *care* about the mental states of others. Theorizing uses cold theories about stimuli and responses—if shocked, then pain—but simulation uses our own feelings to predict those of others. In terms of our two dimensions of mind perception, simulation is grounded in our own experience (*feeling* their pain), whereas theorizing is grounded in our own agency (*reasoning* about their pain).

It is simulation that gives rise to empathy. People have long struggled to define empathy and to determine whether it differs from sympathy or pity.[28] However, a look at the German word for empathy clears this all up: *Einfühlungsvermögen!* Empathy is simply when you *fühlung* someone else's *vermögen*—nothing more and nothing less. Now, the satisfied reader may skip ahead a few pages. But for the rest of you (and for us!) some explanation may be required.

This German word actually translates to "in-feeling" and articulates the notion of sharing in another person's feelings: feeling their pain when they are injured, feeling their anger when someone slights them, or feeling their embarrassment when they botch their big presentation. It is illustrated by Blaise Pascal, who said that "we know truth, not only by the reason, but also by the heart."[29] Empathy is about more than just dispassionately recognizing others' suffering; it is about suffering alongside them. Because suffering is aversive, empathizing with another person's pain compels you to help alleviate it. Empathy is why charity campaigns don't simply report statistics but instead show us the doleful eyes of orphaned children, so that we can connect to their minds, simulate their suffering, and open our wallets.[30]

If mental connection is necessary for empathy, then maintaining it is easiest when someone is nearby, as anyone in a long-distance relationship can attest. Skype-ing or talking on the phone is fine, but physical closeness uniquely increases caring. You can still empathize from a distance when your partner is fired, but touching their tears drives it home. The power of proximity in empathy is exemplified by this thought experiment from philosopher Peter Singer: Imagine you are walking by a pond, wearing a new three-hundred-dollar suit, when you see a drowning child.[31] Should you save the child even if doing so will ruin the suit? You likely wouldn't hesitate to dive in.

Now imagine a different scenario. You are walking down the street after payday when a charity canvasser tells you that twenty dollars will save the life of a starving African child. Chances are you would keep your money and let the child die, even though saving the child costs a fraction of the cost of the suit. Why the difference?

Empathy evolved when people lived in small groups of close relations, and so we care mostly about the visible suffering of those we know—similar others whose minds are easily simulated.[32] Such empathy is poorly suited to the modern world, in which the neediest are people of different races and religions who live far away. Simulating the mind of a Muslim goat farmer is hard, and so we care little when he suffers. To solve this problem, charities try hard to represent the minds of the needy, highlighting their hopes and dreams—and their similarities to you: ten-year-old Ebele may live in faraway Sierra Leone, but she loves school and sometimes gets annoyed with her younger brother—just like American girls!

Expressions of vulnerability are another way to compel empathy.[33] As we saw in chapter 2 on animals, expressions translate internal experiences into external signals. Pain-related expressions include screaming, yelping, grimacing, and crying, which is why babies and puppies—with their big eyes and high-pitched cries—make perfect moral patients. Both babies and puppies are also very vulnerable; they are small and have soft skin and limited mobility. They couldn't stop you from harming them and lack the agency to harm others, both characteristics of vulnerability that evoke feelings of tenderness and compassion.[34] This link between vulnerability and compassion is likely endowed by evolution to guard against frustrated parents leaving their screaming (but helpless) infants in the woods.

Our compassion for vulnerable moral patients translates into rage when they are harmed. People care when adults are injured, but they are incensed when children or animals suffer. People for the Ethical Treatment of Animals (PETA) has allegedly attacked fur-coat owners,[35] and some activists have even advocated killing scientists who experiment upon animals.[36] Even the moral righteousness of incarcerated criminals is piqued when children are harmed: they will injure or murder fellow prisoners who are convicted of crimes against children.[37] Vulnerable moral patients compel moral emotions because they fit so well into the moral dyad of "thinking doer plus vulnerable feeler."[38] Everyone looks like a culpable moral agent when standing next to a vulnerable baby or whimpering puppy.

There is a limit on empathy, however, as we can simulate only so much suffering. Consider the once-popular commercial for the SPCA in which limping dogs and disfigured cats are paired with Sarah McLachlan's slow, sad singing. In mere seconds you are instantly overwhelmed with feeling via an empathy sucker punch.

The SPCA commercial illustrates two ironies. First, people, blasé in the face of genocide, are overcome with pity for a vulnerable dog, which not only lacks the intelligence of the least capable human but also enjoys the taste of garbage. Second, while some empathy is helpful, too much is counterproductive. In a study on the "collapse of compassion," psychologists Daryl Cameron and Keith Payne presented participants with pleas from either one or eight suffering victims.[39] Despite the objectively greater total suffering of eight victims, people were overwhelmed by it and demonstrated *less* compassion. One dying puppy is sad, but a whole football field of suffering puppies is—hey, did you see that new movie about vampires in space?

Even more extreme than seeking distraction, empathy overload can make us wish for others to die. In one unpublished study from our lab led by Anna Jenkins, we described victims of horrific suffering, such as a bedridden elderly woman being engulfed in flames while her synthetic sheets melted into her skin. We varied whether the victim was awake or unconscious and asked participants whether the victim should live or die. We predicted that the active minds of awake victims would compel participants to simulate their pain, causing so much empathy that participants would recommend death.

Our results confirmed this "better off dead" prediction—people recommended death for awake victims—as did a second unpublished study in which we gave some participants energy drinks before they read about suffering. These participants were especially likely to advocate death for conscious victims because their caffeine jitters added to their emotional overload. If excess empathy makes you hope for the death of moral patients, is less empathy better? Modern medicine seems to think so.

In her poignant account of bipolar disorder, Linda Logan talks of familial disruption, of brief manic episodes with breathtaking productivity, and of longer depressive spells where she could barely rouse herself from bed. Despite these symptoms, she suffered most from losing her sense of self in the modern medical system, which downgraded her from person to mere patient—a passive recipient of care, characterized only by symptoms and suffering. Doctors ignored her complicated inner life, focusing instead on the mechanical details of neurochemistry and medication. Rather than simulating her experiences, her doctors simply relied on their explicit theories about her condition. She writes, "The moment the psych-unit doors locked behind me, I was stripped of my identity as wife, mother, teacher and writer and transformed into patient, room number and diagnosis."[40]

Unsurprisingly, medical patients are excellent examples of moral patients: they suffer and are vulnerable to harm. More than that, hospitals and clinics often treat people as *only* patients, stripping away the thoughts and plans of agency and leaving only raw experience. Think about the last time you went to the doctor's office. Were you able to explain your illness-related thoughts and opinions, or did you simply list symptoms and wait for a diagnosis and prescription? One study revealed that doctors interrupted a patient an average of twelve seconds after meeting him or her;[41] without listening to the words of patients, physicians have no hope of understanding their experiences.

One of us (Kurt) recently went to the doctor for persistent daytime sleepiness. He recalls:

> I needed a daily nap and could easily sleep twelve hours at a stretch. Colds arrived every month and lingered long, and the slightest stress further destroyed my already weak immune system. My mom had many theories about this feebleness— low vitamin D, antibiotics at birth, allergies—but one day my wife discovered the culprit. As she lay awake one night, listening to the house settling, she noticed me rasping, gasping, going completely silent, and then suddenly choking on my throat— classic signs of sleep apnea.
>
> When I explained this hypothesis to the doctor, he smirked and replied, "Well, that's for me to figure out." Sleep apnea typically plagues overweight folks, and as I am slim the doctor assumed I was mistaken. After all, he was the one with the MD.* He was the agent with the ability for action and thought,

....

* Of course, Kurt technically has a "doctorate," but when someone calls out, "Is there a doctor!?" they are rarely looking for some emergency help with experiments on mind perception.

and I was the patient with the ability only for suffering. Nevertheless, with enough information about symptoms and family history—my grandmother's snoring could destroy concrete foundations—the doctor agreed to a sleep study, which revealed that I stopped breathing once every five minutes (or approximately one hundred times a night).

It appears that sometimes patients—and their spouses—have some insight. After all, they are the only ones to experience their problems from the inside.

Of course, doctors obviously care deeply about helping others, but medicine trains them to detach in order to think rationally.[42] Too much compassion or grief clouds objective clinical judgment and can lead to emotional burnout,[43] so physicians often embrace insensitivity—especially specialty surgeons, who literally hold patients' lives in their hands. In the operating room, the patient's thoughts and feelings are irrelevant at best and paralyzing at worst as surgeons work on the delicate minutiae of the human body. This explains why surgeons hide under a sheet everything but the relevant square foot of flesh; peering into the tender faces of patients as you prepare to slice them open cannot make the job easier.

Not all doctors are surgeons, and if any physician should be concerned with thoughts and feelings, it should be psychiatrists. The root of the word "psychiatry" is *psyche*, the Greek word for "soul" or "mind," and historically psychiatrists, including Carl Jung and Sigmund Freud, have taken a deeply psychological and philosophical approach. However, recent advances in neurobiology focus attention away from human suffering and feelings and toward drugs that influence brain circuits and neurotransmitters. Psychiatry has been famously described by Thomas Szasz as *mechanomorphic*, treating patients like "defective machines" rather than feeling human beings.[44] Paradoxically, physicians of the mind may fail to see their patients as members of the mind club.

In treating mental illness, pharmaceuticals are undoubtedly powerful, but so is understanding a patient's mind from the inside, as Logan's account of bipolar disorder suggests. Research has shown that relatively mild mental illness can be improved simply by talking to empathic listeners, whether they are trained PhDs or nonpsychologist university professors.[45] This "talk therapy" can result in benefits identical to those of drug therapy and even cause identical brain changes.[46] So when a friend comes to you feeling blue or anxious, remember to listen carefully and respect both their patiency and their agency.

You could also encourage them to help others. Continually receiving help reduces self-esteem and feelings of control, leading to feelings of helplessness and reduced agency.[47] To reestablish this agency, patients need to become the givers of care, transforming into agents with increased self-confidence and personal power. It is no coincidence that twelve-step programs—whether for alcoholism or gambling addiction—involve sponsorship, in which senior members become shepherds for new members. By taking responsibility for another, you break through the mantle of victimhood, moving from one side of the mind-perception fault line to the other. Helping others turns you from a vulnerable feeler into a thinking doer.

Beyond conferring feelings of agency, a study by Stephanie Brown at the University of Michigan revealed that helping others can add years to your life. Brown examined the mortality of older people who were the primary caregivers of their ill spouses. This is an incredibly stressful role because caregivers must manage every aspect of their spouse's treatment and take ultimate responsibility for the spouse's life. As stress is linked to an early death, the obvious prediction would be that caregivers would die earlier than noncaregivers—but they lived significantly *longer*, presumably because of increased feelings of agency.[48]

Even taking care of plants can increase longevity. In one study, nursing home residents given responsibility for a houseplant outlived those who had plants that were looked after by nursing home staff.[49] This may also explain why parenthood transforms the cowardly into the brave—children are the moral patients who turn moms and dads into powerful moral agents.

Just how powerful do you become when you help others? Strong enough to lift a car, suggests the story of Alaskan teenager Riley Anderson. When Anderson arrived home from school, he found his father—the family mechanic—pinned underneath the family station wagon. The 1.5-ton Volkswagen had slipped off the jack and was now suffocating his dad. With help far away, Riley did what was needed: he took hold of the bumper and, with his bare hands, lifted the car off his father.[50] Of course, Riley was likely helped by adrenaline, but we have experimentally confirmed the link between helping others and physical strength—participants can hold a five-pound weight longer if they first donate to charity.[51]

These results suggest that personal power is not only a cause of heroism but also a consequence of it. Consider Mahatma Gandhi, who heroically helped India gain its independence from colonial rule in 1947. An examination of Gandhi's early life suggests that he was born with no more agency than anyone else, with an unremarkable merchant-class childhood.[52] However, as he strove for national freedom, he became able to endure hunger strikes that few of us can imagine. These feats of agency are even more amazing considering that Gandhi was first a moral patient, suffering discrimination and beatings at the hands of the European ruling class. By committing himself to helping others, he turned from patient to agent, a process we call *moral transformation*.

Even if you're not fighting colonial oppression, the link between moral agency and personal power tells us how to better run marathons (do it for charity) and how to focus better at work (help your colleagues).[53] Of course, moral agents include not only heroes but also villains—does evil also increase agency? Studies from our lab suggest that the answer is yes.

We asked participants to write fictional stories about themselves either helping others (hero), harming others (villain),* or just getting work done (neutral), all while holding a five-pound weight. Compared with the neutral condition, we found *both* our experimentally induced heroes and villains could hold the weight longer. Of course, there are many reasons to prefer goodness to cruelty, but if you want to establish your own agency, evil appears to do the trick. We can't condone real cruelty, but try vividly imagining cleaning the toilet with your lazy roommate's toothbrush or giving your boss's BMW a quick swipe with your keys.

Throughout this chapter the savvy reader may have noticed a general rule. It seems that being a moral patient reduces agency, and being a moral agent reduces patiency. When we see others—and ourselves—as vulnerable feelers, it is hard to see them as thinking doers; and when we see others—and ourselves—as thinking doers, it is hard to see them as vulnerable feelers. This inverse relation

----

* Did "villains" write about true evilness? You bet. One person wrote about taking the pen, stabbing the male research assistant in the neck, and then sexually assaulting the female research assistant. Add one point for experimental validity, and subtract a million points for human nature.

between perceptions of agency and patiency (i.e., experience) is called *moral typecasting*. Moral typecasting is a reflection of the mind-perception fault line we revealed back in chapter 1, the border that splits the mind club into two, separating thinking doers from vulnerable feelers.

Typecasting is a frequent phenomenon in Hollywood, where the lovable jokester can't be taken seriously in a dramatic role and the goofy best friend can't be the main love interest. Perhaps the most powerful example of this was Leonard Nimoy as Spock. In real life Leonard Nimoy was passionate and playful, but people forever saw him as a cold and unfeeling personality because he played a Vulcan on *Star Trek*. Chafing against this typecasting, Nimoy entitled his first autobiography *I Am Not Spock*, but in the end he resigned himself to the role's power and entitled his second autobiography *I Am Spock*.

Just as we typecast actors into enduring character roles, so too do we often typecast people in enduring *moral* roles, seeing them as *either* those who do moral deeds *or* those who receive them. More succinctly, we see others as *either* moral agents *or* moral patients. It is hard to imagine Joseph Stalin as a victimized moral patient because of all the evil he committed. Likewise, it is hard to imagine a poor orphan as a responsible moral agent because of all the suffering she feels. As a more visual example, take a look at figure 20. When you see it as a duck, you cannot see it as a rabbit; when you see it as a rabbit, you cannot see it as a duck. Moral typecasting is this phenomenon applied to morality and mind perception: when you see someone as a moral agent, you are blind to their patiency, and when you see someone as a moral patient, you are blind to their agency.

Given the tight link between morality (agents and patients) and

Figure 20: Either Duck or Rabbit, but Not Both
One can be a moral agent or moral patient, but not both.
(Translation: Which animals are most like each other?
Rabbit and duck.)

mind perception (agency and experience), moral typecasting means that agents are seen as especially capable of agency but especially *incapable* of experience. Typecasting also means that patients are seen as especially capable of experience but especially *incapable* of agency. Of course—unlike the rabbit-duck—perceptions of people are seldom all or nothing, but moral typecasting suggests that heroes and villains should seem relatively insensitive to suffering, and victims should seem relatively incapable of responsibility. Studies in our lab confirm this idea. Both good moral agents (e.g., Mother Teresa) and bad moral agents (e.g., Hitler) were seen to be relatively impervious to pain, whereas victimized moral patients were seen as relatively blameless for misdeeds.[54] Each of these aspects of

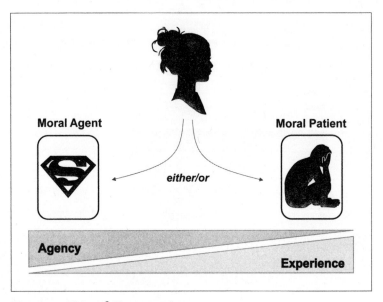

Figure 21: Moral Typecasting
We see heroes and villains as insensitive to suffering and we see victims and beneficiaries as incapable of earning blame.

K. GRAY, L. YOUNG, AND A. WAYTZ, "MIND PERCEPTION IS THE ESSENCE OF MORALITY," *PSYCHOLOGICAL INQUIRY* 23 (2012): 101-24.

moral typecasting—agents seeming insensitive and patients seeming blameless—has important implications.

That heroes and villains seem insensitive to pain can make us treat them poorly. For very evil criminals we demand proportionately harsh punishment—not only to atone for their sins but also to overcome their perceived toughness and ensure they suffer enough. That we are especially cruel to the especially cruel is not surprising, but we sometimes seem to mistreat those we admire, easily forgetting the sacrifices of our heroes. We neglect the feelings of our parents, the trials of our mentors, and the suffering of our leaders.

Going back to the idea of schemas (i.e., mental models) from chapter 3 on machines, our schema for heroes is grounded in moral typecasting—those who do good seem tougher than us and better able to endure life's tribulations. This "moral agent only" schema means that the suffering of heroes is less salient and less demanding of empathy than that of others. When a normal person is punched, our heart leaps, but when Superman or Batman gets punched, we shrug it off because we expect them to do the same. If heroes seem tougher than most, then we may be more likely to give them pain. Admittedly, people seldom enjoy betraying the saintly, but often when push comes to shove—when *someone* has to be harmed— people harm their heroes.

We tested this idea in our lab, asking people to imagine possessing pain pills—not pain-relieving pills but pain-*causing* pills—with one pill causing mild discomfort and four pills causing excruciating (but temporary) pain. Participants divided three pills between pairs of people, which included good agents (Mother Teresa), bad agents (serial killer Ted Bundy), neutral targets (a bank teller), and moral patients (an orphan). In many pairs the division of pills was unsurprising: people gave more pain to Ted Bundy than to the orphan.

The key pair was the bank teller versus Mother Teresa, because it contrasted two competing predictions. Giving less pain to the nun would reward her good deeds, supporting the idea of karma and just deserts (i.e., good things happen to good people). Alternatively, giving Mother Teresa *more* pain would support moral typecasting, revealing that people allocate pain based on mind perception and moral roles.

Typecasting won the day: people gave more pain to Mother Teresa than to the bank teller. Admittedly, they weren't happy about it. While making these decisions, people laughed nervously and asked questions like "Are you sure I can't just split a pill in half?" But at the end of the day, people stuck it to the elderly nun who'd devoted her life to helping others.[55] How's that for justice?

Of course, you might reason that Mother Teresa can actually handle the pain, but imagine a meeting at work where someone is being selected to develop client relationships in Siberia. Chances are the person packing her parka will be the person who has a history of doing previously thankless tasks. If you've done past good deeds, others see you as capable of handling terrible burdens that no one else wants to bear—whether that perception is true or false. So next time your selflessness is praised in front of others, beware: making sacrifices for others makes it easier for them to sacrifice you.

That moral agents seem incapable of being vulnerable feelers is the first principle of moral typecasting. That moral patients seem incapable of being (blameworthy) thinking doers is the second principle. For its illustration we again turn to celebrities.

When the rich and famous run afoul of the law, they follow a predictable script. The opening act is the crime itself: Mr. Celebrity is pulled over for swerving all over the road in a car that costs more than your house. After attempting to hide a bag of drugs under the passenger seat, Mr. Celebrity stumbles out of his car and eloquently explains to the police that the drugs are not his fault but instead that of a convenient ethnic group, such as Canadians or leprechauns. The next act is their mug shot, indictment, and the predictable Twitter explosion.

The following act is the victim act. The celebrity's spokesperson provides a statement such as "Mr. Celebrity has long been a victim of drug use, alcoholism, and depression arising from difficult childhood circumstances. Mr. Celebrity extends a sincere apology to all leprechauns and those of leprechaun descent and will be spending the next couple of months out of the public eye, recovering from this terrible constellation of diseases." In other words, although Mr. Celebrity seems like a rich, entitled racist, that's just not true! Instead he or she is a victim who, despite all the cars, money, and fame, feels only pain. Of course, celebrities—like everyone else—do struggle with mental-health and addiction issues, but these patient-oriented qualities are trotted out only to dodge blame. The key is that this strategy works—victims *do* escape blame!

Typecasting provides the basis for this winning strategy. When someone is cast as a victimized moral patient—a vulnerable feeler— it is difficult to simultaneously see him or her as an agent responsible for wrongdoing. This explains why defendants on trial often testify to the suffering or abuse they experienced in their lives,[56] such as in the case of Lorena Bobbitt. More recently a wealthy Texas teen who killed four people while driving drunk avoided jail time because he was a victim of "affluenza." His lawyer successfully argued that his impaired judgment was a result not of his blood alcohol content of 0.24 but of his sheltered and privileged—and therefore difficult—upbringing.[57]

Studies from our lab confirm victims' ability to escape blame. Participants gave less blame to moral patients (e.g., a victim of crime) than to neutral targets or even good agents (e.g., a life-saving doctor) after committing a bad deed such as vandalism.[58] Consistent with moral typecasting, this reduced blame was driven by mind perception, such that victims were seen as vulnerable feelers, and these perceptions of victimhood led to clemency.

The most surprising extension of this side of typecasting is that highlighting past good deeds can be counterproductive, at least when guilt is certain. Past good deeds reinforce agency, responsibility,

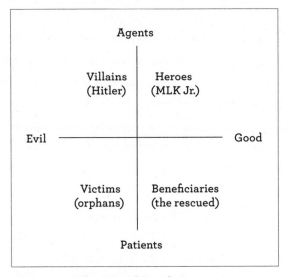

Figure 22: The Moral Landscape
We often divide morality into good and evil, but
typecasting suggests that whether someone is
seen as a moral agent or patient can sometimes be
even more important.

and control, explaining why it is all but impossible to forgive the
misdeeds of priests and presidents. On the other hand, victimization turns people into blameless moral patients, explaining why we
discount the transgressions of the abused and afraid. In this sense,
although it seems that good is the opposite of evil, the mind-
perception gap between agents and patients creates a different moral
landscape: good and evil are both the opposite of victimhood. It
may be relatively easy for a do-gooder to turn evil or for a victim to
become a beneficiary, but it is much harder to turn—at least in the
eyes of others—from a victim to a villain or from a villain to a victim.

Typecasting also explains why children receive less blame for
misdeeds: their reasoning and self-control are not fully developed
until adulthood, but their capacity for suffering and harm exists

from birth. Even looking like a child can lead to less blame. In a series of studies on facial structure, researcher Leslie Zebrowitz found that those who have "baby faces," with big eyes and round cheeks, were given less blame in small-claims court for intentional wrongs.[59]

Typecasting has a limit, however, when the deed is sufficiently evil. When two ten-year-old boys lured British toddler James Bulger away from his parents and then tortured and murdered him, the public saw the boys as agents, demanding that they be tried as adults.[60] Despite the young age of the offenders, the murder was so heinous, and the victim was such an extreme patient—a helpless two-year-old—that our minds cannot help but see them as agents. Just as in the case of the evil pig and the dead peasant baby in chapter 2 on animals, dyadic completion compels us to see as villains those typically lacking agency when someone even more helpless suffers.

Dyadic completion can also induce perceptions of suffering in the face of sin. So far we have explored dyadic completion from patient to agent—when vulnerable victims compel us to see thinking doers—but it also happens in reverse. When someone commits an evil act, a dyadic template compels us to see suffering victims, even if the act is objectively harmless. For illustration consider the case of Anita Bryant.

Anita Bryant used to be a country singer. In the 1950s and 1960s she had a couple of Billboard hits, including "Till There Was You" and "Paper Roses." As a former Miss Oklahoma, she was also pretty and charismatic, which helped her become the spokesperson for the Florida Citrus Commission.* Anita also had strong views on

....

* Her catchphrase was "Breakfast without orange juice is like a day without sunshine."

homosexuality: she was horrified by the advancement of gay rights and particularly incensed by the passage of a Florida law that forbade discrimination on the basis of sexual orientation. She vowed to repeal it, sensing a slippery moral slope: "If gays are granted rights, next we'll have to give rights to prostitutes and to people who sleep with Saint Bernards and to nail biters."[61] She was eventually successful in repealing the law, but her campaign of homophobia had irreparably damaged her reputation, costing her her singing career, her marriage, and the goodwill of Florida citrus farmers.

To Bryant homosexuality wasn't simply wrong; it was also *harmful.* She believed it would lead to the destruction of America as she knew it and titled her autobiography *The Anita Bryant Story: The Survival of Our Nation's Families and the Threat of Militant Homosexuality.* In her mind, because homosexuals couldn't easily have their own children, they would recruit the sons and daughters of God-fearing heterosexual parents. These recruits would be brainwashed by the charismatic gays and become gay too, eventually leading to the demise of the family.

Decades later many still believe that homosexuality spells disaster for America. In 2012 North Carolina pastor Michael Barrett suggested that failing to ban gay marriage would be "equivalent to a nuclear holocaust." And when the U.S. Supreme Court struck down the Defense of Marriage Act, a Christian newspaper heralded the decision as a harbinger of Armageddon.*[62]

To those who see sexual orientation as a matter of biology and

....

* Bryant and Barrett were prescient: History shows that gay rights lead to famine, nuclear war, and anarchy. Or perhaps instead to reduced crime and rising property values. D. Christafore and S. Leguizamon, "The Influence of Gay and Lesbian Coupled Households on House Prices in Conservative and Liberal Neighborhoods," *Journal of Urban Economics* 71 (2012): 258–67.

not morality, claims of its harmfulness seem hyperbolic, but the moral dyad suggests that *perceptions* of harm are legitimate, even if disconnected from objective harm. Just as—despite many cues to mind—the objective criteria for mind-having are unclear, objective criteria for harm are also often elusive. Of course, there are some obvious cues to direct physical and emotional harm, such as bloodshed, crying, and death, but not all harm is so transparent. Gay marriage seems not to cause death and dismemberment, but how are we to objectively disprove the idea that gay marriage causes "societal decay" or "spiritual damnation"? These kinds of harm are a matter of perception and are perceived when people see immorality. Such harm may seem nebulous, but people often see a direct link between this abstract harm and more direct suffering—a weakened America is more vulnerable to terrorists or race riots. Evil deeds inevitably create perceived suffering victims.

The researcher Peter DeScioli has an elegant name for this kind of "agent to patient" dyadic completion—the "indelible victim effect"—and it is ubiquitous.[63] Those who see drug use as wrong think it harms teenagers; those who see flag burning as wrong think it harms disabled veterans; and those who see masturbation as wrong think it harms children. Suffering children are actually a common theme in moral uproar, because their status as vulnerable feelers makes them obvious moral patients.

Research from our lab conducted with Chelsea Schein shows that perceptions of victimhood arise not from effortful justification but automatically from our dyadic moral minds. In one study participants read about "harmless" misdeeds, such as defiling a corpse or using strange masturbation techniques, and then rated their harmfulness. Participants not only saw these wrongs as generally harmful but saw even *more* harm when given a strict time limit that precluded conscious reasoning. Another study in the same set revealed that people perceived more suffering in the faces of children—within milliseconds—after reading about masturbation and necrophilia.[64]

If harm automatically accompanies judgments of immorality, then dyadic completion casts doubt on the very existence of "victimless wrongs." Harmless wrongs may be a logical possibility but—psychologically speaking—are exceedingly rare; only those who fail to see immorality fail to see harm. Because perceptions of harm are ever present in moral judgments, harm provides a powerful way of understanding morality across cultures.

It is clear that different people have different morals. Muslims believe it's immoral to eat pigs but happily eat hamburgers, and Hindus think it's immoral to eat cows but happily eat bacon. Conservatives believe it's immoral to burn an American flag, whereas liberals think of it as an expression of free speech.[65] These and many other differences in morality often lead to disagreement and conflict, and sometimes even war. Some suggest an unbridgeable moral chasm between different cultures—like conservatives and liberals[66]—but mind perception suggests a bridge of understanding.

People may disagree over what exactly is wrong, but our studies find that all people have the same dyadic moral mind. Both liberals and conservatives agree that immorality causes harm, and this similarity may be the key to finding other common ground. We often talk of "perspective taking" as a way to understand moral disagreements, and the moral dyad provides a specific way for taking others' perspectives. When confronted with an opposing moral viewpoint, try to understand how this act could be seen as harmful. If nothing else, remember that the "other side" isn't inventing harms merely to inflame passions and fearmonger—those who oppose something on moral grounds legitimately see it as causing suffering.

The slipperiness of suffering has been the theme of this chapter. Out of all mental capacities, the ability to feel pain is the most crucial for admission into the mind club. Those who seem capable of suffering are moral patients and deserve moral rights. Unfortunately, out of all mental capacities, the ability to feel pain may be the most cryptic. To understand this very internal sensation, we rely on both simulation and theories about other minds—both of which are flawed.

Although we never like our pain to be ignored, when it comes to define us, we become a true patient, stripped of agency and seen only as a vulnerable feeler. This tension between being seen as doer and being seen as feeler stems from moral typecasting, our tendency to view others as *either* moral agents *or* moral patients. Being cast as a patient can help us escape blame and compel others to protect us, but it can also weaken us and even shorten our lives. Moral patients not only form the natural complement to moral agents but also provide a powerful way to understand moral disagreements, as people everywhere link immorality to perceived harm.

One thread running through our discussion of moral patients is that we *care* about them. Whether they are children, animals, or adults, and whether they suffer physically, mentally, or spiritually, we want to alleviate their pain. The same can't be said for our next cryptomind. This cryptomind is one whose suffering we shrug off with cold indifference and whose torture we often embrace: the enemy.

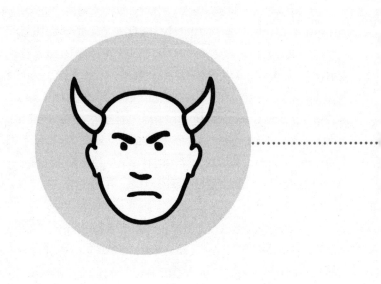

Chapter 5
THE ENEMY

Michael Johnson enlisted in the U.S. Army after high school because of his love of country and belief in democracy. On his very first mission, he was captured by Muslim extremists and held for more than ten years. He was imprisoned in a small, cold cell, and when his captors wanted information, they beat him, punching him in the mouth, ribs, and back. Once, they blindfolded him, threw him into a powerboat, and beat him while driving in circles. One extremist would make him drink salt water and slam his head against the side of the boat while another kept punching him. He received only enough first aid to survive for the next day of torture. His captors would stop at nothing until he revealed everything he knew—even if he knew nothing.

This account likely filled you with empathy for Johnson and rage toward the Muslim extremists, but it isn't quite true. In the real account, it wasn't Michael Johnson who was captured but a Muslim man named Mohamedou Ould Slahi,[1] who was suspected to have some connection with the events of 9/11. To allay these suspicions, Slahi voluntarily presented himself for questioning shortly after the attacks, and although he was cleared by Jordanian intelligence, he somehow found himself shipped to an American air force base in Afghanistan before ending up in Guantanamo Bay, Cuba. Once there, he experienced the torture outlined above, all at the hands of Americans who presumably have stories similar to that of the fictional Michael Johnson—who loved their country, democracy, their friends, and families. How could these otherwise caring men and women[2] torture an innocent man for an entire decade?

In previous chapters we've seen that people have difficulty *not* perceiving minds, seeing thoughts in animals, goals in robots, and emotions in inanimate objects. Accordingly, you might think it inevitable that we see minds in other people, who almost certainly have the ability to think and feel. This is true when it is *our* people— our inner circle of friends and family. But when people lie outside this circle—especially when they are our enemies—we easily strip away their minds, seeing them not as human beings but as dumb beasts, cold machines, or insensate objects. We are only too happy to expel those we dislike from the mind club.

In contrast to anthropomorphism, which involves the ascription of human qualities to animals and objects, this chapter explores dehumanization, the denial of human qualities to other people. At its most extreme, dehumanization enables systemic discrimination and genocide, but it also occurs in everyday life, such as when we ignore the experience of the homeless or the agency of the beautiful. The most reliable predictor of dehumanization is antipathy—seeing someone as your enemy.

Some enemies are a matter of blood, such as in the feud between the Hatfields and the McCoys, which left eleven family members dead from shootings, stabbings, and beatings.[3] Some enemies are a matter of religious belief, with many killed in the battles of Muslims versus Hindus, Christians versus Muslims, and Catholics versus Protestants. Perhaps the most intractable conflict today is between Israelis and Palestinians, two peoples separated by culture, race, religion, language, and history. With so many differences and so much historical antagonism, conflict seems all but inevitable. People have divided into "us versus them" based on much less. How much less?

To answer this question, social psychologists have created the "minimal-groups paradigm," in which people are divided by arbitrary criteria such as shirt color[4] or modern art preference.[5] One study (randomly) divided participants into two groups—Kandinsky lovers and Klee lovers—before they distributed resources among themselves.[6] As predicted, the "Kandinsky" people took more for themselves and sabotaged the "Klee" people, and vice versa, despite their meaningless and made-up division.

Even more arbitrary, another related experiment showed participants hundreds of dots and asked them to guess the number.[7] Conforming to laws of probability, half underestimated the number and half overestimated the number, and researchers labeled participants either dot "underestimators" or "overestimators." As before, people were kind to their own group but cruel to the other group: "Sure, he may look friendly, but I don't want my taxes going to a dot overestimator!" This favoritism may seem absurd, but likely no more absurd than arguments between Catholics and Protestants sound to atheists or debates between academics sound to nonacademics.

Perhaps the most elegant minimal-groups study was conducted

in 1968 by Mrs. Jane Elliott, a third-grade teacher in rural Iowa. Following the assassination of Martin Luther King Jr., she wanted her students to learn firsthand about the pernicious effects of prejudice. As her students were all white and Christian, she made a new racial distinction—proclaiming that children with brown eyes were inferior to children with blue eyes. In no time the blue-eyed children grew smug and powerful and treated their brown-eyed classmates with condescension and cruelty, seeing them as less than human. Many dark-eyed children took this mistreatment to heart, believing that their eye color justified the callousness of their cerulean-eyed masters. Other brown-eyed children chafed under this subjugation, acting out against the society that devalued them. Based on one simple statement about the value of iris pigmentation, Mrs. Elliott had created a robust racial structure remarkably similar to that of modern America.[8]

Along similar lines, social psychologist Muzafer Sherif conducted the classic "Robber's Cave" study at a boys' summer camp. The camp had two clusters of cabins divided by a small forest, and boys were randomly assigned to one side, "the Eagles," or the other, "the Rattlers." In short order the boys had bonded strongly within their own groups and held nothing but contempt toward the other group, despite being fundamentally all the same.[9] In real life, boys no older than those of the Robber's Cave study are told that they are a Crip (blue) or a Blood (red) and are expected to show unwavering allegiance to their brothers and ruthless cruelty to their rivals. The boys from Sherif's study used sticks and stones to claim the forest as their own, whereas those in gangs use handguns to claim drug-distribution territory, but the psychological underpinnings are the same. Superficial differences grow to be extremely meaningful, leading group members to deny their rivals minds and moral rights.

Whether in real life or in experiments, intergroup conflict arises from different identities. You and your friends are black, French, atheist dot overestimators, whereas "they" are all white, Russian, religious dot underestimators. The divisive power of identity suggests that its elimination might erase the conflict between people. If people were truly "color-blind," as well as "religion-blind" and "dot-estimation-blind," would they still form "us" and "them"? Our research suggests that they would. Even without identity, group formation is as easy as 1-2-3.

To get groups to form in a population of people, you need only three elements. The first is the *opportunity for kindness or cruelty*, situations in which two people can interact either nicely or nastily. The second is *reciprocity*, the technical term for paying people back. Reciprocity is when you are friendly to people who treat you nicely and unfriendly to people who treat you nastily. Over time reciprocity can make for best friends or mortal enemies. Imagine that the first time you meet someone, they compliment your clothes. This leads to a feedback cycle in which you compliment them and the two of you talk about your common interests, grab coffee, see movies together, and become lifelong friends. Conversely, imagine that the first time you meet someone, they insult your clothes. This starts a very different feedback cycle in which you insult their clothes and the two of you spread vicious rumors about each other, vandalize each other's homes, and seduce each other's spouses.

To move beyond individual friends and enemies to groups of "us" and "them," we need the third element, *transitivity*. Transitivity means sharing your friends' opinion of others—liking your friends' friends and disliking your friends' enemies. Transitivity is typically established via gossip, in which two people discuss the deeds of mutual acquaintances and align their perceptions accordingly. "Did you hear about Becky?" "She's so sneaky." "I hate her!" "Me too!" When transitivity doesn't hold, awkwardness results—just try making fun of your best friend's spouse or your spouse's best friend.

With an interdisciplinary crew including evolutionary biologist Dave Rand, sociologist Kevin Lewis, and social psychologist Mike Norton, we programmed a computer simulation in which mindless, identity-less agents interacted with reciprocity and transitivity. As expected, these simple agents robustly clustered into stable groups characterized by in-group cooperation and out-group cruelty.* Of course, the agents in our computer simulations are far less sophisticated than real people, but that's the point. If simple computer agents inevitably cluster into groups, there is no doubt that real humans—with entrenched identities, races, and religions—will also form groups.

There seems to be no avoiding "us" and "them," but some group landscapes encourage more ruthlessness than others. Competition for resources is the catalyst that turns "them" into "enemies" and transforms dislike into cruelty. In the land of plenty there is no need to fight, but when resources are tight, competition becomes a matter of survival—and it's easier to win if you have a group backing you up.

The link between resource competition and intergroup hostility is neatly demonstrated by comparing chimpanzees with bonobos. Both primates are evolutionary cousins of humans, but they have very different temperaments and social structures. Chimpanzees (*Pan troglodytes*) have a male-dominated society, are quick to aggress, and form gangs that mercilessly eliminate enemies.[10] If a male stumbles alone into enemy territory, rival chimpanzees will

....

* To see for yourself, you can visit www.mpmlab.org/groups.

attack with overwhelming force, often ripping off his face and testicles (so he won't have any vengeful heirs).[11] Chimpanzees will also cannibalize the babies of rivals[12] and have been known to bite off the fingers of humans who study them.[13]

In contrast to the male-dominated chimpanzees, bonobos (*Pan paniscus*) are female dominated and solve problems with sex instead of violence. In fact, they have sex all the time, not only standard female-with-male but also other combinations. Female-with-female genital-on-genital rubbing is a popular way to cement power alliances and demonstrate bonds of friendship and is certainly more exciting than meeting for coffee. Of course, bonobos still have conflicts and will sometimes act violently, but much less so than chimpanzees.

The difference between these two species lies in resource competition across evolutionary history. Chimps live on the north side of the Congo River, a territory shared with gorillas, which eat much of the same food.[14] Bonobos live on the south side of the Congo River, without gorillas and therefore with less competition for food.

Figure 23: Chimps (left) and Bonobos (right)
Increased resource competition means that chimps are more aggressive than bonobos, who often solve problems with sex.

The perennial dearth of food on the north side compels chimpan-zees to band together in ruthless gangs, fighting for the meager remaining resources. The abundance of food on the south side allows bonobos to instead spend their days indulging their insatia-ble nymphomania.

Humans share an evolutionary legacy with both chimpanzees and bonobos, but news headlines suggest that we may be more like chimps than bonobos. Humans often face resource competition, form gangs, and act ruthlessly toward enemies. Recent research shows that resource scarcity deepens divisions between "us" and "them," leading people to endorse stereotypes of other races and deny them resources.[15] This potential for cruelty is facilitated by the ambiguity of mind perception; just as we can give mind—and moral rights—to the relatively mindless, so too can we can take it away from the minded, seeing "them" as less than human.

When we dislike, fear, compete with, or even lust after other people, we *dehumanize* them, stripping perceived mind and casting them out of the mind club. Just as we perceive mind along the two dimensions of agency and experience, so too can we deny mind along them. Stripping away agency moves people away from the top right of the mind map we revealed in chapter 1 (high agency, high experience) toward the top left (low agency, high experience). As this location is occupied by animals, this form of dehumanization is called "animalizing."

Stripping away experience again moves people away from the top right of the mind map and toward the bottom right (high agency, low experience). On the farthest right we have God, but this is too exalted a position for "them." Instead we must drift some-what left to the robot; when we deny others experience, we dehumanize by likening them to machines, a process called "mechanization."

These two forms of dehumanization were coined by Australian psychologist Nicholas Haslam[16] and his colleagues Stephen Loughnan and Brock Bastian. They should remind you of the mind-perception fault line revealed in chapter 1 and the idea of moral typecasting we covered in chapter 4 on patients. Animalizing and mechanizing reinforce the idea that people are often seen as *either* vulnerable feelers (when they are animalized) *or* thinking doers (when they are mechanized). Dehumanization typically turns "them" into either unfeeling doers or unthinking feelers.

Perhaps the clearest example of animalizing—of stripping agency—is found in early accounts of Europeans who explored Africa; they regaled Victorian Britain with stories of barbaric "savages." These Africans were portrayed as animals or children, as emotional, fearful, angry, and joyous but seldom capable of self-control, rationality, or morality.[17] White men believed that it was in the best interests of the "savages" to have white men keep them safe but subservient, much like pets. The same sentiment existed in America, with Secretary of State John Calhoun stating in 1844, "The African is incapable of self care and sinks into lunacy under the burden of freedom. It is mercy to give him the guardianship and protection from mental death."[18] This paternalism helped to rationalize partitioning sovereign states into colonies, waging war against resistance, and raiding natural resources. Even more pernicious, animalizing was used to justify slavery; just as ranchers kept a stable of helpful livestock, so too did white landowners keep a stable of helpful humans, often treating them no better (and sometimes much worse) than actual livestock.

Colonialism is now out of vogue, but animalization is still present in modern society, if more subtly. In America it manifests itself most powerfully with stereotypes of black people, as research finds that people are quicker to associate images of apes—and apelike descriptions—with black people than with white people.[19] Some of these qualities, such as aggressiveness, toughness, and strength, may seem positive in contexts such as sports, where fans praise the ferocity of linebackers and the hunger of basketball players, but can have insidious effects upon racial equality—who wants to hire an animalistic CEO?[20] Of course, these stereotypes ignore

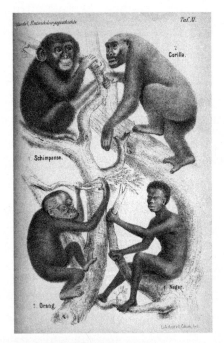

Figure 24: Historical Animalization
Anti–civil rights propaganda links African Americans to apes.
ILLUSTRATION FROM A NATIONAL STATES' RIGHTS PARTY PAMPHLET.

powerful agentic exemplars such as President Barack Obama and anti-Apartheid revolutionary Nelson Mandela, but they still persist. In 2012, at the Republican National Convention, two people were thrown out for tossing handfuls of peanuts at a black CNN camerawoman, saying, "This is how we feed animals."[21] There were clearly animals there, but they weren't the camerawoman.

As a form of dehumanization, animalizing leads perceivers toward paternalism and condescension. As we've seen in previous chapters, perceiving entities as vulnerable feelers makes people want to protect them and extend them at least some moral rights. On the other hand, mechanizing leads perceivers toward fear and outright hatred. Perceiving entities as unfeeling and robotic thinking doers makes people want to blame them, not protect them. If you remember the "Baby vs. Robot" thought experiment—and the mind survey—from chapter 1, we both hold machines morally responsible and allow them to be destroyed.

Anti-Semitism often exemplifies mechanizing, portraying Jewish people as powerful but unsympathetic, as wealthy but ruthless. One quote by Martin Luther, the sixteenth-century Protestant reformer, is revealing: "But the Jews are so hardened that they listen to nothing. . . . It is a pernicious race, oppressing all men by their usury and rapine. If they give a prince or magistrate a thousand florins, they extort twenty thousand from the subjects in payment. We must ever keep on guard against them."[22] To use the terms of the mind survey, Luther portrays Jewish people as high in agency, emphasizing their capacity for intending and planning complex conspiracies regarding business, politics, and banking.

Similar mechanizing stereotypes of Asian Americans have been recently bolstered by Amy Chua, the Chinese American who wrote *Battle Hymn of the Tiger Mother*. Chua believes that Western mothers focus too much on their children's feelings and not enough on their deeds, thereby limiting their capacity to succeed. In contrast, she minimizes the feelings of her children and focuses exclusively on their agency, driving them toward perfection. One instructive quote from Chua to her children: "If the next time's not perfect, I'm going to take all your stuffed animals and burn them."[23]

As these examples begin to show, people feel threatened by those they mechanize, because machines are solely thinking doers, invulnerable and unstoppable. For example, the animated Disney World War II propaganda film *Education for Death: The Making of the Nazi*

Figure 25: WWII Mechanizing Propaganda
American propaganda implying that the Japanese are not only evil but—unlike Americans—will never feel the need for relaxation.

describes a young man raised to be a fearsome Nazi soldier. As he goose-steps monotonously to a drum, the narrator intones, "In him, there is no seed of laughter, hope, tolerance or mercy. For him, only heiling and marching, marching and heiling."[24] The frightening picture of relentless, killing robots means that mechanized peoples are separated from the general population, such as Japanese Americans in the internment camps of World War II or Jews in the concentration camps of the Holocaust.

Both mechanizing and animalizing are paths to dehumanization, but they are paths to *partial* dehumanization. In both these cases people still keep half their minds, just as they do in moral typecasting, and—as in moral typecasting—there are often compensatory perceptions. Stereotypes of black people that deny their agency also highlight their experience as more emotional, more filled with sexual desire, and more in tune with their bodies. Mechanizing people denies their experience but simultaneously emphasizes their agency. In contrast to this partial—and compensatory—dehumanization, the most extreme dehumanization involves total stripping of mind, the denial of both agency and experience. Rather than animalizing or mechanizing, we can call this dehumanization *objectification*, seeing someone not as an animal or robot but as an object without any mind at all.

This most extreme form of denied mind and dehumanization is best exemplified by genocide. Although other Nazis may have seen the Jews as threats, Adolf Eichmann, the SS *Obersturmbannführer* (lieutenant colonel) who implemented Hilter's "Final Solution," saw them as a mere logistical challenge. He wondered how to design train schedules to most effectively move the Jews to concentration camps and how to best execute them and dispose of their bodies. Likewise, gas chambers were designed not to inflict maximum suffering but instead to be maximally efficient, killing the most people in a way that was both time and cost effective.

Beyond the extreme example afforded by the Holocaust, we ignore the minds of others in everyday life—such as homeless people—because they hold no instrumental value. In daily life different people can fulfill different goals. A librarian can help you find an old book, a friend can help set you up with a date, but a homeless person seems to help you with nothing but feelings of guilt. This renders them not only mentally invisible but also physically invisible. Studies by Jazmin Brown-Iannuzzi and Keith Payne at the University of North Carolina reveal that people completely fail to see homeless people in a visual scene unless the homeless people can fulfill a specific goal for the perceiver. As we saw in chapter 3 on machines, we see minds when they are useful to us; it also seems that we ignore them when they are not useful.

Not only can hate, fear, and indifference lead to dehumanization, but so can love—or at least lust. If you and your friends discussed the talents and characteristics of adult film stars, words that likely wouldn't come up are "intellectual," "cerebral," "perspicacious," and "generously endowed." Okay, maybe that last one, but the key is that we seem not to associate sex with mental characteristics. In fact, there seems to be a tension between seeing someone as a beautiful mind and seeing someone as a beautiful body.

Sex makes us think of concrete parts of someone—chest, abs, butt—whereas a mind is the whole of a person, an abstract identity. Sex seems to focus our attention on the physical and lead us to ignore the mental. This fact was not lost on the eighteenth-century philosopher Immanuel Kant, who wrote, "Sexual love makes of the loved person an Object of appetite; as soon as that appetite has been stilled, the person is cast aside as one casts away a lemon which has been sucked dry."[25] Of course, lemon sucking and sex may seem to differ in enjoyability,* but the point is clear—people who are sexualized are seen as simply a means to achieving satisfaction and not as people themselves.

A more contemporary philosopher, Martha Nussbaum, makes a similar point, suggesting that sexualizing others objectifies them, stripping them of their autonomy and their subjectivity—i.e., their perceived agency and experience.[26] Technically, both men and women can be objectified, but research on sexual objectification typically centers on the objectification of women by men, such as via the "male gaze," that lingering, up-and-down leer bestowed upon professional women as they walk by construction sites.[27]

Objectification not only unnerves recipients but also systematically undermines gender equality. A woman seen in terms of her body is unlikely to be first in line for a promotion, although she may have intelligence and ambition in spades. We want an incisive mind to lead and manage, not a shapely behind, and the more we focus on the latter, the less we think of the former. Unfortunately, norms of fashion and appearance mean that there is no easy way out of this problem; a woman who wears a burlap poncho to work may avoid the leers of her male colleagues but will also seem strange and unattractive. In infuriating unfairness, women are punished both for being too attractive and for being too unattractive.

For an obvious example of the objectification of women, just open a magazine. It doesn't even have to be a men's magazine; you can use a women's magazine or even a current-events magazine.

....

* Rumor has it that Kant died a virgin.

Figure 26: Objectifying Women
In advertising, women's bodies are often shown, whereas men are often depicted solely by their faces, a phenomenon called "face-ism."
CREDIT SHAWN DALEY.

You'll immediately notice that while men are often depicted by just their faces, women are often depicted as full bodies, sometimes fully clothed but more often revealing substantial skin.[28] The difference between depictions of men and women is called "face-ism" because women's faces occupy much less space in ads than men's faces.[29] Face-ism reduces perceptions of agency because it is the face—and not the chest—that conveys our thoughts and goals.[30]

It's clear that seeing someone as a body strips away perceived agency, but is the same true about experience? When you wear a revealing outfit, do people deny you both the ability to think and act *and* the ability to feel and sense? To answer this question, we teamed up with philosopher Joshua Knobe and psychologists Paul Bloom and Lisa Feldman Barrett. There were two competing hypotheses. The "object" hypothesis, advanced by centuries of philosophy, suggests that focusing on the body strips away *all* mind—both agency and experience.

The other hypothesis will be familiar to you from chapter 4 on patients. It is the "typecasting" hypothesis. Instead of stripping away all mind, the typecasting hypothesis suggests that seeing someone's body will actually *increase* perceived experience. Reflecting the fault line between agents and patients, typecasting predicts that the less you are seen as a thinking doer, the more you'll be seen as a vulnerable feeler. More skin equals more sensation.

To test these competing hypotheses, we asked participants to rate the minds of male and female models, judging their capacities for thought, planning, and self-control (agency), and for pain, pleasure, desire, and fear (experience). These models were depicted by face only or by both face and (toned) body. As predicted by both hypotheses, people ascribed less agency to models when their bodies were visible. Importantly, a visible body also led to the increased perception of experience. Half-naked men and women were seen as more capable of sensation and emotion—consistent with typecasting.

Another test of these hypotheses used stimuli from the portrait book *XXX: 30 Porn Star Portraits* by Timothy Greenfield-Sanders. This book is an experimental psychologist's dream because it contains identically posed, identically made up, and identically lit adult film stars photographed either clothed or completely naked, enabling researchers to isolate the precise effect of nakedness. When people rated the minds of the exact same adult film star either naked or clothed, they saw the naked version as less capable of thinking but as *more* capable of feeling, again consistent with typecasting.[31]

This nakedness-induced typecasting applies not only to men viewing women but also occurs when women view men's bodies, when women view women's bodies, and when men view other men's bodies, suggesting that it might be more general than objectification. As people generally see bodies in terms of experience and not agency, it suggests that—whether you are male or female—you should wear conservative clothing on job interviews and show a little more skin if you want someone to pay attention to your experience, sexually or otherwise. Just as with those "savages" we encountered earlier, our research suggests that we animalize those who show skin. However, we should note that—as occurs often in science—some other studies provide some evidence for objectification.[32] What distinguishes times when we typecast and animalize others from those when we completely objectify? One possibility is faces. In all our studies people could see the face of the target (whether they could see the person's body or not), whereas in some other studies, people might see *only* the body, with the head out of the frame. If you are staring at a headless body—a collection of shapely legs, breasts, or buttocks—you might forget that it belongs to a person capable of agency or experience. Minds belong to people, not to body parts.

Another factor that may flip the switch between typecasting and objectification is sexism, which comes in two flavors. One kind of sexism is "benevolent sexism," which characterizes women as good and kind but also emotional and vulnerable—just as typecasting suggests. Benevolent sexism provides the basis for chivalry, putting women on a pedestal and seeking to protect them from the cruel world of men. The other kind of sexism is "hostile sexism," which is more fitting in this chapter on the enemy. Hostile sexism holds women as incompetent and inferior but also as manipulative and conniving. When someone calls a woman a "shrew" or a "bitch," they are exhibiting this overtly negative form of sexism.

It appears that hostile sexism involves withholding both agency and experience from women depicted as bodies. In one study psychologists Mina Cikara, Jennifer Eberhardt, and Susan Fiske placed hostile-sexist men in an MRI scanner and showed them pictures of bikini-clad women. Normally, pictures of other people activate neural regions associated with mind perception, but these brain areas were conspicuously silent in these hostile-sexist men. Instead, the active neural regions were associated with *tools*, like hammers, screwdrivers, and saws: these men saw scantily clad women not as people but as something to be used and manipulated to satisfy their own desires, just as Kant suggested centuries ago.[33]

Nakedness can reduce mind perception, but some people—those with autism—have trouble seeing mind even when others are full dressed. Autism affects one out of eighty-eight children and is defined by "difficulties in social interaction, verbal and nonverbal communication and repetitive behaviors."[34] Informally, autism has been called "mindblindness"[35] because it reflects an inability to simulate[36] or theorize[37] the minds of others (the two processes of understanding minds we discussed in chapter 4 on the patient). Whereas people typically cannot help but see personality in pets and emotions in robots, those with autism have difficulty understanding these mental states even in other people.

The most eminent autism researcher is Simon Baron-Cohen.*

....

* He is also the cousin of the entertainer Sacha Baron Cohen, aka Ali G, aka Borat, aka Brüno.

He has designed many tests for assessing this disorder, which have revealed that autism is not a matter of "on" or "off." Instead there is a continuous dimension of impaired mind perception, called the "autism spectrum." Those moderately high on the spectrum can understand minds with effort but often fail to miss subtle social and conversational cues. However, people on the spectrum are often better than average at understanding complex systems such as car engines, computer programming, or philosophical logic.[38] This helps to explain why holiday parties at engineering firms are often a bit daunting; few people like being trapped in a conversation about the finer points of Java versus Perl, especially when your conversational partner mistakes your dead eyes and binge drinking for signs of interest.

Although those on the spectrum have an amazing ability to remember things like license plates and phone numbers, they have difficulty linking facial expressions to emotions. This is nicely illustrated by Baron-Cohen's "Mind in the Eyes," in which participants must label ambiguous emotional expressions. Look at the face in

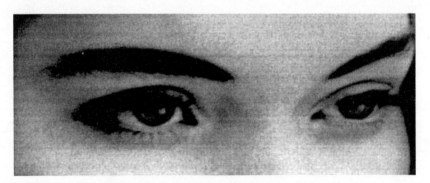

Figure 27: An Image from the "Mind in the Eyes" Test
What is she feeling? Encouraging, sympathetic, or thoughtful?

S. BARON-COHEN ET AL., "THE 'READING THE MIND IN THE EYES' TEST REVISED VERSION: A STUDY WITH NORMAL ADULTS, AND ADULTS WITH ASPERGER SYNDROME OR HIGH-FUNCTIONING AUTISM," *JOURNAL OF CHILD PSYCHOLOGY AND PSYCHIATRY* 42 (2001): 241-51.

the picture below: is it encouraging, sympathetic, thoughtful? If you are low on the spectrum, you likely picked "thoughtful" (even though you may have second-guessed yourself). If you are higher on the spectrum, this may have posed a greater challenge. This is partially because those higher on the spectrum simply do not look people in the eyes and so are less likely to catch face-based cues to emotion.[39]

Despite their difficulty in deciphering the exact nature of others' experience, those higher on the spectrum *do* recognize that others generally have experience. They cannot tell you whether someone is encouraging or thoughtful, but they know that others are capable of feeling *something*. This was demonstrated by a study in which we (together with Anna Jenkins and Andrea Heberlein) gave participants the mind survey while also testing their location on the autism spectrum.[40] We found that those higher on the autism spectrum saw less agency in adult humans, consistent with their difficulties in recognizing the intentions of others.[41] However, we found no association between participants' level of autism and their perception of experience. Those higher on the autism spectrum still recognize that others can be in pain or experience pleasure and, moreover, they care when others suffer.[42]

One example of the dissociation between caring about other minds and being able to accurately gauge their contents is provided by NPR's *All Things Considered*. This episode featured Kristen Finch, a woman who worked with autistic kids and whose marriage was in trouble. It seemed to her that her husband, David, was selfish and insensitive, rigid and reactive, and that he was taking her for granted. She was quickly becoming resentful of him, but one day she had an epiphany, realizing that David was uncannily similar to the autistic children with whom she worked.

She dragged him to a computer and made him do an online test.

Did he notice patterns in things? Yes. Did people comment on his unusual mannerisms and habits? Yes. Consistent with her intuitions, the test revealed that David was high on the autism spectrum (very high—scoring 155 out of 200). David cared very much about making his wife happy but his lack of mind perception denied him an intuitive grasp of how to achieve that. So he approached his wife like a complex mechanical system and made a notebook of explicit rules to follow. The marriage tips in this handbook may seem obvious to most people but not to him; for example, "Don't change the radio station when Kristen's singing along."[43]

Autism is one disorder of mind perception; psychopathy is another. Psychopaths are the dark cousins of those with autism; whereas those with autism are confused but caring, those with psychopathy are cold and calculating. Those with psychopathy typically *can* understand other minds but seldom care enough to bother. They lack empathy for others, viewing people as mere tools to achieve their own goals, and will harm others without compunction—they truly belong in this chapter on the enemy.

Psychologist Hervey Cleckley, who documents many cases of psychopathy in his book *The Mask of Sanity*,[44] tells the story of Gregory, a child who first came to the attention of a psychiatrist at the age of thirteen after setting fire to the local cathedral. Young Gregory had once walked into his mother's bedroom carrying a gun, aimed it at her, and pulled the trigger. The gun malfunctioned and his mother survived to witness Gregory's life of crime, including his theft of a police cruiser and his threatening to commit suicide by jumping off a bridge unless the police stopped pursuing him (he didn't and was arrested). Gregory had an easy time seducing women and convincing his friends that he cared, but his mother knew that beneath his charming facade Gregory would always be an unfeeling monster.

Psychopaths can often recognize the thoughts and feelings of others—if only to manipulate them—but they do have trouble understanding when others are in distress. Psychologist Abby Marsh has studied this phenomenon in children with antisocial behavioral patterns, including children with conduct disorder, who are likely to grow into full-blown psychopaths.[45] In a typical study she presents participants with pictures featuring actors making different posed emotional expressions, such as disgust, anger, and fear. Children with conduct disorder are usually quite good at identifying various emotional expressions, except when it comes to fear, where they seem to lack insight.[46]

An instructive story comes from Essi Viding, a professor at University College London who performed a similar study, asking one teenager with conduct disorder to identify the emotional state of someone who appeared distressed and afraid. The teenager said, "I don't know what that expression is called, but I know it's what people look like right before I stab them." This insensitivity to the distress of others may stem from their own inability to feel this emotion. Psychopaths are notoriously calm in the face of danger, which may explain why some amount of psychopathy helps people succeed in high-pressure environments. You may not be surprised to learn that CEOs are four times more likely to qualify as psychopaths than the general population.[47]

Of course, being a psychopath is not really a choice, as psychopaths are born with different brains from the rest of us. Exactly how different is not entirely clear, but there are two neural regions that seem to matter: the ventromedial prefrontal cortex (vmPFC) and the orbital prefrontal cortex (OPFC), which sit roughly behind your forehead and eyes, respectively. People with normal vmPFCs experience emotional twinges when contemplating doing harm or even taking risky gambles, but those with damaged vmPFCs do not—just like psychopaths.[48] Likewise, people with normal OPFCs control their impulses, whereas those with damaged OPFCs act out their desires, even if antisocial—also just like psychopaths.[49] The biological basis—and the relative innateness—of psychopathy poses a problem, as we typically don't hold people responsible for innate biological differences. If you were born without fingers, no one would hold it against you if you couldn't play the piano, so should we hold it against psychopaths that they were born without empathy?

This question divides the legal system, with answers depending on how psychopathy is framed. One study with real judges as participants revealed that psychopaths were given more blame than nonpsychopaths, unless psychopathy was framed as a biological disorder—and then they were given less blame.[50] In the terms of mind perception, the question is whether a psychopath is an agent or a patient. Certainly psychopaths are capable of acting and planning, but they are also victims of their own miswired brains.[51]

Either way, psychopaths seem very different from normal people, but before you get too smug, consider the example at the beginning of the chapter, in which "normal" people perpetrate torture on innocent victims. How can someone who loves his wife, his mother, and his dog not only be comfortable with the suffering of others but be happy to cause it?

The suffering of others typically makes us pity and protect them, but not when it confronts us too closely. When the injustice of harm is overpowering, we react by denying its injustice and seeing harm as justified and deserved.[52] Take the case of rape, in which people often look to blame the victim and rationalize the crime, asking whether she was drinking or what she was wearing. People have a deep need to see the world as fair and just, and so they believe that people have gotten what they deserve, even when the harm is fundamentally undeserved.[53] They want to know that terrible things won't happen to them, that there is method in the world's madness. With torture, a just world entails that victims deserve their suffering, and so we look for reasons to blame the victim. In the case of Mohamedou Ould Slahi, the Guantanamo Bay detainee we met at the beginning of the chapter, we imagine there must be reasons for his treatment—perhaps he hung out with the wrong people or made some poor early-life choices.

Belief in a just world predicts that the more someone suffers, the more they will be blamed. This prediction of "more pain = more blame" directly contradicts the predictions of moral typecasting, which predicts that the more someone suffers, the *less* they will be blamed. Moral patients are generally not seen as moral agents, so what explains the blaming of victims? We suspected that the key difference between situations of typecasting and situations of just-world belief is whether a victim's suffering directly relates to the observer. With rape it is often those who are most similar to the victim who blame her most. Other young women want to think, "If I simply wear sensible clothes and watch my drinking, then this could never happen to me." Just-world belief means that even more than those who are similar to victims, those who are complicit in someone's suffering will blame the victim. People want to believe themselves to be good people, and good people don't harm others unless they deserve it.

To compare the predictions of typecasting (suffering leads to perceived innocence) and those of the just-world belief (suffering leads to perceived guilt), we designed a study in which participants listened to an episode of torture. This "torture" consisted of putting the hand of a female confederate into a bucket of ice. Importantly, she reacted in one of two ways. In the *nonpainful* condition the confederate endured the ice bath stoically and displayed no real discomfort. In the *painful* condition the confederate whimpered, groaned, complained, and begged to have her hand taken out of the icy slurry.

These two conditions were crossed with another distinction: *uninvolved* and *complicit*. In the *uninvolved* condition participants listened to a previous recording of the torture (either *painful* or *nonpainful*) over headphones. In the *complicit* condition participants first met the confederate and then sat right across the hall from her while the torture was happening, listening in on a one-way intercom.

All participants then evaluated the guilt of the confederate, estimating how likely it was that she had cheated on some prior task. We predicted that in the *uninvolved* condition—when people only listened to a recording of torture—typecasting would apply, such that less blame would be assigned in the *painful* condition than in the *nonpainful* condition. This prediction was confirmed: when people were physically, temporally, and psychologically distant from the torture, they linked more pain to less guilt, just as moral typecasting suggests.

Conversely, in the *complicit* condition we predicted that more pain would be linked to *more* blame. When participants are closely involved in the torture—and could have stopped it—there should be motivation for them to see it as justified. This prediction was also confirmed: when people were physically, temporally, and psychologically close to the torture, they linked more pain to more guilt.

Although this lab study was done miles away from Guantanamo Bay, these psychological processes help explain the debate on torture. When people feel distant from torture, such as when reading about it in the *New York Times* over breakfast, they judge its victims as relatively innocent. But when people feel complicit in torture—whether they are prison guards, CIA decision makers, or simply citizens who voted for a prointerrogation government—they justify it by judging its victims as blameworthy and deserving of pain.

The case of torture demonstrates that we are all conscientious objectors until we pull the trigger, when psychological processes engage to justify our behavior. The upshot is that people are generally unwilling to initially pull the trigger, because of the power of empathy. As we discussed in chapter 4 on the patient, empathy can be suppressed or exhausted but is often powerful even in a theater of war. In the American Civil War, it is rumored that many soldiers either fired over the heads of their enemies or just continually loaded their muskets without ever firing.

Modern military training programs grapple with how to turn empathic people into killing machines, often instilling unquestioning obedience to authorities and a powerful sense of loyalty toward your comrades. If the commands of superiors do not move you, then you are moved by the knowledge that failing to shoot might spell death for your friends.

Using the social psychological principles we've revealed in this chapter, the American military also encourages the division between "us" and "them" by using words like "haji" and "raghead" to describe Muslims. Although these terms are dehumanizing, they are often seen as a necessary survival tactic, because a moment's hesitation about the humanity of your enemy could be the difference between your life and death.[54] Finally, these training programs automate killing, bending thoughts of the enemy away from mind perception and toward reflexive aggression.

Leaving aside perennial debates about the ethics of war, one pressing issue is how to readjust veterans to civilian life. What does a killing machine do when there is no killing to be done? Without the clear structure and goals afforded by war, many veterans find themselves adrift in civilian life. Consider one poignant scene from the Academy Award–winning movie *The Hurt Locker*, in which the protagonist, a soldier used to defusing bombs every day in Iraq, stands frozen in the aisle of a grocery store, pondering what kind of cereal to buy. After standing so often in the crucible of life and death, civilian life seems so inconsequential to him that he yearns to return to war, where at least he had a clear sense of purpose.

Another issue for those who return from war is their entrenched views of the enemy. After you have been trained to dehumanize and kill foreign Muslims, it is difficult to reverse that process and see American Muslims as worthy of respect. Even Muslim servicemen have been attacked for their faith—cabdriver and U.S. Army reservist Mohamed Salim was assaulted in 2013 by a passenger who called him a "fucking Muslim" and accused him of being a jihadist. Despite the clear evidence of Salim's patriotism, he was labeled as being "just as bad as the rest of them."[55]

Perceptions of "us versus them" also persist among civilians, especially those touched by conflict. In the Middle East you would be hard-pressed to find someone who has not—at least indirectly—been harmed by the actions of the opposition. Once someone is your enemy, they tend to stay that way forever, making rapprochement all but impossible. Nevertheless, even if conflicts cannot be solved, they can at least be soothed, and one way to reduce intergroup animosity is through common goals that require cooperation.

In the classic Robber's Cave study, the war between the Eagles and the Rattlers was ended by introducing superordinate goals: working together to fix a broken water fountain, pitching in to cover the cost of a movie screening, and cutting down a tree. One especially powerful unifying goal is the defeat of a common enemy, because everyone finally has something they can agree upon. If movies like *Independence Day* and *Starship Troopers* are any guide, the best way to create a harmonious human brotherhood is through the threat of alien invasion. Slight differences in skin tone seem less important when humankind is faced with extermination by ruthless space insects. Of course, once that common enemy is defeated, there is nothing stopping the revival of those suppressed sectarian differences.

Perhaps the best route to intergroup harmony is through soap operas. Yes, soap operas. Working on the ground in Rwanda, Princeton psychologist Betsy Levy Paluck has investigated whether these daytime dramas can reduce the prejudice between the Hutus and the Tutsis. To refresh your memory, the Hutus and the Tutsis are the two largest cultural groups in Rwanda and have clashed ever since the time of colonialism. This conflict spiked in 1994, when the Rwandan government—consisting primarily of Hutus—perpetrated genocide against the Tutsi minority, killing more than half a million of them (20 percent of Rwanda's population).[56] Rwanda has since stabilized, but prejudice and distrust runs understandably deep.

One intervention to address this animosity is *Musekeweya* (pronounced moo-say-kay-way-ah), or *New Dawn*, a radio soap opera featuring cross-group friendships and romances (like a Rwandan

Romeo and Juliet) and also educational messages about the psychological roots of violence. After randomly assigning these radio soap operas to some communities, Paluck found that people in these communities were more sympathetic toward victims of genocide, more positive about the idea of intergroup cooperation, and even more favorable toward intergroup marriage.[57]

Even without mass-media interventions, people can spontaneously rise above their differences and treat their enemies as friends, even on the battlefield. The Christmas Truce is a touching example of this. In December 1914, after months of bloodshed, German and British soldiers started exchanging seasonal greetings, songs, and even some gifts. This warmth increased as the temperatures cooled, and on Christmas Day many soldiers climbed out of their trenches into no-man's-land, where together they sang carols and in one location even played a game of soccer.*[58] Of course, World War I went on to claim millions of lives through brutal trench warfare and poison gas attacks, but it is reassuring to know that the flames of friendship can flicker in hurricanes of hostility. Even the enemy can sometimes be our friend.

Minds are a matter of perception and, as we've seen repeatedly, these perceptions typically follow our feelings. When we feel lonely or confused, we perceive mind to help us out. When we feel love toward a cryptomind such as a pet, we perceive mind to make it human and give it moral status. In this chapter we've seen how the exact opposite can occur. When we dislike someone, we strip them of mind and turn them into a mere animal or machine—or just an object to be destroyed. Casting people out of the mind club robs them of their moral status and justifies our condescension and

....

* German Battalion 371 defeated the Royal Welch Fusiliers, 2–1.

cruelty to them. Unfortunately, it is all too easy for people to become enemies, to separate into groups of us and them, if only on the basis of eye color or number estimation. Coupled with the aggression-promoting effects of resource scarcity, it is no surprise that many people live in fear of religious, political, and gang violence.

Although it may seem like it is always "other people" who commit crimes of hatred and apathy, research reveals that it is surprisingly easy to turn any of us—even you, gentle reader—into a weapon of cruelty. We hope that after reading this chapter you will listen a bit harder for the sounds of mind in those who seem different from you. But sometimes even listening will do us no good—some minds are completely silent.

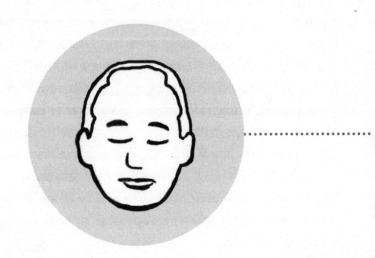

Chapter 6

THE SILENT

In 1986 a young woman and her husband moved to Florida to start new jobs. The husband was a restaurant manager, and the young woman worked at an insurance firm. They led normal lives, but the young woman would obsess over her weight. She would often drink large amounts of water and iced tea to keep her feeling full without the calories of food. Unfortunately, drinking too much water and iced tea can dilute your electrolyte levels and cause hypokalemia—extremely low levels of potassium—which, in turn, can cause cardiac arrest. In 1990 the husband came home to find his wife facedown and unconscious, without a pulse. Paramedics rushed her to the hospital, where doctors quickly restarted her heart, but by the time it had resumed beating, she had suffered permanent brain damage. The young woman—though technically alive—never woke up from her coma, and after a year of unresponsiveness her diagnosis was changed to persistent vegetative state (PVS).

The patient's name was Terri Schiavo, and her case caused a hurricane of controversy. Unlike the typical patients we explored in chapter 4, Terri was completely silent and all but unresponsive. After a number of unsuccessful attempts at rehabilitation, ranging from occupational and speech therapy to experimental brain implants and simple walks in the park, it became clear to Michael Schiavo—Terri's husband—that her vegetative state was permanent.

Terri was kept alive only by a feeding tube that skipped her unresponsive throat and delivered nutrients straight to her stomach. In 1993 Michael signed a DNR, a "do not resuscitate" order, which meant that if Terri stopped breathing, doctors would not try to revive her. Five years later Michael petitioned to have the feeding tube removed, a move opposed by her parents, who were convinced both that Terri would recover and that euthanasia was immoral.

Michael argued that Terri would not have wanted to be kept alive in this state, and doctors agreed that recovery would be extremely unlikely. The dispute between Michael and Terri's parents pulled in state and federal judges, legislators, and lobbying groups. One side argued for Terri's right to die and the other for her right to stay alive. As in other debates about life and death, liberals argued in favor of the right to choose, whereas conservatives argued for the right to life.

The case peaked when then-President George W. Bush signed a law transferring the dispute to the Supreme Court, which upheld the previous ruling to let Terri die. This was not the verdict he was looking for, however, and his brother—the governor of Florida, Jeb Bush—planned on disobeying the court order. The only thing stopping Jeb Bush was a Florida judge who had charged the local sheriffs with guarding Terri while she died. As intervening would have meant a fight of force between the sheriff and the National Guard,

Jeb Bush relented; fifteen years after falling into cardiac arrest, Terri finally died.

Whether you see Terri's death as merciful or merciless depends upon what kind of mind you believe she had. Terri was undoubtedly a medical patient, but was she a true moral patient with an inner life? Those who believe that Terri was relatively mindless see her death as a kindness. From their point of view, letting her die was simply allowing an unfeeling mass of biological cells to stop functioning. Conversely, those who believe that Terri was a relatively mindful moral patient see her death as cruelty. Although her mental capacities may have been masked by her damaged body, they believe that Terri was still "in there." As we have repeatedly seen, mind is the key to moral rights, but in vegetative patients its perception is especially ambiguous.

Typically we assess other human minds through conversation, such as in the Turing test. However, not everything can talk, and this silence is what makes cryptominds like robots and animals so ambiguous. If only cows could say, "Please don't eat me!" then we would know they have minds and would stop eating them—or would at least feel much guiltier about doing so. While we are well accustomed to languageless animals and machines, we expect humans to talk, and it is very strange when they cannot. Without verbal abilities, how can we know whether other people belong in the mind club? Is a PVS patient a vulnerable feeler, a thinking doer, or merely a collection of muscle twitches and nerve pulses?

Silence can be problematic for understanding agency, because we often discuss our future plans and past deeds, but it is especially problematic for experience. Actions can be externally observed, but feelings and sensations must be put into words to be understood by others. Was Terri Schiavo afraid or hopeful? Was she angry or calm?

These are questions to which we can never know the answers. The most extreme kind of silence is suggested by a famous philosophical thought experiment—the brain in a vat. Imagine that your brain— i.e., your mind—is placed in a vat, along with all the nutrients it needs to survive. While resting there, you might have a rich mental life, filled with lush landscapes of imagination, but without some way of communication how would anyone else ever know about it?

More than any other entity the silent represent an interesting counterpoint to the philosophical zombie that we accused your mother of being in chapter 1. A philosophical zombie is someone who can talk but who ultimately lacks conscious experience, whereas the silent may still have experience, despite being unable to communicate it. Without the typical cues to mind, how do we decide whether a silent entity has a mind?

Historically the answer often came down to a heartbeat. Ancient (and not-so-ancient) peoples long struggled with what separated the living from the dead. The heart is the only organ that pulses rhythmically and is immediately essential for life. You can live for some time with a pierced liver or a punctured lung, but harm your heart and you're soon dead. This is likely why the heart was seen as the seat of feeling and cognition; one of the Latin words for heart is *animus*, which is the spirit or animating force of the human body, or what we might call "the mind."

Grounding life in the heart provided a sharp line between the living and the dead: if you had a heartbeat, then you were living, and if you didn't, then you weren't. Of course, even with this criterion people still made mistakes. If the heart was beating too feebly to detect, then death was often pronounced prematurely; as burial preparations were being made for these "corpses," they would sit up and ask about all the digging.[1] More gruesome to consider are those who came alive an hour or two later, trapped in a coffin six feet underground.

The heart was so identified with the mind that it was often thought to be imbued with power even after the rest of the body was cast aside. In Edgar Allan Poe's "The Tell-Tale Heart"[2] the protagonist is driven mad by the imagined heartbeat of a man he has just murdered, and in many stories[3] consuming a person's heart earns you their power. Despite this imagined power, we now know the heart to be a mere machine, if a stunningly reliable one. A person's heart can not only be made to beat artificially through a pacemaker but can also be completely replaced with an artificial heart. In fact, almost all your organs can be simulated by a machine (e.g., kidney dialysis) or replaced with another version, whether synthetically constructed or naturally donated. The only organ that we cannot bolster with a machine or substitute entirely is the brain. The brain is essential for both life and mind, and so current legal definitions of life are tied to brain function—someone is dead when they are "brain-dead."[4]

The mind is obviously linked to the brain. At the coarsest level, if you were to remove someone's entire brain, they would certainly die. At a finer-grained level, removing parts of people's brains also reduces their minds, such as in the famous case of the railway worker Phineas Gage. After losing a cylinder of his brain, the once kind and pious family man turned into a drinking, sex-crazed, authority-hating thunderstorm of a man, prone to fights and cruelty.

Losing even more mind can make you not violent but gentle. Consider the lobotomy, a medical procedure used to reduce mental illness for which Portuguese neurologist António Moniz won the 1949 Nobel Prize in medicine. To perform this procedure, one need only slip an ice pick behind the eyes and into the brain and then wiggle it around until the frontal lobes are thoroughly muddled.[5]

Without these brain regions intact, people become calm and docile and also relatively incapable of independent functioning, initiative, and inhibition.[6] In the words of a prominent doctor, "through lobotomy an insane person is changed into an idiot."[7] Thankfully, not all those who suffered lobotomies are "idiots": Howard Dully, the boy pictured in figure 28, led a remarkably productive life and cowrote the fascinating memoir *My Lobotomy*. Nevertheless, the general correspondence between brain and mind is undeniable.

The link between brain and mind can help inform decisions regarding the silent. In the case of Terri Schiavo, autopsies revealed that she had suffered massive brain damage,[8] perhaps providing some vindication to those who advocated for her right to die. But

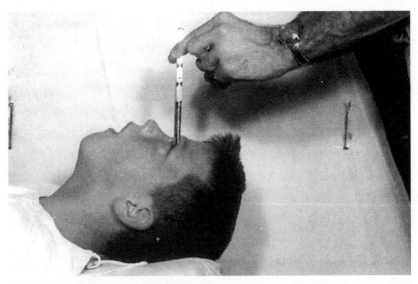

Figure 28: Depiction of Lobotomy
A twelve-year-old boy undergoes prefrontal lobotomy in 1960.

even damaged brains can think and feel, and so questions of both brain and mind turn on nuance.

To get a more detailed understanding of the mind, researchers study not only static brain structures but also the dynamic patterns of neuronal activation. These so-called functional techniques can assess thinking and feeling more directly because they examine how brain cells act in different situations, such as when trying to read, when listening to scary sounds, or even when perceiving the minds of others. Plus, functional analyses give researchers pretty pictures of colored brains, which lends them scientific weight in the eyes of the public.[9]

Two of the most popular functional techniques are functional magnetic resonance imaging (fMRI) and electroencephalography (EEG). fMRI relies upon the simple fact that active cells, whether in the brain or in the kneecap, use up oxygen in the blood. The harder a cell is working, the more oxygen it consumes from the blood, so if you can measure regional blood oxygenation, you can observe brain activity. However, measuring brain-cell oxygenation requires sticking heads inside a very powerful magnet, typically with a field strength of at least three teslas. For comparison, three teslas is one thousand times stronger than a refrigerator magnet but not powerful enough to levitate a frog (which would take sixteen teslas). Nevertheless, a magnetic field at that strength will tear your smartphone out of your hand and tug suggestively on underwire bras.

Magnetic fields are useful for brain imaging because oxygen-rich blood has different magnetic properties from oxygen-poor blood (oxygen binds to hemoglobin, which contains iron, which is magnetic). By looking at the BOLD (blood-oxygenation-level-dependent) signal in a powerful magnet, researchers can detect where fresh, oxygen-rich blood is being sent. This technique gives a fairly precise spatial location of brain activity (within one or two millimeters) during tasks. For example, when people think about the thoughts and intentions of others (i.e., perceive minds), fMRI reveals activations in the ventromedial prefrontal cortex,[10] lateral parietal cortex, and medial parietal cortex.[11] We can use these maps of brain activity to reason about what silent minds might be doing. If a PVS patient shows similar brain activity to that of a healthy person, it hints at someone "in there" and recommends the patient as a mind club member with moral standing.

As a brain-scanning device, fMRI is very useful, but it has two main limitations. First, it is costly: an hour in a scanner typically runs about eight hundred dollars, which means only the richest kids get fMRI-themed birthday parties. Second, although fMRI has good spatial resolution (i.e., location identification), it has poor temporal resolution (i.e., time-course identification). Blood takes a few seconds to flow to brain structures, which is too long to reveal the dynamics of many mental events.

Electroencephalography (EEG) is another brain-imaging technique that can assess these temporal dynamics; it does so by measuring the brain's electrical activity through a network of electrodes affixed to the scalp. Although the brain does not produce a lot of electricity—you couldn't power a television simply by thinking hard—firing neurons release electrically charged particles, causing a current. Just as the current that powers your appliances runs at certain cycles (in the United States it cycles back and forth between positive and negative current at sixty times a second, or sixty hertz), a functioning brain also has certain electrical cycles.

When you plot these up-and-down cycles over time, they look

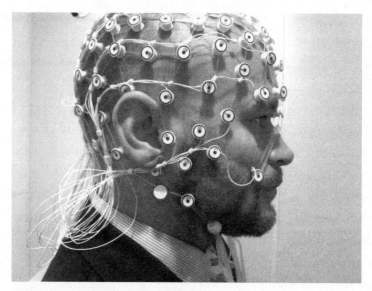

Figure 29: An EEG Electrode Cap
EEG offers the ability to record "brain waves."

like waves, so one cycle is called alpha waves (8–13 Hz) and others include beta waves (14–40 Hz), delta waves (1–3 Hz), and theta waves (4–7 Hz).[12] Alpha waves are the medium-sized waves that characterize wakeful relaxation, beta waves are fast waves that are characteristic of concentration and problem solving, and delta waves are slower and observed during periods of deep sleep or uninterrupted meditation. As these brain cycles correlate with mental states, EEG is usually the method of choice when investigating cryptominds, and it has proved especially useful in examining silent people with disorders of consciousness such as coma, vegetative states, and sleep.

Sleep? Like vegetative states, sleep is a state of silence and altered consciousness. If two people—one sleeping and one in a vegetative state—were next to each other, you would be hard-pressed to tell the difference at a glance. Both would have their eyes closed, be breathing rhythmically, and be unable to speak; the main difference would be found in the mental functioning behind their closed lids.

When people sleep, there is a wealth of neural activity in their brains.[13] As you fall asleep, alpha waves of awakeness give way to the lower-frequency theta waves of light sleep. If you are woken up during theta waves, you likely will not even realize you were asleep. As your sleep deepens, your brain activity is characterized by delta waves—big, slow, rolling waves—and it becomes harder to wake you up. During the delta stage of sleep, the body repairs itself and flushes out neurological waste products. If you manage to wake someone up during this stage, they are typically groggy and disoriented.[14]

The final stage of sleep, called rapid eye movement or REM, is actually quite similar to wakefulness in terms of brain waves; there are alpha and beta waves but also lots of crazy eye movement. Most important from the perspective of mind, REM is when dreaming occurs.[15] Whether you are speaking in front of a large crowd sans pants, falling to your death, or making out with your old high school crush, it all happens during REM.

The vividness of dreams is one reason it is hard to label vegetative patients as "mindless." We know that if *we* were lying with our eyes closed, we would be experiencing the rich inner life of dreams. The idea that coma patients are simply dreaming is a frequent topic in literature and film. One especially clever take on this idea was in the Canadian television show *The Odyssey*, which captivated one of your authors (Kurt) as a child.

In this show a boy falls from a tree house and into a coma. While in the coma, he finds himself in a parallel world devoid of grown-ups and ruled by a fifteen-year-old militaristic dictator. The boy spends three seasons battling the secretive and ominous forces of this dictator (who, in a nod to Kafka, lives in "the tower") and trying to regain consciousness and return home to his family and friends. Even if you've never seen this show, its theme has universal appeal—we like to think of people in comas or other disordered states as simply trying to get home through an odyssey of inner life. Whether people in these disordered states actually have an inner life is a question neuroscience can help answer.

EEG reveals that not all states of silence are the same. At maximum consciousness is our normal awake self, and one large step below is sleep. Sandwiched between awake and asleep is the "minimally conscious state," in which people are aware of stimuli but little else. Minimally conscious patients can follow a pointer on a screen but are unable to complete purposeful behavior; in other words, they have experience but not agency. This state is characterized by slowed theta and delta waves and by weaker brain activity than during wakefulness, and it is usually induced by some kind of traumatic head injury, just like the coma, which is one step further down the consciousness ladder.

Like a minimally conscious state, a coma state is characterized by slowed theta and delta waves, but also by more intermittent delta rhythms, and generally weaker EEG signals.[16] Patients typically recover from a coma after a week or two, which makes it an ideal plot device in television and movies. In a coma you can be out of commission just long enough for your fiancée to fall in love with your brother, despite the fact that she is not really your fiancée at all and, in fact, you have never really met. This is the plot of the movie *While You Were Sleeping* (starring Sandra Bullock and Bill

Pullman), a title that emphasizes the intuitive link between comas and sleeping.*

Below comas are vegetative states, which are characterized by significantly more brain damage and poorer overall functioning. In these states vegetative functions, like breathing and swallowing, remain intact, but people are unresponsive to stimuli and unable to complete voluntary behavior.[17] Vegetative states are further categorized by how long they have lasted. After four weeks, patients are classified as being in a "persistent vegetative state" and have a significantly reduced chance of ever recovering. Patients in vegetative states may still look like they're sleeping, but they're not—and they're not dreaming either. Researchers at the University of Wisconsin at Madison have used EEG to compare brain functioning in healthy, minimally conscious, and vegetative-state patients. They found that the behavioral signs of sleep (e.g., eyes closed, relaxed muscles) co-occurred with sleep-related brain-wave patterns in minimally conscious patients but not in PVS patients.[18]

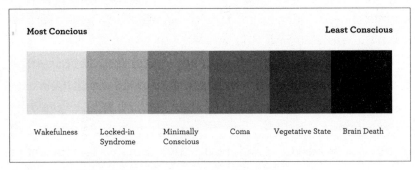

Figure 30: Chart of Disordered Conscious States
Each state involves different EEG patterns.

· · · · · · · · · ·

* It is also a universal truth that plots involving comas are always elaborate and confusing.

Patients in vegetative states, however, do appear to have a neural response to their own names. A study conducted by European researchers recited a list of names to participants, who included normal adults, minimally conscious patients, and vegetative patients.[19] Using EEG, the researchers found that normal adults showed a special neural reaction when their own name was mentioned and— after a significant delay—so did both the minimally conscious and vegetative patients. It is seductive to imagine that these patients were consciously recognizing their names, but this neural response could be completely unconscious, representing only a tenacious mental reflex.

The important question across these states is whether the minds of patients continue to exist, or at least whether they have minds that can be recovered. Is there someone home in there—even if they are trapped in the basement—or have they left to travel abroad, never to return? To address this question, researchers examine not only the brains of patients but also their behaviors, testing whether they interact meaningfully with the world. Do patients respond to the touch of their doctors and their loved ones? Do they care who wins the World Series?

In 2009 the Phillies returned to the World Series, hoping to win back-to-back titles. One unlikely fan who followed their quest for the pennant was Terri Schiavo—or so it seemed. In a video clip taken in October of that year, Terri lies in her hospital bed while a nearby radio broadcasts the game. During what was to be the final play of the final game of the National League Championship Series against the Dodgers, the announcer calmly starts describing a Phillies pitch and subsequent hit by a Dodger, but as the ball climbs high into the air, he becomes more and more excited—it's a pop fly. The crowd explodes as the fly ball drops into the center fielder's glove, and the announcer exclaims that the Phillies are returning to the World Series.

Back in her hospital bed, Terri starts to lift her head, turns it toward the radio, and opens her eyes widely. To all appearances it seems that Terri is *excited* about the Phillies' victory—at least, that is the explanation we would give for that behavior in a healthy adult human. Did Terri have a mind capable of understanding the baseball victory, or was something else going on? Perhaps she was just excited by the excitement, in an unconscious contagion of arousal.

Whether vegetative patients can interact with the world is essential to their diagnosis. Terri Schiavo was diagnosed as being in a vegetative state when doctors realized that she had "absence of voluntary action" and the "inability to communicate or interact purposefully." In the parlance of mind perception, she lacked agency, the ability to impose her intention onto the outside world,[20] but the Phillies clip gives us pause. Isn't this a clear example of mindful behavior? It certainly feels compelling, but one of psychology's lessons is that appearances can often be deceiving. People can perceive complex minds in behaviors that actually have simpler explanations, such as a horse doing math.

This particular horse was named Hans and earned the nickname "Clever Hans" for his uncanny numerical abilities. His trainer, Wilhelm von Osten, would ask him a series of math problems, such as $2 + 4$ or $5 + 3$ or $\frac{dy}{dx} \tanh^{-1} e^x$,* and Hans would cleverly clop out the answer with his front hoof, earning himself a carrot in the process. Audiences were amazed at this ability, and Hans quickly became a celebrity, but a psychologist named Oskar Pfungst needed further

. . . .

* Only kidding—his ability in calculus was untested.

proof. His experimental method was straightforward: he placed a sheet between the trainer and Hans, so that Hans could still hear the math question but couldn't get any other cues from von Osten. With this intervention Hans's performance fell apart and he was no better than your average horse, which is to say, terrible.

Why did this manipulation destroy Hans's ability? Did he have nightmares about sheets, for which he needed his trainer to comfort him? It turns out he did need his trainer, but not for comfort. What was truly clever about Hans was that he had learned to associate body language with clicking his hoof. When von Osten asked a question, he would lean forward expectantly, and the horse would start stepping. Once the correct answer was reached, von Osten would rock back on his heels, satisfied, and the horse would take this as a cue to stop stepping.[21] So Hans was clever, but in a different way from what people thought.

Whether PVS patients' behavior is "clever" or reflexive depends upon whether it responds flexibly to changing task demands. Clever Hans always clopped out the same answer based on body language, regardless of the specific math question. Do PVS patients show more flexibility? In one study researchers in Tel Aviv addressed this question with fMRI scans of four vegetative states (VS) patients who looked at pictures of strangers, friends, family members, and themselves. The researchers examined brain regions tied to face recognition and emotion, since healthy people both recognize and react to pictures of their friends and family and of themselves.[22] All VS patients showed activation in these brain regions, and the activation was strongest in those patients who would eventually recover. But is this contingent behavior *conscious*? Membership in the mind club depends on actually "experiencing" various experiences. As we saw in the beginning of chapter 2 on animals, even plants react to themselves and their environment,[23] and they certainly don't have minds worthy of our concern.

A research team led by British neuroscientist Adrian Owen investigated the mind of a twenty-three-year-old woman injured in a car accident. After five months of treatment, the woman met all criteria for a vegetative state: her reflexes were still intact, but she produced no voluntary or intentional motor behaviors and couldn't follow a moving stimulus with her eyes. She did, however, have intact sleep and wake cycles, and EEGs revealed the presence of some alpha and beta waves, both of which are characteristic of conscious thought. The researchers developed a clever task using fMRI to determine if she could intentionally direct her thinking.

They asked her to imagine one of two scenarios. The first was walking around her house and the second was playing tennis, which she did often before the accident. An fMRI revealed that her brain activity during these tasks was indistinguishable from that of neurotypical people: when asked to imagine moving around her house, her "navigation" areas were activated, and when asked to imagine playing tennis, her "arm motions" areas were activated.[24] Although she couldn't talk, this young woman was responding flexibly to the researchers—almost like a conversation, she was speaking through her brain scans. The researchers concluded that she was imagining the scenarios vividly enough that it counted as purposeful behavior and hinted at a thriving inner life. She wasn't a vegetative patient at all but was instead *locked in.*

Locked-in states are very different from vegetative states, and we will begin our exploration of them with a simple question: how many blinks does it take to write a book? The answer is 200,000, the number of blinks it took Jean-Dominique Bauby to write his memoir *Le scaphandre et le papillon*, or *The Diving Bell and the Butterfly*. The more expedient choice would have been to write it, but Bauby lacked that option. On December 8, 1995, he suffered a stroke, and after twenty days in a coma he awoke to find himself a prisoner of his own body. He was fully aware of his surroundings and himself; he could see, listen, and understand; he could dream, think, and feel; but he couldn't move a muscle. That's not completely true, of course, as he could move one muscle—his left eyelid. Otherwise, he was fully locked in.

Bauby was a writer (he was editor of the magazine *Elle* when he suffered his stroke) and he wanted to tell the world about his experience, so with the help of his assistant, Claude Mendibil, he wrote the 139-page book one letter at a time. The assistant would simply say the letters in order of their frequency, which in French would be *E, S, A, R, I*, and so on. When the correct letter was reached, Bauby would blink and they would move on to the next one. If you haven't read the book, it is a poignant picture of being trapped in one's own body state. Even the title is touching: his useless body is the diving bell, an impenetrable steel casing that sits alone at the bottom of the ocean, but his spirit—his mind—is a butterfly, as light and free as ever. Unfortunately, Bauby did not live to see the success of his book or the host of awards that its film adaptation won, as he died from pneumonia three days after the book was published. We can only hope that his butterfly still flutters somewhere.

Locked-in states are exactly as they sound. Victims finds themselves confined to the prison of their obstinate body, which refuses to obey the mind's directives. It is the most severe kind of paralysis. Rather than paraplegia (paralysis of two limbs) or quadriplegia (paralysis of all four limbs), those suffering from locked-in states are unable to move more than one or two muscles. In terms of the two dimensions of mind, experience is usually unaffected, but agency is extremely curtailed. Locked-in states are feeling without doing; they are input with no output.

Locked-in states can arise gradually, precipitated by diseases such as amyotrophic lateral sclerosis (ALS),* which involves a progressive loss of motor neurons connecting the brain to the muscles. Stephen Hawking is one person who suffers from ALS, and over the course of many years he has become almost entirely paralyzed, except for a few small movements. He currently speaks through a voice synthesizer attached to a wheelchair that he controls with his cheek muscle. For evidence of the preservation of one's mind in this state, one need look only at Hawking's contributions to theoretical physics and mathematics, including his book *A Brief History of Time*, which remained on the *Sunday Times* bestseller list for more than four and a half years.

As ALS progresses, the key challenge is to find ways to preserve agency along with experience. As walking becomes difficult, you can use a cane, a walker, and then a wheelchair. Helpers can cook your meals and dress you, and friends and family can pitch in for everything else. But this reliance on others comes with a psychological cost—as we saw in chapter 4 on patients, relying so much on others can breed feelings of powerlessness and resentment. These feelings are reinforced by a cruel trick of the disease: while motor neurons are dying, sensory neurons are still alive and well, meaning that ALS patients can continue to feel discomfort as their body twists and buckles, without being able to do anything about it. The only saving grace of ALS is that often the patient's voice is preserved

....

* Also often referred to as Lou Gehrig's disease, after the baseball player who died from it at age thirty-seven.

until almost the very end, allowing him to speak and connect with others.

ALS not only represents a powerful example of locked-in states but also has personal significance for your authors. Dan was diagnosed with this disease in November 2010 and passed away from it in July 2013. Initially, we all believed he was suffering from the "slow-progressing" variety and had at least five years to go, but unfortunately nature chose to ignore that lenient diagnosis.

Dan often spoke to others about the difficulty of living with the disease and his looming mortality, but with your other author (Kurt) he spoke mostly about positive aspects of his new life. His diagnosis brought an endless stream of friends and family to his house, and time for thought, reflection, and deep personal connection. He took joy in being able to see the narrative arc of his life from beginning to end, and to live his final days without regret or reluctance. For the sake of maintaining his appetite, he also had an unlimited supply of marijuana pills, and though he refused to share them with his coauthor, he appeared to greatly enjoy their predictable side effects.

We spent many great afternoons talking about mind perception and morality and looking out the picture window at the little sailboats on the lake below. Kurt always wanted to ask Dan about ALS but was too afraid to ask and was having too much fun talking about science. But other people have written eloquently about living with ALS, such as Tony Judt, who was an esteemed thinker, writer, and professor of European history. The excerpt below is from his essay "Night" and describes the experience of greeting the morning after spending the night awake, alone, and motionless on his back.

I wake up in exactly the position, frame of mind, and state of suspended despair with which I went to bed—which in the circumstances might be thought a considerable achievement. . . . This cockroach-like existence is cumulatively intolerable even though on any given night it is perfectly manageable. "Cockroach" is of course an allusion to Kafka's *Metamorphosis*, in which the protagonist wakes up one morning to discover that he has been transformed into an insect. The point of the story is as much the responses and incomprehension of his family as it is the account of his own sensations, and it is hard to resist the thought that even the best-meaning and most generously thoughtful friend or relative cannot hope to understand the sense of isolation and imprisonment that this disease imposes upon its victims.[25]

Living with ALS is a heart-wrenching ordeal, but at least most patients, like Tony Judt, are not fully silent. More troublesome are cases of complete silence, where people have progressed past twitching and blinking. With them, the only route to communication is direct readouts of brain states using fMRI or EEG. As we saw earlier, one group of researchers inferred the presence of one woman's mind by having her imagine playing tennis or navigating her house, but the trick is to harness these scans to enable flexible communication. How do you turn tennis and navigation into conversation? People must control their brain states, using them as "words."

In the case of tennis and navigation, you could think about playing tennis to indicate yes and house navigation to indicate no. This sounds easy in principle but is extremely hard in practice. Thinking of tennis may have some detectable neural correlates, but thinking of tennis as a proxy for yes may have very different correlates. Moreover, these neural signatures are very noisy and often detectable only after dozens and dozens of trials. This would require someone being asked the same question again and again and each time thinking about tennis or navigation. Only then might we be able to discern their answer, after complicated analyses of fMRI data. Hardly the kind of back-and-forth we expect in conversation—and never mind that MRI magnets are amazingly expensive and incredibly loud.

But people can—if only indirectly—control their brain states in real time. Researchers at MIT put chronic-pain patients into an fMRI magnet and connected their brain activity with an image of a flame, which glowed brighter as their pain (and neural activation) increased. Patients were instructed to mentally try to dampen or extinguish it, and seemed able to control their "pain flame"—and feel less pain as a result.[26]

If healthy people can control their brain states, perhaps locked-in patients can do the same. This was the hope of Professor Niels Birbaumer, who traveled to South America with an EEG machine to help Mr. Elías Musiris Chahín communicate with his family. Mr. Chahín was a Peruvian casino magnate who was fully locked in by advanced ALS. Professor Birbaumer hooked up Mr. Chahín to the EEG machine, which was connected to a monitor showing a floating ball, a device Birbaumer called the Thought Translation Device (TTD). Some brain states were programmed to move the ball up, and some were programmed to move the ball down; the trick was for Mr. Chahín to learn to consciously control these brain states and hence the movements of the ball.

If the ball went up, Mr. Chahín would be saying yes, and if the ball went down, he would be saying no. At first the ball just moved randomly, even when Mr. Chahín was repeatedly asked the same question, but one day he flawlessly spelled out his entire name. Despite his immobilized body, his mind still appeared to be intact.[27] In the few years since Professor Birbaumer began working with Mr. Chahín, brain-scanning techniques have advanced in sophistication, and it is hoped that they will soon allow locked-in patients to have richer conversations—patients like Erik Ramsey.

On November 5, 1999, Ramsey was returning home from the movies with a friend. Ramsey was in the passenger seat and his friend was driving well above the speed limit. Their Camaro struck a U-turning minivan, flipping the vehicle and trapping Ramsey inside. The injuries were catastrophic and the pain unbearable—but the worst came when Ramsey developed a blood clot in a section of his brain stem called the pons.* Ramsey woke up to find himself unable to move any part of his body save his eyes, which could be moved only to look up or down. In what could be called a blessing or a curse, Ramsey remained fully conscious.

The plan for Ramsey was more ambitious than Birbaumer's approach with Mr. Chahín. With Ramsey the goal was actual language—the researchers believed they could insert wires into Ramsey's brain that would allow him to spell out words on his computer, similar to Birbaumer's system. Until about 2004 this actually worked. Then one day Ramsey had a bad bout of pneumonia, and his ability to spell disappeared, along with his ability to communicate beyond a simple yes or no. They had to find a new system, and what they developed is remarkable: Ramsey thinks about making simple sounds, such as vowels, and the wires from his brain to the computer translate this activity into *sound.* Slowly his inner voice

....

* Latin for "bridge," this brain region helps relay signals from other neural areas.

is finding a way to express itself, even if he is currently limited to simple vowel sounds.[28]

These neural-interface techniques hold much promise, especially for those who descend slowly into locked-in states, such as through ALS. However, many people become locked in suddenly through a stroke or accident, and their lack of movement is assumed to reflect a lack of mind. Without the appearance of agency, brain-scanning techniques are seldom used, and patients are diagnosed as comatose or vegetative and left to lie forever in hospital beds. Take the case of Julia Tavalaro, who at age thirty-two suffered two strokes and a brain hemorrhage. Lying motionless, she was assumed to be in a vegetative state for six years until her speech therapist, Arlene Kratt, noticed the trace of a smile after the telling of a joke. This small expression proved to be her salvation. With attention from doctors and therapists, she learned to communicate with eye movements (like Bauby) and control a wheelchair with cheek movements (like Hawking). More impressive, Tavalaro also published a collection of her poems, all communicated using a switch she could touch with a small movement of her cheek.[29]

Communicating with others may be lifesaving to some locked-in patients, but others simply want to die. One such patient is Tony Nicklinson, a British man who suffered a stroke and found himself almost fully locked in. Although he could communicate by blinking, he found his life so frustrating and empty that his one great wish was to be allowed to die. Unfortunately for Nicklinson, suicide—like getting dressed or going to the bathroom—is an action that requires some amount of agency, if only to overdose on painkillers. Without any of his own agency, he needed someone else's help, and so he petitioned the British government to allow him assistance. They had to decide whether this would be suicide or murder.

In a statement prepared for the court, Nicklinson described his daily life:

> My life can be summed up as dull, miserable, demeaning, undignified and intolerable. . . . It is a misery created by the accumulation of lots of things which are minor in themselves but, taken together, ruin what's left of my life. Things like . . . constant dribbling; having to be hoisted everywhere; loss of independence . . . particularly toileting and washing, in fact all bodily functions (by far the hardest thing to get used to); having to forgo favourite foods . . . having to wait until 10:30 to go to the toilet. . . . In extreme circumstances I have gone in the chair, and have sat there until the carers arrived at the normal time.[30]

The idea of consensual killing has always posed an ethical problem, because it represents a slippery slope. We might sympathize with Nicklinson, but what about the case of Bernd Brandes, who allowed himself to be eaten by German cannibal Armin Meiwes? Brandes was certainly happy to die—before he bled to death, he and Meiwes shared a meal of Brandes's cooked genitals—but is the simple wish to die sufficient justification for being killed? Is cannibalism okay when the victim expresses a desire to be eaten and have his kneecaps used as fertilizer, as Brandes suggested?[31] In their original decision the German courts wrote that Meiwes had no "base motives" and therefore was not guilty of murder, although he did get eight and a half years for manslaughter.[32]

Of course, Brandes—unlike Nicklinson—could have killed himself. The British court's decision on Nicklinson's case followed precedent, ruling that it was illegal for even a suffering, locked-in patient to be killed. One justice commented, "No one could fail to be deeply moved by the terrible predicament faced by these men struck down in their prime and facing a future bereft of hope . . . but the short answer is that . . . any change [in assisted suicide laws] would need the most carefully structured safeguards which only Parliament can deliver."[33]

What was Nicklinson to do? The court forbade assisted suicide, but it couldn't force him to eat—he still had control over his ability to swallow. Immediately after receiving the court's verdict, Nicklinson vowed to stop eating his spoon-fed meals. In his already weakened state, this lack of nutrition soon led him to catch pneumonia, and only days later he finally got his wish.[34] Whether you believe Nicklinson's death was a merciful release from suffering or a tragic loss of life likely depends upon how you imagine yourself in a locked-in state.

Trying to predict how much you would like or dislike the experience of a different state is called affective forecasting. Affective forecasting is exactly what people do when they make statements such as "I would rather die than be locked in" or "My life would be much better if I won the lottery" or "Giving birth won't hurt enough to need an epidural." In affective forecasting, people in one state (e.g., health) imagine what it would be like to be in a different state (e.g., locked in). Unfortunately, our imaginations are unreliable guides to altered states, which means that most people fail to accurately predict their future feelings.*

....

* For a full discussion of the inadequacy of imagination, we encourage you to read Daniel Gilbert's *Stumbling on Happiness*.

In a classic demonstration people imagined their happiness after hypothetically winning the lottery or becoming paraplegic. Unsurprisingly, people believed that lottery winning would make them ecstatic and that paraplegia would make them miserable. They were half right: immediately after these respective events, people who actually experience them are indeed much happier or sadder than usual, but within a year they basically return to their pre-event happiness level.[35] This means that lottery winners are often no happier than those who are paralyzed from the waist down. "Impossible!" you may scoff, believing with cold certainty that gaining millions of dollars is better than losing the use of your legs.

While it is true that your *imagined* experiences of these events are vastly different—sitting in your yacht drinking piña coladas versus sitting alone in a wheelchair—it turns out that the *actual* experiences of these events are not so different. There are many bad things in lottery winning and many good things in paraplegia. Winners of the lottery have to contend with scheming family members, the resentment of their friends, the loss of meaning in their lives after quitting their jobs, and the endless parade of strangers trying to use them for their money. Paraplegics still have their friends and family, and misfortune serves to strengthen social bonds, allows people to find meaning in their lives, and even helps them find God.[36]

Faulty affective forecasting often leads people to overestimate the misery of medical conditions. You may think that it would be better to be dead than to be both blind and deaf, but Helen Keller had these two disabilities, and not only did she want to keep living but she lived an incredibly rich and important life. You may think it would be better to be dead than to be locked in, but locked-in patients—Nicklinson excepted—seldom advocate for suicide. On the other hand, it is very difficult to simulate experiences such as pain and discomfort, which may make locked-in states *worse* than what we imagine.

In an everyday example, pregnant women often wish to have a natural birth, despite the imagined pain, but when the actual pain of labor arrives, many are quick to abandon that wish and go for the relief of an epidural. So it seems that the only rule when it comes to understanding the experiences of different states is that we seldom truly understand them. The inaccuracy of affective forecasting is ultimately rooted in the problem of other minds, which we introduced in chapter 1. You can ultimately never fully understand other minds, even when that "other" mind is your future self.

Your inability to accurately predict your future experiences is okay concerning giving birth or even paraplegia, because you can decide in the moment and communicate your wishes. In contrast, when you are silent, you end up being bound by your past wishes or the wishes of your family.

Imagine you had a loved one who suddenly suffered a massive stroke and showed no signs of agency but some ambiguous signs of experience via an fMRI scanner. They could be locked in, or they could be in a vegetative state. What would you choose for them? Would you keep them alive in case they could think and sense the world, if only from the solitary confinement of their broken body? Or would you allow them to die, freeing them from suffering and snuffing out any lingering experience they might have? Many people are terrified to make such a stark choice about life and death, wishing instead that the patient in question had given some hint to their wishes through a living will.

Living wills—also called advance directives—are similar to normal wills in that they communicate your wishes when you are no longer able to do so. Rather than applying after death, living wills apply after extreme misfortune, such as strokes, accidents, and neurological diseases. One example of a living will guiding decisions is told by Dr. Pauline Chen in an article she wrote in the *New York Times*. Her father-in-law woke up with coldness in his right arm. It was caused by severe clots in major arteries blocking blood flow to his arm and major organs. Surgery was a possibility, but its chance of success was small, and even if it was successful he would have been condemned to years of suffering and hospital visits. Chen's family struggled with the decision, but her father-in-law had made his wishes known in a living will—he wanted to die.

Despite the misgivings of the family, her father-in-law died happily, surrounded by those he loved—a decision Chen seems at peace with.[37] However, even when there are living wills advocating death, the family's wishes to keep patients on life support often prevail. Technically, the living will should take precedence, but with the patient silent and the family threatening to sue for malpractice (or even press charges for murder), doctors are often quick to capitulate and maintain treatment. Because of moral concerns, some hospitals even keep patients alive when the family agrees with the will's decision to cease treatment.[38]

Knowing about the inaccuracy of affective forecasting might also give us pause about relying on living wills, as the wishes of the healthy past self may not be the same as those of the locked-in future self. Imagine that at age eighteen you make your friend promise to kill you if you ever buy a minivan. Twenty years later you have forgotten this pledge and lost touch with your friend, and so you are surprised to see him arrive at your house with a handgun after you buy a family-sized automobile. Would he be excused for murdering you? Unlikely. The courts recognize that people can change their minds. One way to interpret "change their minds" is to say that the same mind merely shifted its opinion, but the more interesting way is to say that the *mind actually changed*—it's a different mind than it was in the first place. This more literal sense of "mind changing" suggests that someone's wishes in a living will are no different from the wishes of their family: they are both the wishes of people who are fundamentally different from the patient sitting in the bed. The writer of the living will just happens to have the same name as the person who is now silent.

That moral judgments depend more on mind perception than on objective mind is especially true with the silent. We had a thesis student named Annie Knickman who, after spending time in hospitals, noticed something funny about the mind perception of PVS patients: people spoke of them as if they completely lacked minds. In a biological sense PVS patients are somewhere in the limbo between living and dead, but people seemed to see them as *more dead than dead*. In her thesis studies, participants rated the agency and experience of normal people, PVS patients, and dead people. Unsurprisingly, people rated the living person as having more mind than either the PVS patient or the dead person, but PVS patients were also seen as having *less* mental functioning than dead people.[39]

The reason for this strange reversal is something called dualism, which we explore in depth in chapter 8 on the dead. The short explanation is that when you are in a persistent vegetative state, people focus so much on the mechanics of your body, on your neurons and organs, on the breathing machines and feeding tubes, that they forget that there is also a mind in that body. We saw the same phenomenon in chapter 5 on the enemy: focusing on someone's chest and butt turns them from a person into a mere sexual object. Consistent with "objectification," the silent are often seen as biological machines more than living beings.

The ambiguity of mind poses difficulty not only for end-of-life decisions but also for beginning-of-life decisions. Consider fetuses—do they have minds? Out of all the cryptominds you would be hard-pressed to find one more controversial than a developing human in utero. In contrast to PVS and locked-in states, which are possible only with modern life-support machines, fetuses have been around for as long as humans. But despite eons of familiarity, there is still no consensus about when "life" or mind truly begins. Where is

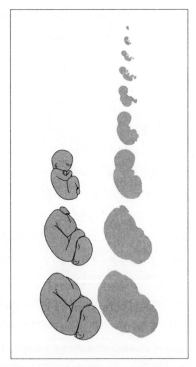

Figure 31: Fetal Development
When does the mind start?

the line between mindlessly replicating cells and a nascent human being?

One straightforward answer to this question is to draw the line at either the very beginning or the very end of development. The Catholic Church takes the "beginning" perspective, claiming that life begins at conception; as soon as an egg and a sperm fuse, there is life—the beginning of a new mind. This perspective is shared by many evangelical Christians, although this is a relatively recent trend. As late as the 1970s many evangelicals emphasized the other end of development and believed that life truly began at birth. Writing in *Christianity Today* in 1968, professors at Dallas Theological Seminary wrote that "God does not regard the fetus as a soul, no matter how far gestation has progressed," and "The embryo is not fully human—it is an undeveloped person."[40]

This "life at birth" position arose to differentiate evangelicals from Catholics and meant that many were relatively comfortable with abortion. A symposium organized in 1968 by the Christian Medical Society affirmed that "the preservation of fetal life . . . may have to be abandoned to maintain full and secure family life," as well as in cases of rape, incest, fetal deformity, and threat to the mother's well-being, whether physical or emotional.[41] Evangelical opinion, however, swung after church leaders such as Jerry Falwell reacted to the 1973 *Roe v. Wade* decision and advocated a "life at conception" interpretation of the Bible.

Between the extremes of conception and birth, there are nine months of gradual change, which makes it difficult to draw any firm boundary. We can all agree on the presence of mind at nine months, and at eight months, but what about seven? Or six? Or five? Or four? Or three? When do cells become people? This question mirrors a long-standing philosophical problem called the sorites paradox, which asks when "grains of sand" become a "pile"?* We can all agree that one grain of sand is not a pile and that a thousand grains is a pile. We can also all agree that one grain of sand never makes the difference between a pile and not a pile. Two grains of sand still isn't a pile and 999 grains of sand still is a pile. But here's the paradox: If you keep adding (or taking away) single grains of sand, eventually you do end up with a pile (or a lack of pile). Somehow, "pileness" emerges from enough grains of sand, even though there is no one single grain that does the trick.

With fetal development no single day is sufficient to transition from mere cells to a minded person, but a minded person eventually does emerge. This problem of vagueness plagues every human category, from newness (how many days until a new car is no longer "new"?) to money (how many dollars does one need in order to be "rich"?) to height (how many inches are required for someone to be "tall"?). The vagueness of fetal minds is particularly troublesome because laws about abortion require precision, such as allowing one during the first trimester but not in the fifty-third trimester when your son drives the family car through the garage door.

One solution to the problem of vagueness is tying mind perception to biological changes, such as the "quickening," when the fetus begins moving on its own. Most pregnant women detect fetal movement somewhere between eighteen and twenty weeks (or somewhat earlier if they've given birth before). The relative precision of the quickening in an otherwise vague developmental process has recommended it as a criterion for the right to life; the British legal scholar William Blackstone wrote in 1765, "Life . . . begins in

....

* In ancient Greek, *sorites* means "heaped up."

contemplation of law as soon as an infant is able to stir in the mother's womb."[42] The quickening was also used as the line beyond which women sentenced to death for crimes could "plead the belly" and stay the execution until after giving birth.[43]

Another potential criterion is viability, the point at which a fetus is able to live on its own. In the dimensions of mind perception, viability can be thought of as agency, the capacity to act upon the world and to achieve one's goals, if only minimally. However, the larger concern in fetal rights—as in most other moral rights—is the capacity for experience. When can a fetus feel pain and suffer? Neurologically speaking, at twenty-three to thirty weeks fetuses develop extensive connections to the thalamus, a brain structure that relays information from the body to higher cortical structures that process pain. EEGs reveal typical "awake" human brain waves a few weeks later in development, along with activations of the somatosensory cortex, which processes painful stimuli. Thirty weeks of development also marks the point at which infants will make facial grimaces in response to noxious stimuli, such as pokes in the heel or extreme heat.[44]

Although this evidence converges to suggest something important happens at thirty weeks of development, it is unclear whether this represents *conscious* experiences of pain. Silent adult patients often have intact thalamocortical connections, exhibit alpha waves in EEGs, and will grimace in response to pokes and prods, but they do not necessarily feel pain. An engineer could easily build a mechanical sensor that reacts to pinches or extreme heat, but we wouldn't say that it could "feel" pain any more than a sensor that detects colors can really "see" a sunset. Feeling requires a *conscious* mind.

Fetal minds are especially ambiguous because perceptions of

current mind are entangled with those of future mind. A fertilized zygote of thirty-two cells is extremely unlikely to have feelings and thoughts but, if left alone, will eventually develop into a person who does have these capacities. For potential parents it can be extremely hard to separate the actual from the potential. When people are bereft after a miscarriage, it is not because of the loss of mere cells but instead the loss of the imagined child, the disappearance of future Thanksgiving dinners and birthday parties. This is why some pro-choice advocates joke that pro-lifers want those contemplating abortion not only to get an ultrasound but also to paint their nursery and pick out a name.[45]

Questions of mind at the beginning of life can sometimes continue even after birth, such as in the horrible case of anencephaly, where normal-looking babies are born missing all of their brain except for the brain stem—allowing them to stay biologically alive despite no other mental functioning.[46] Bioethicists suggest that the most ethical choice in anencephaly is to harvest these babies' organs to save the lives of other infants who need them (of children under the age of two who need organ transplants, 30 percent to 50 percent die before receiving them).[47] Of course, it is incredibly difficult to not see a full human mind within your perfect-looking child, even when their lack of brain proves otherwise.

The allure of a mind imagined and desired exerts its hold even after birth in another kind of silent mind—children with extreme autism. Having a child with any disability can be challenging, but the specific deficits of autism can be extremely trying for parents. Children with Down syndrome may have cognitive delays but easily connect emotionally with their parents, whether through hugs and kisses or by simply saying, "I love you." Conversely, as we saw in chapter 5 on the enemy, autism is marked by difficulties in mind perception and communication that undermine emotional connection. Children with extreme autism may not be silent per se, but without the ability to cogently communicate or reciprocate feelings, they may leave their parents feeling unloved.

This silence is why parents with autistic children were so excited by "facilitated communication" (FC), a technique that seemed to open up their children's otherwise closed minds. In this technique the child sat in front of a computer keyboard while a helper "facilitated" his or her communication by holding his or her hands and sensing where the child wished to type. Ostensibly, these helpers detected minute muscle movements toward certain keys and used them to convey the thoughts and feeling of the autistic child.

Parents were understandably delighted when their previously uncommunicative children would type out long missives of love and longing, such as "Autism held me hostage for seventeen years but not any more because now I can talk."[48] The practice, promoted in the United States by Douglas Biklen, a professor at Syracuse University, spread quickly. Teachers and parents alike were amazed at the messages that were coming from their children—but were they actually coming from their children at all? Suspicions were raised when some of the children began writing poetry and expressing ideas that were not just beyond expectations for an autistic child but beyond expectations for even the brightest children in their age range.

To explain these remarkable children, practitioners of facilitated communication suggested the possibility of "language savants," similar to others with autism who were mathematical or musical geniuses. Others had their doubts, wondering whether the entire practice was simply a way to make money from vulnerable parents. You might think that, either way, facilitated communication caused no harm and gave some parents hope, and so it was a matter of caveat emptor.

Unfortunately, while most children wrote essays of love and wisdom, some children typed graphic accounts of rape and sexual assault at the hands of their parents—often their fathers, but at times extending to siblings, mothers, even grandparents. Courts of law had been accepting FC messages as genuine, but a father accused of brutally raping his autistic daughter demanded that facilitated communication be put to the test. He had lost his family and was facing the loss of his freedom: it was time to finally answer the question of who was really authoring these messages.

A researcher, Dr. Howard Shane, was brought in to investigate the accusations. To determine the true mind behind the message, he designed a paradigm in which the child and the facilitator were asked to identify an item in an image and—unbeknownst to the facilitator—they were each shown a different image. For example, the child might be shown a bird while the facilitator was shown a dog. As the researchers watched, the child's hands—guided by the facilitator—typed out "P-U-P-P-Y"—describing an image that the child had not seen.[49] It appeared that these facilitated messages—whether heartfelt or accusatory—came from the minds of the facilitators and not from the children. These findings were replicated again and again, much to the disappointment of parents who had thought they had finally found a way to bridge the gap of autism.* When it comes to minds, perceptions are strongly biased by what people want to

....

* One of these replications was conducted in our lab and written up in a paper entitled "Clever Hands," in a nod to the power of perception revealed in the case of the horse Clever Hans.

believe. But some things, like facilitated communication, are really too good to be true.

More than any other cryptominds, the silent are characterized by wishful thinking. Whether they are fetuses, autistic children, or vegetative adults, we often perceive the kind of mind we wish (or fear) is present. We want to believe that grandparents without the capacity to talk or walk can nevertheless recognize their own grandchild. We want to believe that our spouse who suffered a stroke isn't living in pain. We want to believe that the mind of a loved child loves us back. The silent provide a Rorschach inkblot of cryptomind, a mute canvas on which we project our own minds and desires.

The silent lead us to wonder whether a body has lost its mind, but the cryptominds we explore next—the group—have the ability to steal our minds without even having a body.

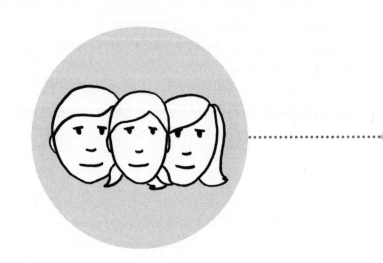

Chapter 7

THE GROUP

E very twelve years the medium-sized Indian city of Allahabad finds itself home to almost 100 million Hindu pilgrims over the course of eight weeks. Originally named Prayaga, "the place of offerings," Allahabad is the meeting place (the Triveni Sangam) of three rivers: the Ganges, the Yamuna, and the Saraswati. The Ganges and the Yamuna are easy to find on a map, but the Saraswati is more difficult, because it has long since dried up. The Hindus believe that this mythical river still flows underground until it reaches Allahabad. They also believe that the gods dropped holy nectar into the Triveni Sangam, gifting this confluence of rivers the power to wash away sins. It is this cleansing power that attracts pilgrims to the Triveni Sangam. In the waters among the millions of others, pilgrims inevitably feel a powerful sense of transcendence. Walking, eating, and bathing as a group, they find their individuality drifting away, replaced by something much grander and more sustaining.

In an article covering this phenomenon for *National Geographic*, writer Laura Spinney met an elderly couple who slept for weeks in an unheated tent at near-freezing temperatures while being constantly bombarded by noise loud enough to cause hearing loss. In addition to these living conditions, bathing in the river meant submersing yourself in frigid water so polluted that it is unsafe to either drink or bathe in. Despite the cold, pollution, and endless crowds, pilgrims nevertheless seem energized and rejuvenated by their experience of losing themselves to the group.

Even in peaceful, spiritual Allahabad, however, the crowds can sometimes spell disaster. On February 10, 2013, at the local train station, pilgrims on their way home started jostling one another. When a few people fell, the police tried to intervene and panic ensued. A stampede crushed, trampled, and otherwise killed thirty-six people.[1] In this kind of crowd the self becomes lost to the group, disappearing into the crackling, screaming energy of terror, and is

Figure 32: Triveni Sangam

regained only once the crowd disperses. Even those within the crowd who recognize the folly of their actions cannot help but push and trample. The group seems to have a mind of its own.

We often speak of "group mind" as some mysterious force that influences people's behavior, but do groups really have a mind? As we saw in the previous chapter, mind is intimately linked to brains, and groups certainly don't have brains. Then again, brains themselves are merely groups of neurons, which themselves are dumb and mindless. So perhaps groups of people—who each have a mind—can make a collective mind. At the very least, groups like corporations, governments, and the Freemasons are *perceived* to have a mind. And as we'll see, they are perceived to have a specific kind of mind, sitting firmly on one side of the moral typecasting fault line. But we are getting ahead of ourselves. Before we investigate the "group mind," we must first discover what it means to be a "group."

The boundaries of an individual are reasonably obvious—you are whatever is inside your skin—but who or what belongs in a group is less straightforward. Consider your family. Who is in and who is out seems clear: mom, dad, sister, husband, and kids are in, whereas distant friends, work colleagues, and acquaintances are out. But what about your uncle who comes only for the holidays, or the biological cousin of your adopted sister, or the brother whom you haven't spoken to for years because of his impossible wife? Do they count as "family"? Groups, like mind, are matters of perception, which further complicates things.

One easy solution for identifying groups is to identify a collection of people in one place. Many groups fulfill this criterion, such as the pilgrims at Allahabad, military platoons, and even nations of people. But this criterion cannot be enough; otherwise the five people waiting at the bus stop are as legitimate a group as the five people who make up the latest pop sensation "All 5-4-Love."* Another potential rule of thumb could be whether a collection of people has the word "group" or "club" or "organization" in its name, like the Sierra Club, the National Organization for Women, or the Pop-Tarts Addiction Group. But these labels exclude folks whose associations are too ephemeral for labels, such as protesters or construction crews of day laborers.

Not only does any definition of "group" yield exceptions, but the more you peer at groups, the more they seem to vanish. We focus on individuals in everyday life, and the more you focus on specific individuals within a group, the more the connections among them disappear. Just as you can "miss the forest for the trees," so too do we often miss "the group" because we think of it from the perspective of any one person. The more you stare at the lead singer of the band or the CEO of a corporation, the more superfluous everyone else seems. Sometimes you just have to take a step back and look at the gestalt.

Gestalt is a German word that translates to "shape" or "form," but it has long held another deeper definition in psychology. Gestalt psychology began in the early twentieth century as a reaction to psychology that examined isolated elements of human perception. Whereas a typical psychologist studied the perception of specific features like shadows or edges or lines, a Gestalt psychologist studied how it all fit together. Although Gestalt psychologists primarily studied visual perception, they revealed five principles of "groupiness" that also apply to perceptions of people: proximity, similarity, closure, continuation, and common fate.[2]

Proximity is the idea that people in groups are typically close to

....
* Not a real pop band . . . yet.

one another. It is easier to be a group when all members are seated in the same basement than when half the people are in Croatia and the other half are in Japan. Bands, sports teams, and reading clubs are characterized by physical proximity and so seem more authentic than Internet groups in which members live all across the globe.* Like proximity, similarity is a relatively straightforward concept. Groups are "groupier" when their members share many similarities, such as the same race, religion, or music preferences. This is why there are more "Black Student Associations" on college campuses than "Black, White, Asian, and American Indian Associations."

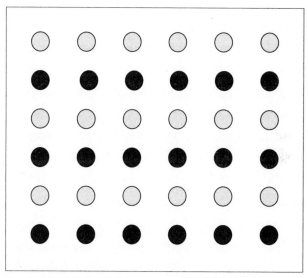

Figure 33: How Do You Group These Dots?
Following the Gestalt principle of similarity, we organize the dots into rows of similar color—not into columns of alternating color.

....

* Proximity within a virtual space, such as in a World of Warcraft guild, is a matter of perception.

Interestingly, we tend to see similarities based on present traits rather than absent traits. We consider Seventh-day Adventists more grouplike than atheists because atheists are unified by the absence of faith rather than the presence of faith. If you looked around your living room, you'd likely see chairs, a table, a lamp, and maybe a rug on the floor and a picture on the wall. But now consider the objects that *aren't* present. Well, probably a car, a monkey, and the Sydney Opera House. In fact, there are an infinite variety of things that could be absent. Absences do a poor job of unifying people because they are much less specific. Imagine a group that thinks Picasso is the greatest painter ever and another group that thinks he isn't— only the former seems like a real group.

The principle of closure suggests that the most obvious shapes— and groups—have firm boundaries. A group seems ill defined if anyone can join and leave, especially if it allows partial membership. Consider the difference between being a Unitarian Universalist and being Jewish. It is easy to become a Unitarian Universalist and easy to leave the church, and there's no clear division between people who are and aren't Unitarian Universalists. In contrast, questions of Jewish identity are much sharper. You are legitimately Jewish only if your mother was Jewish or you undergo an extremely ardu-ous conversion procedure (and even then, it's not really the same). It's also hard to renounce being Jewish—even if you don't believe in God, don't celebrate Passover, don't speak Yiddish, and don't have a mother who makes you feel especially guilty, you're still Jewish, often by virtue of a continuous Ashkenazi bloodline.

Speaking of continuous, continuity is another Gestalt principle. In shapes continuity means that a shape doesn't stop as soon as there is some visual barrier. For example, in a drawing of two over-lapping keys, we expect the bottom key to continue on after it passes

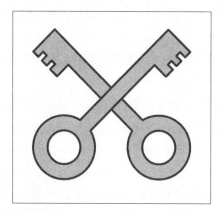

Figure 34: Continuity in Shapes
The bottom key continues even after
it is obscured by the crossing over of
the top key.

under the top key. Continuity is equally important with groups. Temporary flash mobs may technically be groups, but the groupiest groups are those that stick around despite the challenges that they face. To return to the Jewish people, what makes them groupier than many other religions is their continuation through millennia of persecution.

The most important criterion for perceptions of groups is probably common fate. Groups are collections of people that not only are similar, proximate, closed, and continuous but also share a destiny. When a corporation goes bankrupt, everyone is out of a job; when a football team wins the Super Bowl, everyone gets a ring. Groups often fall apart when this common fate comes undone, such as when work teams get rewarded for individual performance rather than group performance.[3]

Combining the principles of proximity, similarity, closure, continuity, and common fate yields a measure of groupiness that is typically given the more scientific name of "entitivity"—how much something is an entity. Perceptions of entitivity—like those of mind—not only are ambiguous but also dictate how we perceive mind in groups and group members. For an obvious example, consider sheep.

Sheep don't appear to possess the most powerful of minds. They've never built a civilization, can't drive, and do even worse at *Jeopardy*. But they are far more intelligent than you might think. In a series of studies, Cambridge University researchers tested the cognitive ability of seven Welsh Mountain sheep in a specially constructed maze.[4] Despite their reputation as fuzzy dunces, sheep are just as smart in these situations as rodents and monkeys.

If sheep are so smart, then why do they seem so stupid? The answer is that sheep are highly entitive—they live in those very "groupy" groups that we call "flocks." Any one sheep appears highly similar to other sheep (at least to our eyes), they remain spatially nearby other sheep, and they have a collective fate. It is the entire flock that is led by a shepherd or stalked by wolves or herded by a border collie, so it's unnecessary to consider the thoughts of any single sheep to understand the behavior of the flock. It is groupiness that strips away mind from individual sheep; when we admonish people for mindlessly following the crowd, we say, "Don't be a sheep."

Research suggests anyone seems dumber in a group, including teenagers, college students, and even the elderly. Consider the difference between talking to your grandmother in her room at the nursing home and watching the sea of gray hairs march down to the dining room for five o'clock dinner. The collective shuffling of the latter seems much less thoughtful. Two psychologists, Adam Waytz and Liane Young, investigated this effect, hypothesizing that it hinged upon the entitivity of the group: the more entitive the group, the less mind individual members should be perceived to possess. To test this hypothesis, participants rated the minds of individuals belonging to low-entitivity groups like Facebook users or golf players and high-entitivity groups like the U.S. Marine Corps or the New York Yankees, which exhibit the principles of similarity, proximity, closure, continuity, and common fate. As predicted, in more entitive groups members were stripped of their individual minds.[5]

Psychologist Carey Morewedge and his team independently found this effect with a creative experimental design. One of More-wedge's coinvestigators, psychologist Jonathan Schooler, had a daughter who owned an aquarium full of brine shrimp, or Sea-Monkeys. At first the aquarium was populated by a large cluster of shrimp, and each individual shrimp wasn't particularly interesting to Schooler or his daughter. But gradually, as happens with pets, the shrimp began to die, until there was just one left.

Suddenly this one remaining brine shrimp was fascinating—Schooler and his daughter gave it a name and began to see it as possessing personality traits. Of course, this same shrimp had been there all along, but it became interesting only once it had shed its surrounding group. Mimicking this Sea-Monkey experience, the researchers showed participants pictures of individuals in groups of varying sizes and also manipulated the individuals' proximity and similarity to the group. They found that the more an individual stood out—by being in a smaller group, being distant from the group, or being different from the group—the more they were perceived to possess mind.[6]

Importantly, the perceived mind stripped from group members in entitive groups doesn't just vanish. Instead it gets ascribed to the group as a whole. Take the case of a squad of marines. Not only do marines all look the same, courtesy of uniforms and haircuts, but they all have the same training and—within a given squad—have the same mission and intertwined fates. Because they act together as one unit, it makes sense to think of the whole squad as a mind, rather than individual marines. The secretary of defense doesn't need to know that Private Jones misses home or that Private Wilson listens to heavy metal music to get pumped up. All she needs to know is that the entire squad is planning on taking the enemy position, collectively believing that they have the tactical advantage.

This mind-perception "trade-off"[7] between groups and their members is reminiscent of the mind-perception fault line seen throughout the book. Just as individual minds are seen as *either* feelers *or* doers, minds are ascribed to *either* groups *or* their members. Groups may derive their perceived mind from their members, but studies reveal that groups are ascribed a different kind of mind from their members.

In one experiment philosophers Josh Knobe and Jesse Prinz asked people to rate the "naturalness" of a number of sentences. Some of these sentences asked whether a company, Acme Corp, believed its profit margins would increase or intended to release a new product. In other words, they asked about Acme Corp's status as a thinking doer. Other sentences asked about Acme Corp's ability to have experience and be a vulnerable feeler, such as whether Acme Corp was feeling joy or pain. The agency-related set of statements were all rated as very natural, whereas the experience set of statements were rated as rather unnatural.*[8]

These results suggest that—unlike the humans who make up

....

* Bryce Huebner, a philosopher at Georgetown University, and her colleagues have found similar results when asking about the nation of China. B. Huebner,

groups—groups themselves are typically seen only as thinking doers and not as vulnerable feelers. A cohesive collection of people has agency but not experience. In another test of this "group as agent" hypothesis, we included Google in our set of mind-survey characters. As predicted, people admitted that Google could think and act but denied it the ability to feel and sense—placing it in the bottom right of the mind survey, together with God.

Corporations seem to lack experience because they lack a body, which is the seat of our passions and the vehicle through which we feel hunger, and lust, and fear. Although you might be willing to grant that Google is feeling a bit disappointed with a Supreme Court decision, you are likely unwilling to say that Google is thirsty or lustful. Experience rests in the body, and only individuals have bodies, which obscures even the experience of individuals within groups.

Because experience is grounded in the individual, people will often spend thousands of dollars to help a single person but nothing to help many people—a fact well noted by Joseph Stalin, who is rumored to have said, "A single death is a tragedy, a million deaths is a statistic."* Take the case of Baby Jessica, an eighteen-month-old who in 1987 fell down a well. Picture a steel pipe eight inches wide, which is just wide enough for a little baby girl to become wedged inside, dozens of feet below the surface. When Jessica's story was featured on the national news, people around the world gave a total of $800,000 for her successful rescue, a heartwarming display of generosity.[9]

But before your heart gets too warm, in the span of time that

....

M. Bruno, and H. Sarkissian, "What Does the Nation of China Think About Phenomenal States?" *Review of Philosophy and Psychology* 1 (2009): 225–43.

* This quote is in fact from Französischer Witz, by Kurt Tucholsky. A French diplomat says, "The war? I can't find it too terrible! The death of one man: that is a catastrophe. One hundred thousand deaths: That is a statistic!"

she was trapped (two and a half days), just under 35,000 children likely died worldwide from malnutrition.[10] How many of these lives could have been saved for the same amount of money? A lot. Those commercials that promise to help out a starving village for just dollars a day aren't lying. It's relatively cheap to give children in developing nations access to clean water, sufficient food, and basic medical supplies—at least orders of magnitude cheaper than rescuing Baby Jessica.

As we explored in chapter 4 on the patient, we help others when we feel empathy, and it is easier to empathize with the story of a single American girl than with thousands of faceless African children. However, people help individuals even when they know nothing about them. In one elegant study conducted at Carnegie Mellon University,[11] researchers evenly divided ten dollars among a group of eight participants by dealing out forty twenty-five-cent tickets (i.e., participants got five tickets each). Participants were then divided into "keepers" and "losers." The losers were told that they had to forfeit all their money, while the keepers held on to their tickets. The keepers were then given an additional option—they could donate some of their tickets to a loser.

Some keepers were assigned a specific participant who would receive their donation (e.g., "participant 4"), whereas others were just told that it would go to "one" of the losers. Importantly, the participants never met and keepers had no clue about the real identity of participant 4. From the keepers' perspectives, their money was still going to some random person out of the eight—but now that person had a name, even if that name was just a participant number. Keepers who had an "identifiable" victim donated an average of $3.42, whereas keepers who had a (more) unknown victim donated only an average of $2.12. If donations increase with simple identification, imagine what happens when we know someone's real name, gender, and specific predicament—as in the case of Baby Jessica.

It pays to be an individual not only when are you are harmed but also when you perpetrate harm. In chapter 1 we saw that minds are typically divided into doers and feelers, an idea expanded upon in chapter 4 on the patient with the concept of moral typecasting. Moral typecasting suggests that we see others as either blameworthy moral agents or innocent moral patients—explaining why it pays to play the victim card in court. This legal strategy works for individual humans, because we all have both agency and experience and can emphasize our experience to garner sympathy. Groups, on the other hand, are seen as possessing only agency and lacking the experience needed to earn sympathy.

We are happy to prosecute companies that dump pollution, lay off employees, or rig the stock market but rarely feel bad when they get dismantled or are the targets of hostile takeovers.[12] This has led psychologist Tage Rai to suggest that "corporations are cyborgs." As revealed in chapter 3 on machines, it is easy to blame robots as moral agents but hard to see them as vulnerable moral patients. The same is true of groups.

Consider when an army squadron commits a terrible crime in the theater of war. Such a crime may be inexcusable, but we could still extend compassion to the young men and women who face danger, watch their friends die, and wake up in sweats from night terrors. But these problems are suffered by *individual* soldiers, and so when a group does something heinous, people feel less overall sympathy and demand punishment. Unfortunately, it is the individual members who bear the punishment for wrongdoing, not the group.

The denial of experience to groups means we fail to extend them the same protections as other cryptominds like babies and puppies. Mitt Romney has challenged this habit, arguing that "corporations are people too"[13] and deserve the right to support candidates in elections. The Supreme Court agreed. In a five-to-four decision it ruled that corporations have the same free-speech rights as individuals.[14] What about other rights? In one lampoon, Stephen Colbert takes seriously the idea that corporations are people, suggesting that Romney's work at Bain Capital, in which he downsized and divided (i.e., dismembered) corporations qualifies him as a serial killer.[15]

We laugh at this idea because even forcibly dividing a corporation seems to cause no real suffering, but the inability of groups to suffer causes consternation to those who wish to see them punished. If a corporation harms the environment, its customers, or its employees, how can we make this group agent suffer in turn? One solution is to levy fines, but does this really "hurt" the corporation? The lack of experience in groups is why mere financial settlements against corporations are so unfulfilling. Consider the $1.9 billion settlement levied against HSBC for allowing the laundering of billions for Mexican drug cartels.[16] Even two billion dollars is unsatisfying when the crime involves supporting organizations that display severed heads along the sides of highways.

The invulnerability of groups coupled with their ability to plan and act can also lead us to distrust them—especially invisible ones built on world domination. To understand what we mean, just look up at the sky. See the soft white lines of jet exhaust crisscrossing above you? You may not have given these condensation trails—or "contrails"—much thought, but consider the pattern they make from space. Each day thousands of planes fly across the world, and their contrails form a tight grid around the globe, an inescapable web of white fog. From your vantage point on the ground, each of these contrails seems to leave only water, but from that distance could you distinguish water from acid or from hallucinogens or other mind-control agents?

Because you've read this far, we feel that we can trust you with an important secret: There is a secret group controlling the highest reaches of government, including the Federal Aviation Administration. Every day this nefarious group impregnates jet fuel with a variety of chemicals that mist out from the engines and float down into your lungs. The white lines above you aren't just contrails—they're *chem trails*—made from chemicals expressly designed to subjugate people, turning normally free-thinking Americans into docile drones who accept without question this group's propaganda. What propaganda? Not only the liberal media but also the subliminal messages embedded in your favorite television programs. With only a 767 passing silently overhead and the right commercial, shadow governments can rob you of your free will.

As you may have guessed, this is an example of a conspiracy theory, broadly called the "chem-trail" theory. Although there is virtually no evidence to support it, that hasn't stopped many people from believing it and attempting to use their innate psychic powers to disperse the sky chemicals. Conspiracy theories are as old as human society. For as long as there have been social ills, people have blamed them on nefarious, high-agency, low-experience groups such as the Illuminati, the Freemasons, or the shape-shifting lizard people known as Reptilians.* Today conspiracies are implicated in

....

* No joke—4 percent of American voters believe in the existence of Reptilians, according to a 2013 Public Policy Polling poll. P. Bump, "12 Million Americans

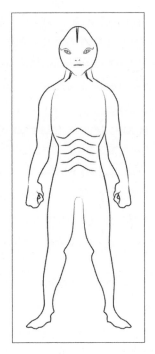

Figure 35: Reptilian
An artist's interpretation of a Reptilian leader of the New World Order,
a legitimate conspiracy theory.

everything from the devastation of the 9/11 attacks[17] to the suffering
caused by the rise of autism.[18]

Why do conspiracy theories emerge so robustly to explain tragedies such as disease, war, and death? The answer—as you may have
guessed from previous chapters—is dyadic completion. When there
is a tragedy, people seldom throw up their hands, say, "*C'est la vie,*"
and accept the inherent randomness of life. Instead they search for
meaning, asking not only *how* something bad could have happened

Believe Lizard People Run Our Country," *The Wire,* April 2, 2013, http://www
.thewire.com/national/2013/04/12-million-americans-believe-lizard-people
-run-our-country/63799/.

but also *who* is behind it. When people feel like suffering moral patients, their dyadic moral template compels them to find moral agents to hold responsible. We first saw this kind of "agentic dyadic completion" in chapter 2 on animals, where people put a pig on trial for the death of a child.

As an easy example, consider rush-hour driving. When a car cuts you off during your daily commute, you likely seldom think, "They must be in a hurry," or even, "They're a little distracted," but instead, "That asshole knew I was there and cut me off just to spite me!!" The link between perceptions of harm and perceptions of evil intention is nicely illustrated by a pair of scenarios designed by philosopher Joshua Knobe.

Both scenarios feature a chairman of the board presented with a new, profitable project by a company vice president. In the first case, the VP says, "We are thinking of starting a new program. It will help us increase profits, but it will also *help* the environment." The chairman of the board then answers, "I don't care at all about helping the environment. I just want to make as much profit as I can. Let's start the new program." The question is whether the chairman intentionally helped the environment. Most people in this case answer no—if the CEO doesn't care about helping the environment, then the help is unintentional. But now consider the second scenario with only one word changed.

The VP now says to the chairman of the board, "We are thinking of starting a new program. It will help us increase profits, but it will also *harm* the environment." The chairman of the board then answers, "I don't care at all about harming the environment. I just want to make as much profit as I can. Let's start the new program." Did the chairman intentionally harm the environment? Most people now answer yes—if the CEO doesn't care about harming the environment, then the harm is intentional.[19] This is a striking reversal. His words and deeds were *exactly* the same in both cases, and in both cases he was motivated only by profit. However, psychologically we perceive the good act to be merely incidental and the evil act to be intentional.

Harm compels us to find a mind to blame, but not all minds are equally blameworthy. You'll notice that the environmental harm was pinned on a business leader and not a puppy, as dyadic completion can only occur with someone or something that possesses a lot of agency. You're not going to blame a little girl for the downturn of stocks or a cancer patient for a plane crash but instead presidents and cabinet ministers and corporations. Agentic dyadic completion often locates specific agents to blame. When the environment is harmed because of corporate policies, we blame the CEO; when a loved one dies from botched surgery, we blame the overconfident doctor; and when someone beats us for a promotion, we blame our biased boss.

However, some events are difficult to pin on any one person, whether because the chain of blame is uncertain or because the magnitude of suffering is too great to imagine its being caused by a single individual. In these cases, such as the day the music died* or JFK's assassination, we seek to blame something even more powerful and mysterious: the agentic minds of conspiring groups. Mass destruction calls for mass intentional evil, which conspiracies— with their collection of calculating senators, bankers, and spies— can easily provide. Perhaps the best example of this is from the show *The X-Files*, in which a group of men smoke in a shadowy room,

....

* That is, the plane crash that claimed the lives of Buddy Holly, the Big Bopper, and Ritchie Valens.

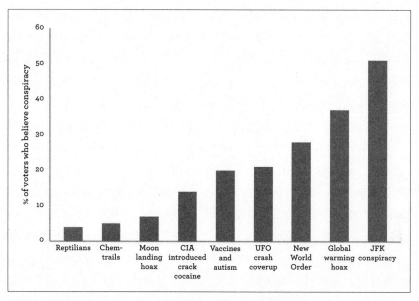

Figure 36: Belief in Various Conspiracy Theories

BASED ON T. JENSEN, "DEMOCRATS AND REPUBLICANS DIFFER ON CONSPIRACY THEORY BELIEFS"
(PUBLIC POLICY POLLING, 2013).

pulling the strings on alien abductions, secret experiments, and mind control.

Conspiracy theories are helped by the complicated nature of causation. The most immediate causes of events are often obvious, but their ultimate causes are unclear. Consider the case of the common cold. The immediate reason for your sickness is a quickly replicating virus, but why did you get the virus at that exact time, and why is it making *you* sick and not your coworkers? Lack of sleep? Lack of vitamin C? Licking too many doorknobs? In the case of JFK's assassination, the proximate cause was a bullet. But less clear is the ultimate cause of these events: How did Oswald get to the depository unnoticed? How did he purchase the guns? Was the CIA involved? With any tragedy there are levels upon levels of causation, and we usually keep going up them until arriving at a sufficiently agentic mind, such as a conspiring group. Typically, the bigger the tragedy is, the larger the conspiracy we perceive. As we've seen, groups harvest their mind from their members, and so the more members are involved in a conspiracy, the more it seems to have agency.

So far we have learned two things about how people perceive the minds of groups. The first is that we take mind away from individual group members and instead give it to the overall group. The second is that we frequently blame groups—and their agentic minds—for wrongdoing. Sometimes this evildoing is perpetrated by collections of überpowerful individuals, but recent movies, television, and books have popularized a very different idea of group evil. Accounts such as *World War Z*, *The Walking Dead*, and *28 Days Later* have depicted groups who do incredible harm but with relatively mindless members. It paints these group members as zombies—not the philosophical kind this time but actual brain-eating monsters.

Zombies illustrate our deep fears about what happens to people in groups. They lose all individual thought and self-control, shuffling mindlessly toward their goal of destruction. Even more than sheep, zombies are completely interchangeable, each of them slackjawed and glassy-eyed in tattered clothes. If this sounds like teenagers, you're right, and the comparison is very apt, as people seem to fear zombies similarly to how they fear groups of youths standing on the corner. Members of both groups seem to lose themselves to the will of the group and to think little for themselves. Although zombification due to experimental viruses is good science fiction, the zombification of people in groups is just good science.

Consider the murder of Michael Roberts, a fifty-three-year-old homeless man, by a group of teenagers. Their motive? Boredom. The boys were looking for amusement, and Roberts was simply in the wrong place at the wrong time. The teens punched and kicked him and hit him with sticks. One boy even dropped a log onto Roberts's ribs, which the boys then jumped on. They left Roberts's body in a woods and the next day invited friends to come see the corpse of the man they had just killed.[20] Who were they? Terrifyingly, they were just normal teenage boys together in a group. Just as groups can strip *perceived* mind from members, they can also strip *actual* mind from members.

Losing one's individual mind to the group collective is called deindividuation, and though it may most easily affect young men, it can influence anyone, regardless of age, race, or gender. Whenever people assemble for a common purpose, whether a sporting event, a religious service, or a political protest, our minds seem to leave us and get taken up by the group. This heady experience, called "we-feeling," is a kind of altered state of consciousness that is not necessarily bad in itself. In fact, it can be a wonderful thing, as we saw with the Allahabad pilgrims, who transcended their individual lives when spiritually connected to millions of like-minded others.

This we-feeling is induced especially through synchrony, when your actions are closely matched to those of other group members. Examples of synchrony include platoons marching in step, concert fans swaying back and forth together, and prayers being jointly said by a congregation—each of which seems to bind people together into a coherent whole. To test the bonding power of synchrony, Stanford psychologists Scott Wiltermuth and Chip Heath had participants walk around campus in groups of three. Half of these groups walked synchronously, marching in step, whereas the other groups walked normally. Each group then participated in an economic game that required a high amount of group trust in order to succeed. Wiltermuth and Heath found that participants who had walked in synchrony were more trusting of one another and out-performed those groups who hadn't walked in synchrony.[21]

Synchrony facilitates not only group goodness but also group evil. In another study by Wiltermuth, participants who walked in step with a leader felt closer to him or her and were therefore more willing to kill at the leader's behest.[22] Of course, as this was a psychology study, participants were tempted to kill only insects, but it is easy to apply the findings to human victims. The link between synchrony and destructive conformity explains why military groups march in step. Nazi goose-stepping may look odd, but it encouraged the soldiers to follow the cruel orders of their leaders.

Synchrony with group members is one way that groups encourage evil against outsiders, and anonymity is another. History has repeatedly shown that groups are especially destructive when members cannot be identified, whether because of masks or uniforms or even the firewalls of the Internet. This anonymity leads group members to identify more with the group and see outsiders as more bound to their rival groups.[23] Cloaked in his uniform, a Nazi soldier sees himself not as an individual but instead as simply a Nazi, while also viewing his victims not as individual human beings but as members of an undesirable group to be exterminated.

Even without a group context, anonymity frees people to be evil individuals. People who feel anonymous are more aggressive drivers,[24] are less willing to share with others,[25] are more likely to participate in racist aggression,[26] and are more likely to commit extreme acts of violence.[27] The liberating thrill of anonymity unleashes those primal passions that Freud consigned to the id, allowing them to riot, loot, and lynch. Take a less extreme example from YouTube user Kaipotainment, who innocently posted a (reasonably entertaining) video of his cat, edited to look like it has X-Man Wolverine's

Figure 37: Anonymous Protesters
Anonymity increases cruel behavior.

claws.[28] Moments after the video's posting, the first anonymous Internet trolls descended with their vitriol. YouTube user Solidest-Stone wrote,

This is RAD! . . . . NOT!
Awe . . . Pointless and Boring!
Dumb
FAKE!
Ghey
Justin Bieber

That last dig certainly crosses the line, but none of these comments is likely to be said face to face between the people behind

Kaipotainment and SolidestStone. We may laugh at the frivolity of this example, but other cases of Internet anonymity are much darker, such as when gay teens are bullied into taking their own lives. Rafael Morelos, a fourteen-year-old from Washington, committed suicide after cyberbullying that included the creation of a fake Facebook page mocking his sexual orientation.[29]

There are two ways to combat these cruel trolls. The first is to unmask them, as one online newspaper found that requiring commenters to list their full names reduced the incidence of racism, profanity, and hate speech.[30] The second way to combat trolls is to fight fire with fire and out-troll the trolls. This is one of the hobbies of the hacker group Anonymous, which uses its impressive computer skills to advance its own brand of social justice. In one case Amanda Todd, a fifteen-year-old Canadian girl, was bullied by a man she had met online. In an early conversation the man persuaded Todd to flash her webcam. He then demanded more nude photos of her under the threat that he would post the original picture all over the Internet. Even more frightening, he had somehow discovered the names of her family members and where she lived and used these details to increase the severity of his blackmail. Because of this cyberbullying, Todd became so depressed that she hanged herself.

The story gained wide attention, thanks in large part to a YouTube video Todd had posted, describing her ordeal and the suffering that followed. It caught the attention of Anonymous, and soon the hunt was on to unveil the identity of her tormentor. Soon enough the name of her alleged abuser was posted online, along with screenshots of his Internet history—and where he lived.[31] Just as anonymity had allowed the man to bully Todd, it allowed Anonymous to pursue effective vigilante justice. Todd's tormenter was arrested and charged with extortion, Internet luring, criminal harassment, and child pornography. As a group itself, Anonymous seems especially formidable, consisting of pure agency and impossible to harm—a conspiracy of do-gooders—serving, one hopes, to remind would-be offenders to think twice.

Of course, even social movements that start with the best of intentions can go awry, such as Reddit's hunt for the Boston Marathon bombers. After the detonation of two improvised explosive devices at the 2013 Boston Marathon, law-enforcement agencies were desperate for information. A group of users of the popular social media site Reddit hoped that crowdsourcing could effectively identify possible suspects and began poring over images of the marathon for suspicious figures. Soon they thought they had found their man—Sunil Tripathi, a student at Brown University. Unfortunately for Tripathi, he bore a close resemblance to the Tsarnaev brothers (the real bombers) and became social media's prime suspect. Despite being innocent, Tripathi could not bear the hateful media attention and the Brown University crew team later found his floating body, dead in an apparent suicide.[32]

Although anonymity can unleash real evil, large Internet groups also undermine more prosaic prosocial behavior, such as donating to charity. In 2007 Facebook launched "Causes," through which charities could raise both online awareness and money. Facebook hoped it would revolutionize online activism through two basic psychological mechanisms. The first was *influence*, that people follow their friends not only in fashion and music but also in charitable activities. Once enough people in a friend group joined a Cause, Facebook hoped it would reach a "tipping point"[33] and start a cascade of helping.

Causes also banked on *consistency*, hoping that once people had joined a cause, they would also donate to it. In a classic social psychological example of consistency, some homeowners were asked to put a small sticker on their door saying DRIVE CAREFULLY, and most acquiesced. Afterward these same folks were willing to place a large and gaudy DRIVE CAREFULLY sign on their front lawn, in order to be consistent with their past behavior. In contrast, those who weren't first given a sticker—and so lacked the motivation for consistency—said no to the ugly sign.[34]

In Facebook Causes people could do two things: they could "join" a Cause, which is the low-cost equivalent of the small sign, or they could "donate" to it, which is the equivalent of the big, gaudy sign. Did the low-cost joining lead to higher-cost donations, further propelled by social influence? To test this idea, Kevin Lewis, Jens Meierhenrich, and one of us (Kurt) looked at the complete records from the Save Darfur Cause as of January 2010.

Save Darfur raises awareness and funds to combat genocide and raised $70 million in offline donations (e.g., through direct-mailing campaigns) in the years measured.[35] For its part, the online Cause raised approximately $100,000 dollars, which sounds respectable until you realize that there were more than one million members, yielding an average of only $0.10 per person. Even more striking, the vast majority of all action was taken by a small number of members—only 28 percent recruited anybody, and only 0.24 percent actually donated.[36] In comparison, direct-mail campaigns usually have response rates between 1.3 percent and 3.4 percent.[37]

This dismal turnout is explained by the old saying "Why buy the cow when you can get the milk for free?" In this case the milk is the social status of being a good person, and buying the cow is actually donating. The Causes app was structured so that you could see when your friends joined a cause but not when they actually donated. This means that you got social rewards from the low-cost option but none from the high-cost options, letting people appear good without actually having to work for it. This has been cleverly called slacktivism, a term that was originally coined in the mid-1990s and has gained popularity with the rise of online petitions.[38]

Donations aside, we generally expect that if you want to get a job done, it's best to have all hands on deck. As the saying goes, "Many hands make light the work." However, this turns out not to always be the case, because groups can lead individuals to contribute less than they might when alone. Just as people have less mind in groups, they also contribute less effort. In the early twentieth century, a French researcher named Maximilien Ringelmann measured the effort of individuals when they pulled on a rope either alone or as part of a team. He found that individuals put in much less effort when pulling as part of a team than when they pulled alone, an effect now sometimes called the Ringelmann effect[39] but more often called "being lazy." Replicating this effect, researchers from Ohio State University found that people who are asked to either shout or clap will do so much more energetically alone* than in a group.[40]

Even when people are very motivated to perform well, groups can lead to suboptimal decisions through "group think." Group think is when people fail to voice their concerns in a group meeting, and it led to the deaths of the seven astronauts on the space shuttle *Challenger*. On January 27, 1986, one day before the launch, the engineers met to discuss the next day's cold-weather forecast. Individually they each doubted that the rubber O-ring in the solid rocket boosters would function in the below-freezing temperatures, but

....

* Despite looking totally crazy.

collectively it seemed that the group wasn't worried. Each engineer erroneously believed that everybody *else* was confident about the O-ring and mistook the group's silence for confidence. The O-ring went in as planned and the shuttle exploded seventy-three seconds after takeoff.[41]

As groups strip away minds from individuals, often the best way to understand group behavior is to entirely ignore individual minds. Consider large, moving crowds, such as the thousands of people who leave a stadium at the end of a game. Everyone in the crowd may have their own thoughts and desires, but safety engineers often treat a large group as a simple fluid, albeit one with psychological regularities. This approach has effectively reduced the death and destruction caused by stampedes as people crush toward an exit.[42] One insight is to *not* provide an easy line of sight or single path to doors, lest the density of the crowd get too high. Instead, doors are placed behind large pillars, so that people must flow around them from both sides and reconvene where the pressure is lower.

The examples so far suggest that individuals within groups, if not totally mindless, are at least best understood as so. But this sells groups short. Although individuals may lack minds in groups, minds wouldn't exist without groups. Why? Because *minds are groups*. Your brain—the basis of your mind—has approximately one hundred billion neurons. Each of these cells is little more than a biological on/off switch made of membranes and metal ions, triggered by chemicals from other neurons, and in turn triggering other neurons with its own chemicals.

Exactly how the mind emerges from a symphony of mindless cells is one of the most difficult questions facing modern science, but most scientists agree that the answer lies in emergence. Emergence is when simple elements at lower levels combine to be more than the sum of their parts at higher levels. Consider your computer, through which you can listen to music, write documents, or play the latest video games. It is hard to believe that all this rich diversity is accomplished with the same basic ingredients—electrons rushing through semiconductors—but it is the number and interconnection of these semiconductors that give computers their power. Low-level electron behavior is translated into machine language, then operating systems, then object-oriented languages like C++ or Java, and then finally the rich experience of cursing at the angry bird who failed its mission.[43]

Consider also the case of ants. Each ant is individually not much more than a little six-legged machine with little (if any) mind. But if you look at the behavior of the colony collectively, it displays surprisingly sophisticated behavior: it reacts to threats,[44] seeks out new food,[45] safeguards its reproduction,[46] and even plans for the future.[47] It does this through a complex system of interactions, pheromones, and specialization. Most researchers agree that the individual ant is simply the wrong level at which to understand the colony, just as the individual organ or cell is the wrong way to understand the human body.[48] We shouldn't expect a single ant to be smart any more than we should expect an individual kidney cell or microchip to be smart. Smartness arises at the level of the group.

Of course, if we put a billion cockroaches or toasters or livers into a huge box and shook it up, it is unlikely a mind would emerge. Instead, elements must be connected correctly, mutually reinforcing and constraining one another in just the right way. Exactly how to connect dumb things into intelligent wholes is one of the most important questions facing cognitive science today.

If sufficiently interconnected elements allow for intelligence, one surprising possibility is that minds may exist at levels above humans. Consider the United States of America. Just like us (and ant colonies), it has millions of individual units (citizens) each of whom is highly specialized, with some acting in defense (soldiers), some acting to transport nutrients across the body (truckers), some acting as neurons to help the central brain decide action (congresspeople). When it is attacked (e.g., the terrorism of 9/11), it responds to eliminate those threats just like any self-interested creature with a mind. It forms close bonds with other countries (e.g., Canada), worries about foreign infection (e.g., illegal immigrants), consumes resources (e.g., food, iron, coal), and excretes waste products (e.g., garbage, CO_2).

Is the United States conscious? It's hard to know. Would your kidney cell know that it is part of a higher-level, conscious organism? It may be that minds can see other minds only at their level or lower. We can see other people as minded and maybe even explain the behavior of our organs or cells as minded but may forever be unable to know if we ourselves are part of a higher-order mind. Perhaps countries are conscious, conversing with one another through us, just as we use our tongues to talk to other people. From the countries' point of view, we may be their dumb cells that enact their higher-level plans for food production and waste disposal, espionage and protection. We may all be the unwitting pawns in the international dance of higher-level minds.

Whether or not we are part of a bigger mind, groups of people can be quite wise, even without communicating. In 1907 Sir Francis Galton attended the annual show of the West of England Fat Stock and Poultry Exhibition. Part of the show involved the audience members guessing the weight of a recently slaughtered ox by writing down their answers on tickets. The lowest guess was less than 1,100 pounds, the highest guess was about 1,300 pounds, and the average estimate was 1,207 pounds, which was very close to the ox's actual weight of 1,198 pounds. Thus, although any single individual guess was unlikely to be accurate, the collective wisdom of the crowd was within 1 percent of the ox's actual weight.[49]

More recently an initiative called the Good Judgment Project has evaluated the accuracy of crowd-based predictions of global events. Preliminary reports suggest that crowdsourcing better predicts world events than do the CIA's trained specialists. For instance, forecasters collectively predicted with much greater certainty than experts the eventual presence of weapons inspectors in Syria.[50] The secret to its success, according to project leader Phil Tetlock, is that the random noise contained in individual guesses tends to eventually cancel itself out. There may be a lot of misinformation and misconceptions about whether or not North Korea will launch a nuclear missile in the next few months, but our imperfect guesses tend to be centered on the truth.[51] As in the parable of the blind men and the elephant, each person may touch only a small piece of the puzzle, but when combined, these limited perceptions can yield the truth.

The examples of this chapter speak to the broader paradox of mind perception: groups are the source of both the most mindless and the most intelligent behavior. This paradox can be resolved, however, if we understand that groups serve to pool the minds of their members. These members are left individually less intelligent, but together they can make something greater than even the sum of their individual minds. Beyond mere intelligence, there are other paradoxes about mind perception in groups. Groups allow us to cooperate and achieve amazing things, but they also cause us to perpetrate egregious harm, especially when we are anonymous. Groups are composed of individuals who feel and suffer, and yet groups as a whole are generally seen as incapable of feeling and suffering, which can make them easy targets for blame—and conspiracy theories.

Of course, our very ability to feel and suffer comes itself from a group—the collection of our neurons. That our mind arises from interconnected brain cells is not only mysterious but also sobering. All cells one day die. When our neurons disintegrate, must too our mind? This is a question we investigate in the next chapter on the dead.

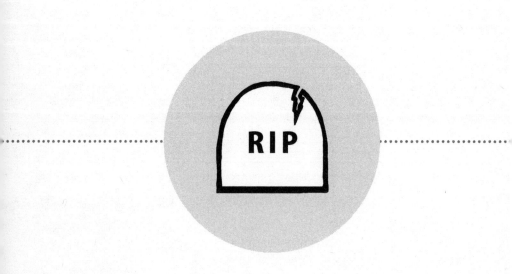

Chapter 8

THE DEAD

John Edward bills himself as a psychic medium, performing his readings in front of a televised audience. In a typical example of a reading, he declares that energy is coming from a section of the crowd where a spiritual connection is suggesting "heart disease" and a name beginning with *J*.

"Where's James or John? Where's heart disease?" A woman we'll call Carol puts up her hand.

"My father," she replies.

"Passed?"

"Yes."

"Heart attack?" Edward asks.

"Yes."

"I thought so," he says, "and he's sending me a message—are you the eldest girl in the family?"

Carol reports that she is the only girl, but when Edward says,

"Right, but he's making me feel like you're the strong one, the one he always trusted most." She nods knowingly, trying to keep herself from crying.

Driven on by the spirit, he continues, "He wants you to know that he loves you, and to tell you to keep being strong." Carol wipes the tears from her face, deeply touched by her connection with her deceased father.

This exchange is remarkable for two reasons. The first is Edward's ability to convince thousands of people that he has a direct connection to the spiritual realm. Edward is likely not communicating with the dead but instead "cold reading," a stage-magician technique of saying ambiguous statements (e.g., "James" or "heart disease") and observing the audience for reactions. The best statement is one bound to be correct but with enough specificity to convince people that it applies only to them. In this particular case the odds of success are high: James and John are the two most popular American men's names,[1] and heart disease is the leading cause of death in America.[2] In an audience of three hundred people, it is all but guaranteed that someone knows somebody named James or John who died of heart disease.

Once these statements become linked to someone, Edward continues to make statements, tailoring them to subsequent information. For example, saying "You were the eldest" was a good guess, but when it turned out to be wrong, Edward simply said that Carol's father treated her *as if* she were the eldest, which means only that he was impressed with her. Even if Edward fails on the details, he generally succeeds because of the predictable emotional bonds felt toward the deceased. He always conveys some heartfelt sentiment from beyond the grave, often that the deceased still loves the audience member and regrets not conveying that before they died. It may be just as likely that the deceased is angry that the audience member pawned an antique ring to buy a sports car, but such a detail never comes up. In the time-honored technique of showmen and hucksters, Edward tells people what they want to hear.

We may marvel at Edward's ability to convince others of his "spirit connection," but it works only because people believe that the minds of others somehow persist after death. You may be saying to yourself, "Of course the minds of others persist after death." But where do they persist exactly? In heaven? In hell? In your cellar, where they drag around their chains on Christmas Eve? Mostly they persist in your own mind. Even without physical reminders, it is exceptionally easy to perceive the minds of people who have long since passed away.[3] You may forget what your dead grandparents looked or smelled like or how their laughs sounded, but you can still confidently say things like "Grandma would have liked it like this" or "Grandpa would be proud." How do you know?

Humans may be unique in the scope and depth with which they perceive the minds of others, but they are especially unique in how they perceive the minds of entities with no physical reality. Our father may be cremated into ashes and scattered over the rugged shores of Maine, and yet, even without physical remnants, we get a sense of his mind. If you died today, you can be sure your dog wouldn't say, "David would be glad that I am eating this treat," but it seems unremarkable when people say, "Rover would have loved this park." Why—and how—humans perceive the minds of the deceased so vividly is the subject of this chapter.

These topics may seem a little freaky, which is why our entrée to the dead will be the movie *Freaky Friday*, released in 2003, about a mother and a daughter who switch bodies. Hilarity ensues when the sedate, middle-aged mother finds herself playing in a teenage garage band and when the insolent, hormone-driven teen finds herself at PTA meetings. Switching bodies is a well-worn Hollywood plot twist, and every few years studios release a movie based on this premise. In *Like Father Like Son* (1987) and *Vice Versa* (1988), fathers switch bodies with their sons. In *Virtual Sexuality* (1999), *The Hot Chick* (2002), and *It's a Boy Girl Thing* (2006), men switch bodies with women. Finally, in *The Change-Up* (2011), two friends named Dave and Mitch swap bodies through some complicated scientific process of electro-urine-mental-transduction: Both of them are peeing in an outdoor fountain when lightning strikes it. Suddenly married Dave finds himself trapped in the body of his single friend Mitch, and vice versa.

Now that the married Dave is in a single man's body, and single Mitch is in a married man's body, we are left to grapple with two profound questions: One, is it cheating if (married) Dave has a one-night stand with an attractive woman while in (single) Mitch's body? Two, does (single) Mitch betray (married) Dave by sleeping with his wife, even though he is in (married) Dave's body? Informal polling suggests that, yes, having sex with these respective ladies is immoral. Why?

The answer is that we identify people as their minds, seeing their bodies as mere containers. Our intuitions about body switching are the same as about car switching—even if Dave drove Mitch's Pontiac Fiero and Mitch drove Dave's minivan, they would still be the same people, despite being in different automobiles. Our bodies often seem little more than our minds' vehicles, easily discarded or traded, which affords the sense that our minds persist after bodily death.

This separation of mind from body not only is a popular plot device but also has deep roots in philosophy. For millennia philosophers have debated whether the world consists of one substance or two. The "one substance" supporters are called monists* and include ancient Greek philosophers Heraclitus and Parmenides and modern philosophers Georg Wilhelm Friedrich Hegel and Baruch Spinoza. Supporters of the "two substances" are called dualists and include the philosophers René Descartes and, more recently, David Chalmers, the champion of philosophical zombies we met on the very first page.

The monists suggest that physical matter is everything, such that the atoms that make up your chair, your car, and your body are also responsible for your mind. For the monist it's not mind *over*

Figure 38: Rene Descartes, Dualist Philosopher

....

* "Mono-," the English prefix for "one," is derived from the Greek *monos*, which means "alone, only, single." Other appropriate uses of the word include "That lady with fourteen cats will forever be a monist."

matter; instead mind *is* matter. In a monist world the death of the body spells the death of the mind, because the mind is simply one (albeit important) manifestation of the physical body.

The dualist, on the other hand, believes that mind is completely distinct from matter. In this view mind is immaterial, with no obvious physical properties, and so cannot be scientifically measured with scales or even EEGs and fMRIs. In contrast to the single world of monism, dualism suggests that there are two distinct but intertwining worlds. One is the coarse, visible world of dumb matter, including atoms, molecules, objects, and bodies, and the other is the pure, invisible world of mind, including thought, reason, and beliefs.

Unfortunately, the dualist version of reality poses some difficult questions, including how an immaterial mind interfaces with a physical body. It is all well and good to have thoughts floating alone in the rarefied ether, but our thoughts are connected with actions in the material world. We think, "Raise my hand," and lo, our hand is raised. Monists have an explanation for this link, involving a chain of neurons from the cortex to the arm. Dualists do not. Descartes thought that the mysterious thought-action link involved the pineal gland, a small volume of tissue buried in the middle of the brain. He believed that this gland was the "principal seat of the soul," but we now know that it simply regulates mammalian sleep cycles.

Modern psychology generally refutes dualism, as the mind *can* be measured through electrical and magnetic activity and relies heavily on physical brain structures. As we saw in chapter 4 on patients, if you destroy someone's brain, you inevitably also destroy their mind. However, modern psychology also tells us that intuitions often diverge from reality, and so dualism persists. For all of us who have thoughts and feelings, it is difficult to reconcile the mental and the physical, and even hardened scientists have to fight the urge to think in terms of dualism. In fact, psychologist Paul Bloom suggests that we are all natural-born-dualists.[4]

As evidence for innate dualism Bloom cites studies involving babies and toddlers. These studies need to be clever because babies respond poorly to verbal questioning. Researchers cannot say, "Please stop breast-feeding for a second. We were wondering, were you born with the fundamental expectation that mind and matter are separate substances?" Instead they often use the behavioral measure of looking time, which is simply the length of time an infant stares at something. The reasoning behind this measure is that humans look longer at surprising things than at unsurprising things. For example, you will look longer at a young girl giving her father a piggyback ride than vice versa, because it violates expectations.

To investigate innate intuitions about the nature of the world, experiments measure how long children stare at examples of either monism or dualism. If children ignore the examples of dualism but stare at examples of monism, that is evidence that they have the fundamental expectation that mind and matter are separate substances.

The most striking of these studies was led by psychologist Valerie Kuhlmeier, who showed infants two videos, each containing an open stage with two sections of wall. In the *continuous* video, objects (e.g., a box) moved normally, progressing smoothly across the stage—starting on the left and heading right, first passing behind one wall, then appearing between the two walls, then passing behind the second wall, then appearing to the right of the second wall, then leaving the stage.

In the *discontinuous* video, objects were strangely teleported across the stage—starting on the left, moving behind the first wall, then emerging to the right of the *second* wall, entirely skipping the space in the middle. Understandably, babies were surprised when an object was teleported, staring longer at the discontinuous than at the continuous video. However, when a *person* was featured in the video, babies looked equally long at the continuous and discontinuous videos. They weren't surprised at all by a teleporting person,[5] perhaps because they expect things with minds to (at least occasionally) disobey the laws of matter.

Of course, human bodies generally are subject to the laws of gravity and momentum, but these facts are often learned slowly and painfully, through falls and collisions. Even after a lifetime of experiencing the physical world, it is easy to believe in the unbounded

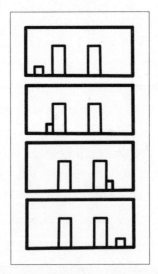

Figure 39: Teleportation of an Object in the Discontinuous Condition
When a human appears to teleport across the stage, infants are not surprised. When an object appears to teleport across the stage, this violates babies' expectations.

power of the mind—how else could we entertain ideas like clairvoyance and remote viewing? It may be *physically* impossible to see maps locked in a cabinet overseas, but is it *mentally* possible? The American military thought so.

At the height of the cold war, the CIA became convinced that the Russians were pouring money into psychic research. In actuality the Soviets were simply spreading misinformation (the equivalent of cold-war trolling) in a successful effort to get the United States to waste money. The Americans, fearing that they would be psychically outmaneuvered, started "Stargate Project," a remote viewing program in which operatives, sitting safely on home soil, projected their minds overseas to steal secrets from the Communists. There were three techniques used by remote viewers: coordinate remote viewing (CRV), which reported sights at a specific location; extended remote viewing (ERV), which conveyed general visual impressions gleaned from relaxation and meditation; and written remote viewing (WRV), which channeled another individual's thoughts into writing.[6]

Initially this project appeared to yield results. In 1979 viewer Joseph McMoneagle "saw" suspicious construction at a Soviet nuclear research center and predicted the debut of a fearsome new class of submarines, two visions allegedly corroborated by spy satellite images. These and other insights earned McMoneagle a Legion of Merit in 1984 for "producing crucial and vital intelligence unavailable from any other source." Unfortunately, these sightings—and the one "confirmation"—could not be corroborated by other sources, and despite $20 million of funding, no information provided by Stargate Project yielded "any value to the intelligence community."[7] The inability of these psychics to predict top-secret Soviet military decisions was perhaps unsurprising, considering remote viewers cannot even guess the identity of an object in a nearby box.[8] Decades of scientific research have made clear that remote viewing is impossible—the mind can sense only through boring bodily routes—but intuitions of dualism make us want to believe in it and other forms of ESP.

Intuitions of dualism are especially powerful in the case of death. Adults from Catholics to Scientologists believe that minds survive physical death; so do children.[9] At the University of Arkansas, psychology professor Jesse Bering and his colleagues confirmed the early roots of afterlife belief with a study involving kindergartners. They performed a puppet play for the children, starring a baby brown mouse and a big green alligator, narrated as follows:

> There's Mr. Alligator hiding behind those bushes. And here comes Brown Mouse. Brown Mouse doesn't see Mr. Alligator. And Mr. Alligator doesn't see Brown Mouse yet. Brown Mouse is having a very bad day. First of all, he's lost! He has no idea where he is or how to get home. . . . And he's very hungry and thirsty because he hasn't had anything to eat or drink all day. Uh-oh! Mr. Alligator sees Brown Mouse and is coming to get him! [Mr. Alligator eats Brown Mouse.] Well, it looks like Brown Mouse got eaten by Mr. Alligator. Brown Mouse is not alive anymore.[10]

Children then answered questions about Brown Mouse's mind, including those about bodily feelings (Was he still hungry?), desires (Did he still want to go home?), emotions (Did he still love his mom?), and knowledge (Did he still believe that he was smarter than his brother?). Kindergartners believed that dead Brown Mouse's mind survived and possessed "mental" states like emotions and knowledge more than "physical" biological states like hunger and thirst. These results square nicely with dualism: when the body dies, so too do pesky biological urges, but thoughts and feelings remain.

Dualism also persists in adulthood, showing itself in surprising paradoxes. As we briefly mentioned in chapter 6 on the silent, our thesis student Annie Knickman discovered that people often see more mind in deceased people than in vegetative patients, despite common sense and biology.[11] The reason for this reversal is that vegetative states focus attention on the body at the expense of the mind. The more we see someone as a mechanical system of fleshy pumps, tubes, and wires, the less we see them as a mental system of thoughts, feelings, and desires. This effect is actually an extension of dualism, whereby the body and the mind are not only distinct but often competing conceptions of others. We often think of others not as bodies *and* minds but as bodies *or* minds.

In contrast to vegetative states, death seems to focus our attention *away* from the body. Corpses disappear quickly, whether they are buried under beautiful grass or cremated and spread across mountain passes. Without a visible body, our thoughts are free to linger on the minds of the deceased in heaven or reincarnated as a small woodland creature. This means that focusing people's attention upon dead bodies should decrease the mind ascribed to them, a theory we confirmed in an extension of Knickman's thesis studies. As before, this study revealed that a patient who "passed away" was ascribed more mind than a patient in a "vegetative state"; however, this death-superiority effect disappeared when we mentioned that the deceased's body was "embalmed at the local morgue and then buried six feet underground." Thoughts of the body interfered with thoughts of the mind, just as dualism predicts.

Our intuitive dualism not only paves the way for the belief in immortality but also prevents us from accepting the equivalence of mind and brain. How can deep feelings of love and hard-learned memories be mere patterns of electrical firing—ones that disappear as soon as the electricity is disconnected? If the mind equals the brain, then someone with a brain exactly like yours would be more than just similar to you—they would be *exactly you.* And if you could replicate your brain and body a million times over, then there would be a million of you, and each of them would have the rightful claim to your identity. Most people shudder at this extreme idea of duplication.

To be fair, people also dislike even mild duplication. We may like similar-minded others, but when a friend likes *all* the same music, books, TV shows, and potential partners that we do, we get a little irked. The best illustration of this phenomenon is "hipsters." Hipsters are typically young white professionals who like independent rock, mustaches, cheap sunglasses, and expensive fixed-gear bicycles. The irony is that they *all* do this, deriving conformity out of "uniqueness." Indeed, nothing enrages a hipster more than labeling him or her a hipster, because it suggests interchangeability rather than individuality.

Someone who shares all your preferences may be irritating, but not as much as another you. In a study conducted in our lab and led by graduate student Chelsea Schein, we asked people to imagine that they had been transported in a *Star Trek*–like transporter but that the original transporter had failed to destroy their old selves. Thus, there was a "you" standing on the *Enterprise* and a "you" standing on the surface of a far-flung planet. People invariably found this duplication of mind unsettling, just as dualism would predict, and were especially irked when imagining their clone sleeping with their spouse. Technically it's not cheating, but it's hard not to feel betrayed: your spouse owes allegiance to *you*—your specific mind—not to a body with your same brain.

Duplicating your mind may be science fiction, but the opposite—its complete annihilation—is not. We call it "death." Part of our discomfort with and confusion about death stems from dualism, which suggests that just as a mind cannot be duplicated, it also cannot be destroyed. Instead, mind seems to be a quantity that must always be conserved, just like energy or matter. Mind may be transformed to other forms—ghosts, spirits, reincarnation, the afterlife—but never truly destroyed. As evidence for this belief in *conservation of mind*, consider the many cultures that treat death as a simple journey between worlds, with funerals serving as preparation. Pharaohs were entombed with gold,[12] Norse Vikings were burned with their swords,[13] and one Ohio biker was recently buried upright on his Harley-Davidson, seemingly riding his hog into the afterlife.[14]

Conservation of mind also suggests the remarkable phenomenon that those with more mind before death—i.e., who seem more capable of agency and experience—will also be ascribed more mind *after* death. Compare the death of an infant with the death of a teenager. Although both are tragedies, it is the teenager's mind that persists among the living because of their richer mental life, including a more developed personality, hopes and fears, mannerisms, and sense of humor. With funding from the John Templeton Foundation, our lab has experimentally tested conservation of mind across death, focusing on the mental states someone possesses at the exact time of death. We hypothesized that minds dying while awake and lucid would persist more after death than minds asleep or otherwise muddled.

Our studies revealed that, as predicted, people have more

postmortem mind when they die while awake (versus asleep) or while on hallucinogens that enrich experiences (versus sedatives that dull experiences) or while in possession of all their mental capacities (versus in the grip of dementia). Highlighting the separation of mind and body, participants judged a victim of ALS (who died with a damaged body) to have more mind after death than a victim of Alzheimer's (who died with a damaged mind). Importantly, these perceptions of mind also predicted moral judgments: participants judged it more important to keep promises made to those who died while awake (versus in a coma). These studies suggest that if you want people to follow your dying wishes, you should die clear-eyed and alert, capitalizing on conservation of mind.

Adding to the many paradoxes about the mind club, conservation of mind suggests that membership is both fluid *and* stable. It is fluid because small differences in mind at the time of death fundamentally change perceptions of mind after death. It is stable because we use the mind in life as a firm anchor for understanding the mind in death.

Speaking of paradox, as hard as it is to imagine your friends and family passing away, it may actually be *impossible* to imagine yourself dead.[15] As we discussed in the section on affective forecasting in chapter 6 on the silent, we are poor at perceiving our own mind in the future. But how do we perceive our own mind at a time when it has completely vanished?

If we assume that monism is true and death marks the disappearance of mind, then imagining yourself dead is like trying to imagine nothingness. You could imagine yourself without any thoughts or feelings, but your imagination (or "simulation"—the process we explored in chapter 4 on patients) is still from the point of view of *you*. In death there is no *you* to imagine, or even any imagination. Trying to perceive your dead mind is paradoxical, because you have to perceive a state that is incapable of perception—which is impossible while you are currently perceiving. It's like trying to make a movie without using a camera. Of course, experiencing death is impossible only if you're a monist, and there are certainly lots of dualists who think they have glimpsed the afterlife, such as Pam Reynolds.

At the age of thirty-five, Pam Reynolds suffered a brain aneurysm that required emergency surgery. The odds of her survival were slim, especially because doctors were forced to induce hypothermic cardiac arrest, lowering her body temperature to fifty degrees so that her breathing and heartbeat stopped and the blood drained from her head. She was clinically dead for almost an entire hour. Shortly after surgery began, Reynolds found herself floating above the operating table, observing the doctors clearly enough that she could later report their conversation with startling accuracy.

Like many of those who have near-death experiences (NDEs), she felt herself being pulled toward a bright light, where she saw deceased family members and even had an experience of God. Ultimately her long-deceased uncle pushed her away from the afterlife and back into her body, at which point her breathing and heartbeat resumed. But before that moment she displayed absolutely no evidence of any brain activity.[16]

More recently, four-year-old Colton Burpo was in surgery for an appendectomy when he ostensibly died and slipped away to heaven, where he was able to confirm much of contemporary Christian thought about the place. In heaven no one was sick, and Jesus has a "rough but kind face, sea-blue eyes . . . a smile that lit up the

Figure 40: *Ascent of the Blessed* **by Hieronymus Bosch**
Some describe this painting of the saved entering heaven as the first depiction of an NDE, with its light at the end of the tunnel.

H. BOSCH, *ASCENT OF THE BLESSED*, 1490, HTTP://UPLOAD.WIKIMEDIA.ORG/WIKIPEDIA/ COMMONS/THUMB/1/16/HIERONYMUS _BOSCH_013.JPG/262PX-HIERONYMUS _BOSCH_013.JPG.

heavens," loves everyone very much, and rides a rainbow-colored horse. *[17]

Unfortunately, Colton's account of a Christian heaven is not an impartial audit, like the ones provided by physicists when inspecting the nuclear facilities of rogue states. Young children are notoriously impressionable, and Colton's father is extremely religious, working as a pastor of Crossroads Wesleyan Church in Imperial, Nebraska. In fact, it was Colton's father who wrote the book

....

* Admittedly, Jesus' rainbow horse isn't in the Bible.

Heaven Is for Real: A Little Boy's Astounding Story of His Trip to Heaven and Back through discussions with him.

We can be sure that Colton's father asked the right questions to confirm his Christian worldview—and reach the bestseller list—such as "And wasn't Jesus bathed in a white light?" and "Was Grandma happy or *really* happy?" One wonders how the book would read if an ancient Greek had been the one doing the writing and interviewing: "Was the river Styx wide or *really* wide?" and "Was the three-headed dog Cerberus terrifying or *really* terrifying?"

Some scientists, including Dr. Sam Parnia at Stony Brook University Hospital, have taken the near-death experiences of Pam Reynolds, Colton Burpo, and others as evidence for dualism because they involve mental functioning without observable brain activity. Many would be more than happy to agree with Parnia, including the Hollywood producers who made millions from the movie adaptation of *Heaven Is for Real*. But others are more reluctant to accept dualism.

One of these dualism skeptics is Dr. Dean Mobbs, who explains the elements of NDEs with boring old biology.[18] The experience of floating over your body can be generated by overstimulation of the right temporoparietal junction. The white light can be generated by retinal ischemia, caused by reduced blood supply to the eye. The mystical meeting of your grandparents may be the result of activity in the angular gyrus or abnormal levels of dopamine in the brain. Meanwhile, the sense of peace and acceptance of death is very similar to the experiences one has under the influence of powerful drugs such as ketamine or amphetamine.[19] With the flood of neurotransmitters released during NDEs, it's no surprise that the experience is similar to that of drug use.

Despite these prosaic explanations of NDEs, a single number once argued in favor of dualism and the continuing life of the soul: twenty-one. This number has nothing to do with blackjack or the legal drinking age but instead is the apparent weight of the soul. In 1907 Dr. Duncan MacDougall placed a man dying of tuberculosis on a very delicate scale and intently watched the dial as his heart slowed to a stop. As the man's body released his last breath, the good doctor noticed that his patient lost twenty-one grams in weight, which MacDougall interpreted to be his escaping soul.

Seeking to generalize this finding, MacDougall put a dying dog on the scale but failed to find the same loss of weight upon its death,[20] suggesting either that the original reading was in error or perhaps that man's best friend is soulless.* Another study rumored to test for the weight of the soul involved earthworms and a blender. The premise was simple: put a blender on a sensitive scale, add some earthworms, and then turn it on and watch for a decrease in weight as their souls escape. Like the canine study, this study didn't reveal any weight changes, but that's unproblematic unless you believe that "all nematodes go to heaven." Alas, the twenty-one-gram loss from human death was never replicated, but even if it were, it wouldn't support dualism. Dualism suggests that we all have an immaterial soul, and immaterial souls don't have weight because weight depends on mass, and mass is a feature of matter.

Whether grinding up innocent earthworms is justified for science, it certainly seems cruel. Nevertheless, it is always possible to be crueler. If you had to guess, what's the cruelest thing you can say to a young child? That the Easter Bunny isn't real? That Santa Claus

··········

* Of course, we know that all dogs go to heaven (just ask Pope Francis), and souls are necessary for this spiritual journey.

is really her parents? That her finger paintings are pedestrian and her ballet dancing mediocre? No, probably the nastiest thing you can tell her is that one day everyone she knows and loves—her mom, her dad, her pet dog, and her best friend—will die. And one day she too will die; her candle will be snuffed out by the fickle wind of fate. The other insults she would eventually forget, but the specter of inevitable death is undeniable and deeply unsettling.*

Of course, children have heard of death before. We have a colleague whose six-year-old daughter was in school when the teacher said, "Remember, class, every problem has a solution."

Since it wasn't a question, the teacher was surprised when Janette put up her hand. "Yes, Janette?"

"I know one problem that doesn't."

"You probably just need help thinking about a solution. What's the problem?"

"Death." A letter was sent home to the parents.

Even when kids know about the inevitability of death, their innate dualism leads them to think of it merely as a transition. Unfortunately, the monist explanation favored by scientists suggests that once your brain turns off, so too do you. This not only violates our beliefs about conservation of mind but also poses a powerful existential conundrum: If we all die in the end, then what does it matter what we do in life? Why bother working hard to get that degree, promotion, or raise when forty years from now, give or take, you will be dead, and in another forty after that, you and everything you've ever done will likely be forgotten? Faced with this terrible truth, what gets us out of bed in the morning?

This very question was pondered by a German sociologist

· · · · · · · · · ·

* These discussions about death ensure that we never get asked to babysit.

named Ernest Becker, who suggested that the knowledge of our own death is a defining characteristic of our species.[21] Animals certainly seem to lack a sense of their impending demise. Take salmon. They are so exhausted by swimming up mountain streams to spawn that they die right after releasing their eggs and sperm.[22] Likewise, the male praying mantis often has his head bitten off during foreplay (before headlessly mounting the female).[23] If you were a male praying mantis, you might think, "That praying mantis lady sure looks fine, but I think I'll stick with back issues of *Play-mantis* and keep my head." However, if animals recognized their impending doom, their species would lose the game of evolution. Without suicidal spawning and sexing, there would be no future salmon or praying mantises, and so species are better off if their members aren't aware of death.

Unfortunately, humans have powerful brains that cannot help but realize the relentlessness of death, a realization that poses a challenge for the propagation of our species. If we each recognize the futility of our lives, then why slave at monotonous jobs to provide for our children, who also require us to forgo sleep and adult conversation? In other words, why bother propagating our species? The very short answer is that we are designed to seldom think of this question. We rarely think, "I want to approach this woman and ask for her number, but what about the inevitable annihilation of my consciousness?" In fact, Becker suggests (echoing Sigmund Freud)[24] that the human mind actively represses thoughts of death.

Becker believed that thoughts of death are terrifying and immobilizing, and how we deal with such terror is the research project of a handful of psychologists who have developed "Terror Management Theory."[25] They suggest that we cope with the terror of death in two ways. The first is by thinking that we—or, more technically, our minds—will literally never die, that our consciousness will persist in the great beyond, perhaps to be contacted by John Edward at a taped psychic reading. The second way of coping with the terror of death is by thinking that we will achieve symbolic immortality through the success of our culture. This route to immortality acknowledges that our consciousness will be snuffed out but takes comfort that at least other similar minds will live on.

Literal immortality was the dream of every conquistador who quested through the Amazon jungle looking for the fountain of youth. Stories of adventurers seeking immortality go as far back as the legends of Alexander the Great, who braved the Land of Darkness in the hope of finding the Water of Life.[26] It is also the dream of every scientist who studies ways to slow the biological process of aging, including resveratrol,[27] low stress,[28] calorie restriction,[29] and social support.[30] But even if we moved our family and friends to a lazy town in Ikaria [*31] and consumed nothing but vegetables, olive oil, and red wine, our bodies would still fail eventually.

As currently slated-for-death humans, we might console ourselves with the idea that somehow, someday, science will succeed in making people live forever. But how much do you really care about your great-great-great-great-great-grandson? That future kid has less than 1 percent genetic overlap with you, so you would rather live forever yourself. Currently the only two possible options for personal immortality are either waiting patiently in cryogenic storage for science to put a stop to aging or spurring computers on to the singularity so that our consciousnesses can be uploaded (as we discussed in chapter 3 on machines).

....

* A Greek island that boasts more healthy nonagenarians than anywhere else on Earth.

Figure 41: Literal Immortality
The Fountain of Youth, as depicted by Lucas Cranach the Elder (1472–1553).

Taking the cryogenic option was Dick Clair, an Emmy-winning Hollywood writer who worked on the most popular shows of the 1970s, including *The Mary Tyler Moore Show*, *The Bob Newhart Show*, and *The Carol Burnett Show*. Clair was diagnosed with AIDS in 1986, and knowing that his remaining time would be short, he contracted Alcor—an Arizona-based nonprofit organization—to vitrify (cool to the point of solidification) his body upon death. Despite fierce opposition from the hospital, a court decision finally allowed Alcor to grant Clair's wishes. He now resides in a custom-designed capsule bathed in liquid nitrogen at −196°C, a temperature that keeps Clair's body in stasis indefinitely, until the technology is available for his resurrection and recovery. Other members cryogenically suspended at Alcor's facility include Jerry Leaf (Alcor's ex–vice president), the futurist FM-2030 (his actual name), and baseball hall-of-famer Ted Williams (and his son John Henry). You

Figure 42: An Alcor "Dewar"
An insulated storage unit for
vitrified patients.

too can join the cryonics club by preserving your whole body for
$200,000 or just your head for only $80,000.

Liquid nitrogen may provide bodily immortality, but most people are content with living on only via their minds in the afterlife.
Studies reveal that just the idea of the afterlife decreases the fear of
death—even in atheists.[32] You might therefore expect highly religious folks to be sanguine about death. If you are convinced of the
existence of heaven—and your qualification for admission—then
death should be no big deal. If anything, it should be *embraced*, as
it allows you to leave this physical world of suffering and head
straight to the ethereal empyrean realm.

Two studies investigated whether the religious embrace death
by examining doctors' decisions regarding terminally ill patients.

Religious doctors, regardless of faith, turned out to be significantly less likely to perform procedures that would hasten the death of terminal patients, even those suffering from excruciating pain.[33] And those who believed most firmly in a paradise-like afterlife— religious fundamentalists—were the *most* likely to request heroic lifesaving measures, even if they were painful and humiliating and were likely to prolong life by only a week or so.[34] These hardly seem like the decisions of those convinced of heaven. Instead these data suggest that people may be religious in the first place because they are terrified of death. In support of this idea, one study found that people made to think about their own death increased their belief in God.[35]

Of course, not everyone believes in God, but even hardened nonbelievers like Richard Dawkins can still cheat annihilation through symbolic immortality. In contrast to literal immortality, which suggests the continued existence of your consciousness, symbolic immortality suggests the continued existence of other similar minds—and those symbols you all believe in, like science, truth, freedom, and the great U.S. of A. When people die for a "cause," they are demonstrating symbolic immortality.

To test this idea, terror-management theorist Tom Pyszczynski and colleagues had people read an essay supporting open immigration either on a normal city sidewalk or in front of a funeral home. They hypothesized that reminders of death would lead people to identify strongly with their nationality—Go America!—and therefore see foreigners as threatening. As predicted, people evaluated the proimmigrant argument more harshly when they read it in front of the funeral home,[36] demonstrating that death makes us protective of our own cultures and values.

This isn't as strange as it may seem. We tell soldiers that even though they may die on the battlefield, they will live on through their deeds and the triumph of their country. This is why many are so offended by the burning of Old Glory: you are destroying not just a piece of fabric but the symbol for which so many have given their lives. To quote Representative Henry Hyde during a 1995 debate on an amendment to ban flag burning: "A young man thousands of miles away from home . . . who died defending freedom. How do you honor, how do you glorify that? You honor Old Glory on behalf of that hero."[37]

In addition to condemning flag burning, death makes us identify with the most dominant cultural group. Reminding people of mortality causes them to accept racism toward an out-group,[38] to criticize those who oppose their political views, to perceive more similarity to those who share their gender,[39] and to punish rule breakers.[40] As reminders of death seem to make people anti-immigration, profamily, and pro–rule following—that is, Republican—it makes sense that people primed with death were more likely to express support for George W. Bush over John Kerry in the 2004 election.

More generally, those who see the world as more threatening lean more conservative,[41] and death is the ultimate threat. The link between perceptions of threat and conservatism provides some perspective on findings that conservatism increases with age[42]—the older you are, the closer you are to death. Symbolic immortality suggests that the fear of death depends upon how you spend your last days—the more you contribute to your culture, the less terror you are likely to feel. To misquote Horace Mann's 1859 address to Antioch College, "You will be afraid to die until you have won some victory for humanity."*

....

* The actual quote begins, "Be ashamed to die until you have won some victory for humanity."

Existential terror can explain why people themselves want to live on, but it leaves open the question of why we continue to see the minds of deceased *others*. Not everyone believes in ghosts, but many people do believe in the continued presence of deceased individuals, if only in their minds. After losing someone we know, we often continue to simulate their minds so vividly that it is difficult to think of them as truly gone. We wonder what they might be thinking, hope that they might be proud of us, and are scared that they might be angry.

Grief and feelings of unfinished business are reasons why close others live on in our minds, but people also see the dead even when they don't know or love them—especially if they are good or evil. Imagine you are sitting around a campfire one night when a local guide starts to tell you about some strange happenings in the surrounding woods, now thick with fog. Apparently, not far from where you're sitting people have reported feeling a brooding presence, heaviness in the air, and an unnatural silence. You begin to feel it too, and out of the corner of your eye you see a flicker of motion, but when you quickly turn, there is nothing there but an ominous swirling of mist. The guide mentions the word "ghost" and you and your friends draw closer together, leaning in toward the fire and away from the expansive darkness. You quietly ask, "Whose ghost?" and the guide tells you that in life the ghost's name was Ed Kowalski, a local plumber who loved reality TV and homemade pierogi. Suddenly the ghost seems much less plausible.

When we think of ghosts, we think of those who have done evil in their lives; our studies bear this out. We asked people to imagine that they were in a place where they felt strange emotions, a sensation of a presence, and changes in the atmosphere. We then asked the participants to describe the kind of spirit that might cause these sensations, and sure enough they often described people who were evil in life, using descriptors like "hateful," "violent," and "psychopathic." This persistence of evil is consistent not only with horror movies but also with conceptions of the afterlife. People believe that good people—and normal people—go on to heaven, whereas the souls—and minds—of the evil remain trapped on Earth.

Good people also appear to live on after death, but not in the same way. When we asked people to rate what happened to heroes such as Mother Teresa, they didn't think that they would be experienced as the same tangible presence. Instead they believed that good people live on more abstractly, within all of our hearts. As most people see themselves as fundamentally good, they are happy to assimilate heroes into their own self-concept. It may be only wishful thinking, but many like to see their own good deeds as continuing the work of their role models. In contrast, villains seem to have so little overlap with us that we think of them as completely distinct and feel them as a brooding threat to us. Good people live on in our hearts, and evil people live on in our basements.

The continued presence of good or evil people is rooted in the phenomenon of moral typecasting, introduced in chapter 4 on patients. Those who do good or evil are perceived as especially agentic and less vulnerable to harm. Not only do heroes and villains seem harder to harm and harder to kill, but even once they are killed, their minds seems to resist complete dissolution.

A thread running through our discussion of the dead is the perceived stability of minds after death. We acknowledge that people can be changed through life-altering events (by definition) and can shift their perspective and priorities after a brush with death. However, minds are perceived as changing little after *actual* death, and the spirits of the dead seem very similar to who they were in life: people evil in life become vengeful spirits, and people good in life provide a benevolent presence. Work by psychologist Scott Allison finds that perceptions of death are forever frozen in time and are even resistant to new information revealed postmortem.

In one study participants learned one fact about a fictional woman named Eleanor Dripp that was either positive (helping a stranger) or negative (cheating on her husband). Participants then learned either that Dripp was still alive or that she had died. Finally, they learned whichever of the two facts about her they hadn't been told before. So if participants first read about her helping a stranger, they then read about her infidelity, and if they had first read about her infidelity, they then read about her helpfulness. Allison found that on hearing the second fact about Dripp, people adjusted their opinions of her much less if they had first learned that she was dead, and the same result was found with other real-life targets.[43]

The minds of others in death stay as we knew them in life, even if we knew them only briefly, which explains our resistance to thinking better of people we knew as villains or thinking worse of those we knew as heroes. Not only do people's moral characters freeze at death, but we also tend to exaggerate who they were—the good becoming truly heroic and the bad becoming truly evil.[44] Minds may be insubstantial and invisible, but they seem to thicken and solidify after death, becoming more concrete and extreme.

This increased extremity after death also occurs in nonmoral domains. If a good musician suddenly dies at the peak of his career, he becomes the best to have ever lived. This is why members of the "twenty-seven club"—musicians who died at age twenty-seven—are remembered as so legendary. Jim Morrison, Janis Joplin, Jimi Hendrix, Kurt Cobain, and Amy Winehouse might not seem as amazing if we could watch them for an additional forty years. Seeing 1969 Jimi Hendrix play the national anthem with his guitar behind his back at Woodstock is incredible. Seeing 2009 Jimi Hendrix shilling for AARP after a sad money-grabbing comeback tour would be less than incredible.

Although people exaggerate and freeze the moral characters of heroes and villains in death, when it concerns more average people there is a tendency to think of them as somewhat kinder. When someone dies, we typically remember the good things about them, such as their smile, their laugh, their love for their family, and their successes at work, and not how they could be petty or selfish or bitter, or how they sometimes hurt those close to them with callous remarks. As proof, just take a look at newspaper obituaries, in which people praise the "warmth," "kindness," and "generosity" of the deceased. People don't want to speak ill of the dead, perhaps because they are afraid of vengeful spirits or because they pity them as moral patients who have suffered the ultimate harm.

The aversion to maligning the dead appears to extend to disrespecting their wishes. When someone makes a deathbed request (e.g., "Avenge my death"), people seem to feel obligated to fulfill it, despite the fact that the person now doesn't care (or certainly cares less than when living). We seem to consider the dead's minds as not only persisting but also having moral rights, as is consistent with the deep connection between mind perception and morality revealed way back in chapter 1. We think that the dead can be harmed through defacing their graves or breaking promises to them, and we try to follow their wills to the letter of the law. When people give all their money away to their cat, society tries to respect that request instead of spending the money on something more useful, like fighting malaria or childhood poverty. That we would respect the agency of the dead over the suffering of the living is one more quirk of mind perception.

Whether in bustling and brightly lit television studios or in the quiet and dim bedrooms we used to share with spouses, we cannot help but perceive the minds of those who have left us. Seeing the minds of dead others not only is a natural continuation of seeing their living minds but also is supported by intuitions of dualism and conservation of mind. With our own minds it is annihilation of mind that we fear most, but luckily we are typically able to suppress this fear with the help of religion and culture.

Try as we might, it is impossible to imagine our minds in death, and this paradox is mirrored by another paradox of the mind club. Minds are insubstantial during life, but after death we somehow perceive them as more solid and less changeable. In the past chapters we have emphasized the importance of cues to mind such as expressive features, language, and purposeful behavior. Each of these are physical manifestations of mind, but the dead suggest that minds can be completely disconnected from physical reality. In death the *less* we tie minds to physical bodies, the *more* they persist.

The club of dead minds seems to hinge more upon how people are remembered in life than on biological fact, but the disconnection of mind perception from externally verifiable mental capacities is true for many cryptominds, especially for the most contentious of all cryptominds: God.

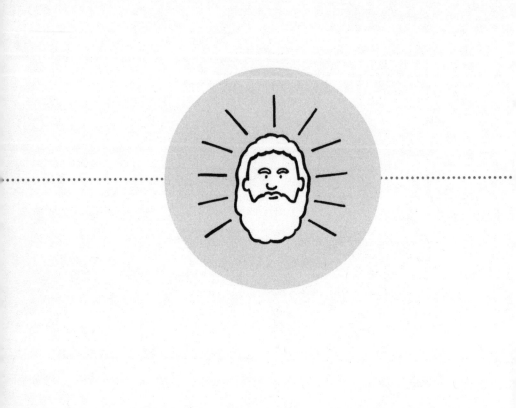

Chapter 9

GOD

In the seventeenth century the French philosopher Blaise Pascal was trying to decide whether he should believe in God. Rather than look skyward for a sign, Pascal looked to logic. He came up with a small table—or matrix—to help him decide. He divided it vertically based on whether he believed in God, with the top row representing "believe" and the bottom row representing "do not believe." He then divided it horizontally based on whether God existed, with the left column representing "does not exist" and the right column representing "exists."

First Pascal wondered what would happen if God didn't exist. If he wrongly believed in Him, he would feel compelled to live a prudish life, missing out on many delightful but sinful experiences, such as Las Vegas and French wine. Then at the end of his ascetic life— without a God to provide an afterlife—death would mean the end of the story. This scenario would be assigned a score of −80, one negative point for every year of austerity. Alternatively, if God didn't exist and Pascal correctly disbelieved in him, then he would have eighty years of delicious debauchery and scintillating sin, giving an overall life score of +80.

If God exists, however, the calculations substantially change, because of the existence of an afterlife. Correctly believing in God still yields a boring, prudish life (−80), but these dull years of following His commandments also yield an eternal afterlife in heaven. If we assign one positive point for every year in heaven, then we have $+1 \times \infty = +\infty$, and if we combine life and afterlife, we get $-80 + \infty$, which still equals $+\infty$. Conversely, failing to correctly believe in God still gives the joy of lusty living (+80) but is offset by an afterlife of eternal suffering in hell ($-\infty$), and combining these values yields $-\infty$, which completes the final cell of the table (see figure 43). The smart choice should now be obvious. If there is any doubt in your mind about whether God exists, you should hedge your bets and act as if He does exist, lest you be sent to hell forever. Pascal argued that believing in God was simply the rational thing to do.[1]

Of course, rational calculation is not what people typically cite as the source of their faith. People don't sit down with their financial adviser and, while picking mutual funds, pause to ask whether they

	God does not exist	God exists
Believe in God	−80	+∞
Do not believe in God	+80	−∞

Figure 43: Pascal's Wager
The numbers count the good or bad years of a decision to believe (or not) given whether God exists (or not).

should believe in the Almighty. God is not something that you approach with cold mathematical logic. Instead, belief is something intuitive, emotional, and—for many people—powerfully obvious. Christian philosopher Søren Kierkegaard is quoted as having said, "Life is not a problem to be solved, but a reality to be *experienced*,"[2] and the same applies to how people perceive God. People don't think about God so much as perceive His presence in their lives. Just as you cannot help but perceive the minds of people—despite the possibility that they ultimately may not exist—people cannot help but perceive God, despite the fact that He might not exist. Even Pascal, with his wager, took the existence of God as a given.[3]

God is many things to many people, but to all of them He is a mind. Just like the humans who believe in Him, God is perceived as being able to think and feel, and people wonder what He intends for the future and feel His love for them. Although His mind is very humanlike, He is also different from humans in many important ways. He is perceived as knowing more than anyone else and as being exempt from many of the emotions and sensations that humans feel, such as embarrassment, hunger, and lust. This explains why chapter 1's mind survey revealed that God is perceived as being very high in agency but relatively low in experience.[4]

As we'll soon see, one reason for God's uniquely agentic mind is His importance in morality. God seems not to care what color socks we wear but to care a lot about our cheating on our taxes and coveting our neighbor's new car. The reason for God's moral preoccupation comes from the idea of (agentic) dyadic completion, which, if you remember, is the idea that suffering compels us to see powerful moral agents. God's moral bent also stems from the fact that large-scale cooperation helps cultures to crush their enemies. But we are getting ahead of ourselves. To understand why people perceive

God's mind, we must begin in the mists of human prehistory—or, more technically, the tall grasslands of human prehistory—with "the mystery of the rustling grass."

Imagine you are a prehistoric man or woman walking through the darkness of the savanna one night when you suddenly hear a mysterious rustling in the grass. You freeze and consider two different options. The first is to run like the dickens, and the second is to continue leisurely on your merry way. If the rustling signals a lion, you should run, but if it's just the wind, then you should keep walking. But what happens if you guess wrong? If you run and it's just the wind, then you'll look pretty stupid when you arrive back in your village flushed and out of breath. On the other hand, if you keep walking and there's a lion, then looking stupid is the least of your concerns because you'll soon be dinner.

If you think about it, this scenario is exactly like Pascal's wager because of a massive asymmetry in outcomes. Just as the threat of eternal suffering makes it rational to believe in God, the threat of death makes it rational to always assume that there is a lion in the grass. This cost/benefit ratio is just the kind of thing upon which natural selection operates, such that "lion assumers" generally live longer and pass on more genes than "lion ignorers." The same principle holds whether we are taking about lions, tigers, or bears.* Evolution has selected for people who in ambiguous situations are likely to perceive agents—those self-directed minds that could eat or otherwise harm them.

More specifically, evolution has endowed our prehistoric ancestors—and us—with a hyperactive agency-detection device (HADD) that makes us acutely sensitive to the possibility of agents

....
* Oh my.

	No Lion	Lion
Run	 Well, that was embarrassing. But you're alive! Your genes may still be passed on.	 Close call, but you made it! Your genes may still be passed on.
Don't run	 Everything is a-ok. Your genes may still be passed on.	 Bad choice, you've ended up lion chow! It's the end of the line for your genetic code.

Figure 44: Pascal's Logic Applied to the "Mystery of the Rustling Grass"
It makes sense to generally assume the presence of an agent.

in our environment.[5] Of course, in today's world we are seldom at risk of being eaten by predators, but the HADD still works as well as ever. When you are home alone at night and hear a strange noise from your backyard, you instantly think of a serial killer and not a gust of wind. And when you feel a soft twitching on your face, you instantly think of a spider and not a stray piece of hair.

This hardwired tendency to detect earthy agents also makes us detect supernatural agents. When a branch snaps in a dark forest, it might be a bear, or it might be the ghost of a murdered camper. As we saw in the previous chapter, people often assume that these supernatural agents are dangerous. For example, Japanese Buddhism speaks of the *jikininki*, spirits of the evil dead who come back at night to devour human corpses,[6] and the ancient Greeks spoke of the Keres, spirits who would fly over battlefields and descend upon wounded soldiers to drink their blood and send them to Hades.[7]

The reason for this assumed supernatural malevolence is the same reason behind the HADD: if you have to guess the intentions of someone, it's best to stay on guard and assume that they're out to get you. Consider again the mystery midnight noise in the backyard. You typically don't think, "Great! Someone is sneaking around to leave me a big pile of money!" Instead you think about a depraved criminal who plans to do terrible things to you and your pets.

Although threatening situations predispose people to see agents, people will also perceive them at more relaxed times, such as when lying on their backs, staring at faces in the clouds.[8] Part of this perception stems from apophenia, the general tendency of our minds to make meaning out of the meaningless. At its most extreme this can be a symptom of schizophrenia, such as when people believe that individuals wearing red ties are part of a vast communist conspiracy to overthrow the government (as in the case of Nobel Prize–winning mathematician and paranoid schizophrenic John Nash).[9] A less extreme form of apophenia involves the idea of divination, in which you can see hints of the future through patterns of tea leaves, tarot cards, or runes. For example, in ancient Rome religious figures known as haruspices performed divination by examining the entrails of sacrificed sheep, particularly their livers.[10] Each of these cases of apophenia typically involves supernatural agents, as people believed that spirits and gods were speaking through the cards (or sheep organs). Even modern people seem to feel the presence of supernatural agents in mundane objects—like a navel orange.

On Christmas morning 2009, Lockport, New York, resident Paul Kulniszewski ate his usual breakfast orange. But on that anniversary of Christ's birth, cutting his orange in half yielded a miracle: Jesus and Mary suddenly appeared. No, they didn't walk into his kitchen to share some slices, but instead they appeared *in* the orange. The cross section of the orange revealed a pattern of slices and pith that looked like Jesus on the cross with Mary kneeling before Him. Although Kulniszewski's interpretation could be disputed, he is not alone in seeing God around him. In fact, there was a woman who belonged to the very same church as Kulniszewski who saw the Virgin Mary in a recently trimmed maple tree. People came from all across upstate New York to behold the arboreal form of the mother of God.

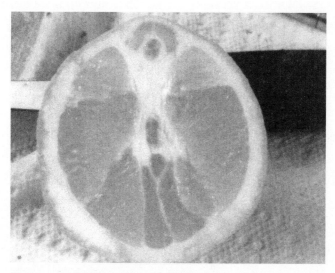

Figure 45: Vitamin D and Divinity
Do you see Jesus and Mary in this orange?
PAUL KULNISZEWSKI

Other examples of this divine apophenia include Linda Lowe, who saw Jesus in a piece of toast;[11] Ernesto Garza, who saw Christ in a breakfast taco;[12] and Jim Mize, who saw Jesus and the Virgin Mary in a Funyun.*[13] Whether any of these objects truly reflect divine presence is debatable, but it is clear that such sightings bring people together and strengthen their faith. People undoubtedly feel a deeper sense of human connection when beholding Jesus toast than when beholding mere toast. The ability of the divine to bring people together is no accident. Researchers suggest that our propensity to detect supernatural agents—especially God—may have evolved for this very reason.

Let's return to the mists of evolution. When we were here before, we discussed how hyperactive agency detection allows us to avoid threats from hungry animals, which better allows our genes to propagate. For prehistoric humans wild animals were only the start of their problems. With no Gore-Tex, hiking boots, or Siri to ask "Which way to the closest warm shelter?" life was pretty grim for *Homo sapiens*. If you want to see for yourself, just take off your clothes and go live alone on the savanna. Unless you have some specialized Navy SEAL training, you'd probably last less than a week. We don't mean to malign your survival skills, but it's difficult for *anyone* to survive anywhere completely alone. Like it or not, humans are a social species, and although that means dealing with body odor on the subway, it also means an increased ability to propagate our genes.

Think about it—how is it that a slow, scrawny, clawless, furless biped with a terrible sense of smell got to rule the world? Our big

----

* An onion-flavored corn snack made by Frito-Lay.

brains helped, but the real reason is that we do things *together*.[14] Any one person alone is pretty pitiable, but put people together into a big enough group and they can do almost anything. Groups of people can build city walls for protection, farms for food, and hospitals for health care, all of which help their genes thrive. Importantly, group living affords these benefits only when people work together, putting aside some of their own selfish desires in the service of others. You may not want to sit in the car's middle seat, but unless someone does, your group will never make it to the concert.

In the terms of evolution, individual genetic fitness requires collective success, which in turn requires collective cooperation. Of course, as team projects, life with roommates, and chapter 7 on groups revealed, groups also encourage selfishness and slacking off. Why work to help others when *they* will work to help *you*? Living in groups allows you to reap benefits without putting in effort. Unfortunately, if everyone recognizes this fact, and everyone is selfish, then everyone is *worse* off. When cooperation dissolves in shared houses, no one pays the rent, no one does the dishes or takes out the trash, and life descends into filthy chaos. When cooperation dissolves in whole societies, catastrophe results, and so evolution needs mechanisms for making people cooperate.[15]

In small societies like individual tribes, these cooperation-inducing mechanisms include gossip, ostracism, and punishment.[16] People who act selfishly in small communities are subject to penalties from simple name-calling to exile. The benefit of small groups is that everyone knows everyone else, and so it's easy to keep tabs on other people, whether by observing them directly or through hearsay. However, the downside of these small societies is that they can't accomplish as much as big societies. When your entire tribe consists of only ninety people, it's hard to build hospitals, roads, and universities. Accordingly, evolution has favored bigger societies, but this has led to a cooperation problem.

In big societies it is impossible for everyone to keep tabs on one another. Anthropological research suggests that we can have stable relationships with only approximately 150 people, which explains why most social groups like fraternities, military companies, and HOAs have no more than this many members. When social groups do grow beyond this size, they typically split by forming a new chapter, another company, or a separate HOA. In fact, this number is so consistent across social groups that it's called "Dunbar's number" after Robin Dunbar, the anthropologist who discovered it.[17] It likely also applies to you. If you made a list of all the people you know (not *all* your Facebook friends, but just the ones whose ongoing life events you know by heart), you probably wouldn't make it past 150.

In terms of cooperation, Dunbar's number means that if you're living in a big city like New York, it is impossible to know who is a good cooperator, let alone informally enforce cooperation. One way big societies get around this anonymity is with laws and police forces that suppress anticooperation tendencies, but they can arrest people only in extremely obvious cases like murder and theft. Even then, many criminals escape blame because of the high burden of proof for conviction. What big societies need to *really* enforce cooperation is a powerful police force that knows not only people's every action but also their every thought.

One possibility is an Orwellian thought police and a secret network of spies, but an even better solution is God. Even if someone can deceive other people and disguise his selfishness to others, God can see directly into his mind—and is able to punish him with eternal suffering. The evolutionary importance of cooperation is why God seems to care more about your morality than about your hobbies. Working together and suppressing selfishness is essential to the success of societies and the individuals living within them. Without close neighbors to observe actions, big, anonymous societies need an all-seeing, all-powerful divine judge. In support of this idea, psychologists Ara Norenzayan and Azim Shariff examined the characteristics ascribed to God across many different human societies, from the small tribes of aboriginal populations to the bustling cities of America.[18] They found that in the small tribes God is perceived as having a very different mind than He does in big societies like ours.

The gods of small tribes are seen as relatively less powerful and knowledgeable than the God of the Western world. These small gods are not omniscient or omnipotent like our Western gods, and often their power is limited to the village borders. You can even trick these gods and hide your sins from them. However, as the size of societies increases, Norenzayan and Shariff found that their gods also increase in power, knowledge, and moral orientation.[19] In the largest and most anonymous societies, such as the United States, God is "big"—He is omniscient and omnipotent and has very strict ideas about what you ought to do.

The concept of sin and punishment features very prominently in Christianity and other Abrahamic religions, and the gravest sins are those that put one's own interests above social harmony, such as murder, adultery, theft, and jealousy. In Dante's "Inferno," the lowest levels of hell are occupied by those who betrayed their families, their friends, and their lords.[20]

Not only does believing in God come with the specter of Hell, but unlike other people, God cannot be tricked. Like Santa Claus, God is always watching your behavior and keeping a list of all your naughty deeds. Feeling watched by God has the same effect on our behavior as being watched by other people—we suddenly feel self-aware and are more likely to act in socially desirable ways.[21] Even more than God, another supernatural mind—the Devil—offers a powerful corrective against wrongdoing, because he most vividly represents the punishment for selfishness: an eternity in hell.

In early thought Satan lacked the supernatural powers—and evilness—he is now seen as possessing. The original translation of the Hebrew word *satan* means something like a stumbling block that stands in the way of achieving a goal. Although this obstruction can be negative, it can also be positive, such as when God places barriers in people's path to imprudent actions. As God became more powerful and moralizing, so too did Satan become more immoral, and the idea of stumbling transformed into "the fall" from grace.[22] A study led by Azim Shariff revealed that across the nations of the world, the more people believe in hell the lower the national crime rate.[23] A loving, forgiving God may make people feel safe and secure, but it is the threat of hell that makes people moral.

Everyday people seem to recognize the link between religious belief and acting morally, because they distrust atheists. Polling data shows that when it comes to electing a president, Americans are less comfortable with an atheist than with someone of a different race, gender, or sexual orientation.[24] They believe that without God to direct their moral compass, atheists are morally depraved.[25] In one study psychologist Will Gervais and colleagues found that people rated the morality of atheists as no different from that of convicted rapists.[26] One conservative Web site claims, "Not possessing a religious basis for morality, atheists are fundamentally incapable of having a coherent system of morality"—which supposedly makes atheists likely pedophiles.[27] Of course, there is no evidence to suggest that atheists are any less moral than believers. In fact, many of the most violent conflicts in history have been perpetrated in the name of the Almighty.

God's ostensible support of war comes again from the importance of group coordination in evolution. In the evolutionary landscape, people and their genes were threatened not only by wild animals and lazy individuals but also by rival groups. As we saw in chapter 5 on the enemy, when resources become scarce or tensions are high, it takes little to prompt one group to attempt the destruction or enslavement of a competing group. The winning group is then free to enjoy the spoils of victory, spreading both their genes and their religion.

The most functional religions, therefore, are ones that encourage not only intragroup cooperation but also intergroup dominance. Consistent with this idea, one study conducted by psychologists Jesse Preston and Ryan Ritter found that although priming people with God-related words makes them nicer to out-group members (consistent with how God would like us to act), priming them with religion-related words leads to an us-over-them mentality.[28] This may explain why the most religious Americans are also the most likely to advocate for violent military conflict, except, again, if explicitly reminded of God's desire for us to behave compassionately.[29]

Although atheists often bemoan religion-induced aggression, consider the point of view of the religion itself. Imagine that you are a god with your own religion and you are competing for believers with lots of other gods, each with their own religions. In other words, you are a religious entrepreneur. How should you design your religion and brand yourself to earn maximum market capitalization?*

First, you want to encourage your members to have a lot of children, because they are easily indoctrinated and typically adopt the views of their parents.[30] Second, you want to encourage missionaries to spread your Word across the land and reach new markets. A religion with no children and no missionaries would die as soon as its current believers die.

Third, you would want to have reasonably unique views—a distinct brand—to ensure that your religion stands out from others. Research in marketing finds that brand distinctiveness is a key to luring customers and outcompeting competitors, and religion is no different.[31] Fourth, you would want to discourage dissent or free thinking, since free thinking could lead people to believe in gods other than you. Fifth and finally, you would want to destroy any other competing religions, whether through marketing campaigns, lawsuits, or outright violence.

Regardless of their ultimate truth, religions that have many or all of these features tend to outcompete rival religions. Consider the world's most popular religion: Christianity. Both Catholicism and Evangelical Protestantism encourage kids and missionaries, the reliance on authority—whether through the pope or the unchanging Bible—and the occasional use of violence against threats. These principles can also explain why Mormonism is one of the fastest-growing religions in the United States, with an increase of 45.5 percent from 2000 to 2010.[32]

....

* This idea is called memetics, treating ideas (i.e., memes) through the framework of genetics and natural selection.

Mormonism encourages many children, formalizes missionary work by sending young men abroad to spread the Word, and also takes a large annual tithe (10 percent of income) to help build the church's influence and support group projects. Although Christian, Mormons also have unique views, believing that Jesus came to the New World after his crucifixion and that the angel Moroni revealed a set of golden tablets to Joseph Smith in upstate New York.[33] Mormons have also used violence to protect their views, such as in the Mountain Meadows massacre, which left dead a hundred men, women, and children.[34]

The spreading power of Mormonism makes sense if you consider the environment of intense religious competition in which it was formed. During the years 1790–1840, America was in the midst of what scholars now call the Second Great Awakening.[35] The number of religious movements in the young country exploded, as did the number of new converts. Mormonism was engaged in intense competition with other new faiths, including those of the Baptists, Shakers, Adventists, and Presbyterians, and it survived only because it was well structured to survive in the religious marketplace.

One general rule for helping supernatural ideas stick is "minimal counterintuitiveness," when religious concepts are surprising but not *too* surprising. Consider two different hypothetical supernatural agents. The first is a seemingly normal man named Kitus, who can make himself invisible, hear any conversation on Earth, and be killed only by making him eat a plant grown deep in the Amazon rain forest. The second is a life-form named R443TTS that frequently looks like a thick paste but can also transform into a feathered hat. It speaks only in clicks and whistles, eats only nickels from 1979, and visits other universes every other Tuesday in months that end with -*er*.

Which one would you guess has more cognitive staying power? If you said the first, you are right (and might consider calling yourself "prophet"). People tend to believe in agents that are mostly normal—Kitus is just a person with a couple of special characteristics, whereas R443TTS is abnormal in every respect. Minimally counterintuitive agents are those that fit squarely into our category of "agent" (or person) but are just a bit different, which makes them emotionally evocative. A similar process was at work in chapter 3 on machines with the uncanny valley, where robots that looked almost human were the most attention grabbing.

Minimal counterintuitiveness can help explain why more people are Christians than are Scientologists: Jesus was a reasonably normal guy who died for your sins, whereas Xenu was an alien dictator who came to Earth (aka "Teegeeack") 75 million years ago and used hydrogen bombs to obliterate millions of his people near active volcanoes.

Religions may have qualities that help them spread from mind to mind, but they must also help their believers in return. One important benefit of believing in a powerful supernatural agent is that belief furnishes people with a sense of control in an otherwise random world. As we saw in chapter 3 on machines, uncertainty makes people see mind because minds are relatively easy to understand. Consider the question of why earthquakes happen. One reason, provided by geophysicists, stems from the instability of subduction zones, in which one tectonic plate dives under another and releases a tremendous amount of energy. While technically true, a better explanation for earthquakes—psychologically speaking—is that they are expressions of God's anger. This explanation also affords a sense of control, as earthquakes can be avoided as long as God stays happy.

The need for control and the belief in God may help explain why the wealthy are the least religious. Of Americans making under $10,000 a year, 83.8 percent report some belief in God, with 64.7 percent being strong believers. In contrast, only 68.7 percent of Americans making over $150,000 report some belief in God, with only 40.2 percent being strong believers.[36] The wealthy feel control and agency in their day-to-day lives and so have little need for divine order. In contrast, those struggling with poverty face a number of challenges in their day-to-day lives, and the comfort of a caring creator may serve to create order in an otherwise chaotic world.[37]

Even children look to the supernatural when they are uncertain. In an amazing study psychologists Jesse Bering and Becky Parker had children aged three to nine play a forced-choice game in which they were told to select between two boxes. In this design one box was the correct choice, and the other was the wrong choice, but this fifty-fifty chance of success was boosted by some supernatural help. Half the children were told that they were going to be aided by Princess Alice, an invisible princess who would be "telling them, somehow, when they chose the wrong box." The other children did not receive this notice.

As the children reached to select a box, a sudden, spooky event would occur, like a light switching on and off or a picture falling off a wall and clattering to the ground. Researchers then recorded whether or not the children switched the box they had selected—a sign that they had heard Princess Alice's message and were acting accordingly. They found that many kids changed their selection, making the connection between the unexpected event and Princess Alice.[38] This study suggests that our attention to the agency of supernatural entities emerges relatively early in life and is likely a prerequisite to acquiring full-fledged religious belief.

Figure 46: Supernatural Communication
A child receives Princess Alice's message and changes his choice.

Supernatural agents not only give you confidence about picking boxes, jobs, and spouses but also provide meaning to the world more generally. Consider this deep and eternal question: what is the purpose of a can opener? It's not a trick question. Can openers are for opening cans. Consider a similar question: what is the purpose of a rock? This question has no clear answer. You might answer "nothing" or "whatever you use it for." The purpose of a rock might be to hold open a door, to make a splash in a river, to bring down Goliath, or, in a pinch, to open a can.

The difference between can openers and rocks is that, unlike a rock, someone made a can opener, and they had a specific goal in mind when they did so.* Rocks aren't made to do something; they just *are*. Of course, that's what most adults think, but kids are a different story. In one study led by developmental psychologist Deborah Kelemen, seven-year-old kids and adults were asked why one particular rock was pointy. Adults mentioned erosion or chance, but kids mentioned a purpose. One suggested that it was pointy so that animals could scratch themselves on it, and another suggested that the point was designed to prevent animals from sitting on it. Just as we are natural-born mind perceivers, it appears that we are natural-born purpose perceivers[39]—and these may be the same thing.

People may not often think about the purpose of rocks, but they often think about the deeper meaning of their lives. People want to know what they are meant—or designed—to do. Being designed to do something requires a designer, a mind that has a plan about your life. This mind is typically held to be God. In his book *The Purpose Driven Life* Christian pastor Rick Warren provides five purposes to the big question "What on Earth am I here for?" all of which involve serving God.

The mind of God is seen as designing not only individual lives but also recently creating the Earth. Although the idea is considered absurd in scientific circles, 46 percent of Americans endorse creationism, believing that the Earth was created only a few thousand years ago, basically as is.[40] This account has difficulty explaining the fossil record and the relatively high levels of argon in rocks of the

·········

* In the terms of philosopher Daniel Dennett (mentioned in chapter 1), we can take a "design" stance with the can opener.

Canadian shield* but does seem much more intuitive than how the Earth actually formed. For many creationists, the sticking point with an old-Earth theory appears to be evolution, which suggests that not only sharks, cacti, and butterflies evolved but also humans. As one nineteenth-century antievolution tract wrote,

> If a man prefers to look for his kindred in the zoological gardens, it is no concern of mine; if he wants to believe that the founder of his family was an ape, a gorilla, a mud-turtle, or a moner, he may do so; but when he insists that I shall trace my lineage in that direction, I say No Sir! . . . I prefer that my genealogical table shall end as it now does, with "Cainan, which was the son of Seth, which was the son of Adam, which was the son of God."[41]

There are many reasons that people oppose the idea of human evolution, and our lab has explored one that has to do with mind perception. Recall from chapter 8 on the dead the idea of "conservation of mind," in which people found it difficult to imagine a mind being created or destroyed. Conservation of mind means that it is difficult to imagine the powerful human mind coalescing out of a set of intrinsically mindless processes. The mutation and recombination of genes is a process with no more mind than a rainstorm, and yet science suggests that it is responsible for our entire mind, both our agency and our experience. To explore people's resistance

....

* Potassium, a relatively common element in rocks, decays over millions of years into the gas argon, which remains trapped in the crystal lattice of rocks until cracked open by geochronologists (geologists who specialize in dating minerals). Kurt majored in earth science before switching to psychology.

to the idea of mind evolving, we and Chelsea Schein ran a pilot study in which people rated the likelihood that various physical and mental human traits evolved.

As predicted, people were happy to describe physical processes (e.g., having an immune system) as the result of evolution, but they were far less comfortable with ascribing mental processes to evolution—especially love. If you believe in God, however, there is no amazing creation of mind ex nihilo, as He can merely pass on a small piece of His own mind to others, like lighting a torch from an eternal central flame. This belief is reenacted symbolically in Catholic baptism, when infant children are presented with a candle lit from the flame of the Paschal candle, representing the light of Christ now burning in the newly baptized child.

As important as God is in the beginning of life, He is even more important at the end of life. God's plan is often invoked when car accidents kill people in their prime, when children are diagnosed with terminal cancer, and when natural disasters destroy entire villages of families. Why does God hold such an important role in situations of suffering? As we discussed earlier, people dislike randomness and lack of purpose, and believing in God can give a sense of control. However, there is another powerful reason why times of intense suffering lead people to see God: dyadic completion.

As we have seen many times throughout this book, our cognitive template of good and evil includes two minds, a moral agent and a moral patient. This template leads people to infer the presence of victims when they observe an isolated moral agent, such as when those who see homosexuality as immoral point to the irreparable damage it causes to children (patientic dyadic completion). This dyadic template also leads people to infer the presence of agents when they observe an isolated moral patient, such as when environmental destruction by corporations is seen as intentional. This agentic dyadic completion happens all the time. When children become obese through so many Big Macs, parents search for an intentional agent to blame (not themselves, of course) and sue McDonald's. Yet there is often suffering so grand that even McDonald's can't take the blame. When there is massive suffering in the world, people don't just ask, "Why?" Instead they drop to their knees, look skyward, and shout "Why, God!?"

Anecdotal evidence for God's role in suffering comes after every major natural disaster. After the 2004 tsunami that killed more than 280,000 in Thailand, Sri Lanka, Indonesia, and India, Saudi cleric Muhammad Al-Munajjid said it was vengeance for the sinful lifestyle of tourists at coastal resorts, "who used to sprawl all over the beaches and in pubs overflowing with wine."[42] After Hurricane Katrina, New Orleans mayor Ray Nagin also invoked God's wrath, and Pat Robertson suggested that New Orleans was being punished for America's abortion policy.[43]

Going beyond these anecdotes, we wanted to test dyadic completion on a national scale, so we examined whether suffering across the United States predicted religious belief. We obtained the average level of religious belief in each state by using the percentage of people who reported that "they strongly believe in God" in a recent public opinion survey. Next we obtained the average level of suffering in each state by mathematically reversing the score given to each state by the United Health Foundation.[44] This "suffering score" reflects the prevalence of negative health outcomes in a state, such as obesity, diabetes, and infectious disease. Correlating suffering with religious belief yields a value of 0.69, which is extremely high for something as idiosyncratic as religious belief. This link is even higher if you take out the two outlier states—Utah and Nevada.

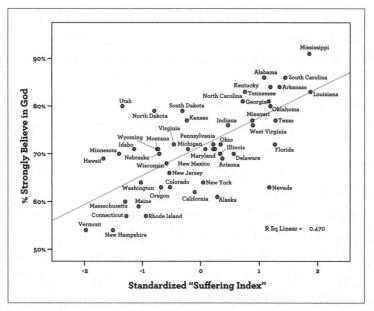

Figure 47: Scatterplot of U.S. States—Mean Belief in God by Suffering Index.

K. GRAY AND D. M. WEGNER, "BLAMING GOD FOR OUR PAIN: HUMAN SUFFERING AND THE DIVINE MIND," *PERSONALITY AND SOCIAL PSYCHOLOGY REVIEW* 14 (2010): 7–16.

Utah is where people are generally happy and religious (i.e., Mormons), and Nevada is where people are generally miserable and have forsaken God (i.e., gamblers and other sinners).

We replicated the link between perceived suffering and religious belief in another study in which people read fictional scenarios about the Millers, a family who decide to hike down to a canyon floor for a weekend picnic. In the story the Millers are eating their lunch when the water level of the canyon rises suddenly and they all either die (in one version) or escape to the parking lot to finish their soggy sandwiches (in another version). We also manipulated whether there was a clear human agent behind the flood, saying either it was caused by a malevolent damn worker upstream of the canyon (in one version) or for some unknown reason (in another version). We then asked how much the events of the story were part of "God's plan." Just as we predicted, people saw God's handiwork only in one specific situation—when the cause of the flood was unknown and the Millers all died. When the family died, people needed to find an agent to blame for their suffering but looked to God only when there wasn't an easy human agent to blame. In other words, people saw God in the "moral gaps" when blame was otherwise unaccounted.

People often see God in goodness as well, such as when they narrowly miss being in a car accident, when their team wins the Super Bowl, when they find a prime parking spot during Christmas shopping season, or when, in 2010, thirty-three trapped Chilean miners were rescued after spending sixty-nine days buried far underground. However, hundreds of studies find that negative information has much more psychological power than positive information.[45] You may thank God briefly at Thanksgiving dinner, but after being diagnosed with cancer, you may think about Him and His plan almost every day. Of course, God is not the only powerful agent that we blame for suffering, and studies reveal that we often look to the government or—as we saw in chapter 7 on groups—conspiracy theories to make sense of misery.[46]

Although there are many agents in the mind club, God is unparalleled in His level of agency. His power, knowledge, and preoccupation with morality make Him the ultimate moral agent. As predicted by moral typecasting—the separation between moral agents and moral patients—His extreme moral agency makes Him seem invulnerable to suffering. God is seen as capable of doing, acting, planning, and thinking but not feeling many of the bodily sensations and emotions that characterize humans. God does not get embarrassed or afraid or hungry, and it would be gauche to think of him needing to go to the bathroom. He is a thinking doer and not a vulnerable feeler.

God's all-agency mind may remind you of the corporations we explored in chapter 7 on groups, and this parallel is even stronger when you consider Google. The mind survey indicated that God and Google occupied the same place on the mind map, and there is already an official "Church of Google,"* which sees the awesome power of Google as (at least somewhat) divine. The church offers commandments, which, like the real commandments, offer both general moral principles such as "Thou shalt not plagiarise or take undue credit for other's work" and Google-specific guidelines such as "Thou shalt have no other Search Engine before me, neither Yahoo nor Lycos, AltaVista nor Metacrawler. Thou shalt worship only me, and come to Google only for answers." It also lists a number of Google prayers, such as this adaptation of Proverbs 3:5–6 by one congregant:

> Trust in the GOOGLE with all your heart
> and lean not on your own understanding;
> in all your ways acknowledge Her,
> and She will direct your paths.[47]

If you believe in the real God, you may scoff at these "prayers" to Google, but the breadth of knowledge housed within the mind of Google is all but incomprehensible, just like the mind of God.

Despite being incomprehensible, God's mind is, conveniently, very humanlike. God supposedly created us in His image, but how

....

* See www.thechurchofgoogle.org.

are we to know that we aren't just creating Him in our image? In one classic study that tested mind perception and God, participants read a story about God doing various tasks, such as helping people. This story was constructed to be consistent with what is called a "theologically correct view of God," such that God could have been in two places at once (omnipresence) or could have heard a conversation over very loud noises (omniscience). Although participants shared this theologically correct view, explicitly ascribing to Him all the appropriate "omnis," a different pattern emerged when they informally recalled the stories. Participants spoke of God as having to stop one thing before starting another (violating omnipresence) and of not being able to see something when it was behind a barrier (violating omniscience). In other words, they saw God as an especially powerful person and not an incomprehensible deity.[48]

This contradiction between the human (anthro) and divine (omni) elements of God—particularly in Jesus—has long been a point of contention in Christianity. How can something be both a mortal man and an immortal God? The whole point of being godly is to transcend humanity, whereas the whole point of being human is to have flaws and limitations. Some early Christians found this "omni-anthro paradox" too hard to take, but this duality may in fact have helped Christianity to spread around the world, as it may be just counterintuitive enough to stick in people's minds. Something fully godlike or fully human may be easily forgotten, but something that is both may capture attention in a powerful way.

An anthropomorphic God not only sticks in our thoughts but is simply easier to think of as someone like us. Western religious images portray Jesus as a white European, despite the fact that a Middle Eastern Jew would look quite different. In Africa Jesus can appear as a black man; in South America, as a Hispanic man. Even more than the physical image of God, we project our individual beliefs onto Him. Ever wonder why people who condemn homosexuality also believe that "God hates fags,"[49] whereas those who think homosexuality is merely a matter of attraction also believe that God loves us all?[50] God seems to share our exact moral belief, even when it contradicts someone else's God-endorsed moral belief.

The root of this phenomenon is known as "the false consensus effect." In almost everything we overestimate the percentage of others who share our beliefs.[51] How many people like Taylor Swift or foie gras or light bondage in the bedroom? Studies suggest that we answer this question by first anchoring on whether we like these things, then adjusting slightly—but always insufficiently. As we discussed earlier, in chapter 4 on patients, we use simulation to understand the minds of others, and God's mind is no different. In fact, this bias is even stronger when estimating the beliefs of God, as a study led by Nick Epley found.[52]

Epley had participants estimate the opinions of the general public and, predictably, participants believed that their own beliefs were more common than they actually were. If a participant supported the legalization of marijuana, they overestimated the percentage of the public that supported legalization. Participants were then asked to estimate God's beliefs. As it turned out, participants who thought marijuana should be legalized also believed that the creator was overwhelmingly in favor of lighting up a doobie. Why? Perhaps because we know that although others may be stupid and not share our love of Taylor Swift, God is infallible, so of course He agrees with us.

People see God not only as an all-access agent who passes moral judgment and accounts for suffering but also as a trusted confidant. Even when your friends don't want to hear about your problems, your spouse pretends to be sleeping, and the family dog plays dead, God is there to listen to you. One evangelical church called Vineyard encourages its members to have a very personal relationship with God. As explored by anthropologist T. M. Luhrmann in her book *When God Talks Back*, congregants are encouraged to schedule time to speak with Jesus.

Because God talks to people through their thoughts, such conversations blur the line between their own minds and God's, and it takes practice to recognize which of their thoughts have divine provenance. This discernment between mundane and divine thoughts also appears to require social consensus, as congregants frequently relay a number of potentially godly thoughts to other members, who then identify which ones seem reasonably divine. For example, thoughts that are self-centered (e.g., God says to buy a new stereo) are often seen as coming from the self, whereas thoughts of compassion (e.g., God says to volunteer at the soup kitchen) are collectively acknowledged as godly.

Once people are able to discern their divinely inspired thoughts, they are encouraged to have even more regular conversations with Him. Vineyard women often speak of setting aside a night to have a "date" with Jesus, sometimes setting their dinner table for two: themselves and Him. During these dates people are encouraged to speak to God as if he were actually sitting there, directing his full attention and limitless love to them. As one congregant told Luhrmann about the Bible, "It's a love story, and it's written for me." This kind of relationship would seem incredible to medieval believers, who saw God as a cold, inscrutable, and distant judge, and likely reflects changing norms regarding not only God but also our parents.

Centuries ago, parents also had a very different role in the lives of children. In ancient Rome fathers were rulers of their families but had no obligation to treat their spouses and offspring kindly. They had the option of abandoning any child at birth and could choose to sell an unwanted son or daughter into slavery. They even possessed the right to kill their children, if they so chose.[53] Today murdering a child is widely frowned upon, and modern fathers face expectations of compassion, caretaking, and guidance—just like God. Why would our relationship with God hew so closely to those with our parents?

Freud didn't get a lot right, but he was right about some of our early-childhood experiences shaping our future lives when it comes to relationships. For example, research finds that many people expect their partners to be like their parents.[54] If your parents were cold and distant, or warm and responsive, you expect your romantic partners to be the same way. Research finds that the same pattern applies to God, such that people respond to God in the same way they respond to their parents.[55] Those with secure emotional bonds to their parents have a similar comfortable, close relationship with God. In contrast, those insecurely attached to their parents worry about what God might think of them and about being abandoned.[56]

If you've read this far, you should understand at least one thing by now, and that is that minds—including God's—are a matter of perception. The religious may see the will of God on a daily basis while the atheist sees nothing but randomness. But what about those who experience God directly, not in a symbolic way but via an intense, personal vision of God, in the style of Moses, Joseph Smith, or Muhammad? One scientist, Michael Persinger, believes that he can elicit this religious experience in anyone, even the staunchest of disbelievers. Persinger helped develop the "God helmet," a device that uses a weak electric current to stimulate a small area of the temporal lobe.

Participants who wear this special helmet are placed in a completely darkened room with zero stimulation. They are seated comfortably in a large armchair and covered with a blanket. The current is turned on, and they spend the next hour alone in complete darkness—but are they really alone? Participants soon report strange sensations, such as spirits in the room, rising out of their bodies, and an overwhelming feeling of a presence. Sometimes they experience God. As Persinger points out, if you know that you're in a lab, this may be simply a fun adventure in tricking the brain, but imagine the consequences if someone were to have the same experience in a mosque, in a synagogue, in a church, or even home alone at night.[57] Such an experience could be a life-changing revelation for a believer or even cause a skeptic to rethink his views.

The God helmet suggests that some of the deepest and most transformative religious experiences could stem from the simple overstimulation of neurons. However, many scientifically sophisticated believers suggest that it cannot be any other way. God—through evolution—gave us the kind of brain that can know Him, not through something magical but through the same neural processes by which we know other truths in the world, such as the love of our children and the freshness of the air after a thunderstorm.

Just because researchers can induce religious experiences, they assert, doesn't mean that the same experiences in a church aren't real connections to God. As an analogy, it is possible to open up your car's dash and move the speedometer with your finger, so that it looks like you are going eighty miles per hour when you are actually parked. However, this doesn't mean that the speedometer is always wrong—sometimes when it reads eighty miles per hour, you are whooshing down a highway with nothing but the open sky before you. And sometimes when you get an exhilarating rush of the divine, it could also be an accurate readout of the spiritual world moving beneath your feet.

Nevertheless, knowing how the brain constructs religion takes at least some of the mystery out of things, which is why psychologists, out of all scientists, are the least likely to believe in God. In a recent study it was revealed that 50 percent of psychology professors are staunch atheists, with only 13 percent affirming a strong belief in God.[58] Some believe that psychology is out of its depth in studying these religious experiences, or even that these questions are generally off-limits to science. The biologist Stephen Jay Gould believed that science and religion have "non-overlapping magisterias"—distinct and circumscribed domains of knowledge.[59] He thought that science could explain how to make better batteries, how black holes work, and how to cure polio, but that only religion could explain questions like morality and the meaning of life. But as we have seen again and again, psychology *can* explain at least how people understand these deep topics. In other words, psychology suggests that the domains of science and religion are actually inextricably intertwined.

Out of all the minds we've covered, questions about God are possibly the most divisive. More blood has been spilled about the nature of God's mind than any other, and debates about whether it exists at all have polarized national discussions. God's mind is ascribed qualities such as immortality, omnipotence, and omniscience—but is also seen as fundamentally human—making it a very interesting case study in mind perception. In truth, God is actually only the *second*-most interesting of all minds. The *most* interesting mind is obvious; nothing is more interesting to people than themselves. In the last chapter we will explore the mind of the self.

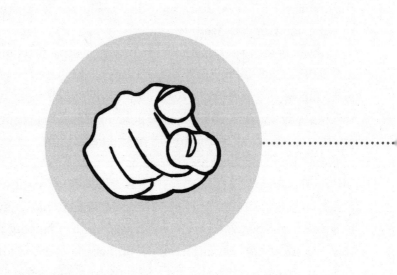

Chapter 10

THE SELF

Kenneth Parks seems to be an unremarkable man. He is middle-aged, lives in Toronto, Canada, and once ran for school trustee, attempting to help shape the system that taught five of his children. Unfortunately for Parks, he lost the trustee election because of an event that happened decades ago. When he was twenty-three and living with his new wife and their five-month-old daughter, Parks started having sleep problems. Of course, anyone with a new baby has difficulty sleeping, but these seemed to go deeper, stemming perhaps from his financial troubles. Parks had a gambling problem that had cost him much of his family savings and even his job, but despite these difficulties he still maintained a good relationship with his wife and his in-laws. Indeed, his mother-in-law, Barbara, took a special shine to her son-in-law, calling him her "gentle giant." It is Parks's close relationship with

Barbara that makes his actions on the night of May 23, 1987, seem so unbelievable.

On that night Parks fell asleep in front of the TV and, *while still asleep*, got up and drove the two dozen kilometers to his in-laws' house. Using the key they had given him, he entered the house and made his way up to their bedroom while they slept. He was holding a tire iron. Parks first walked over to Barbara and bludgeoned her to death before turning his attention to his father-in-law, Dennis, whom he choked and left for dead. Parks then—still asleep and now covered in blood—drove directly to the nearest police station and confessed, saying, "I think I just killed two people."

It is clear that Parks physically killed his mother-in-law (Dennis miraculously survived), but was he guilty? Guilt in the eyes of the law requires both *actus reus* (guilty action) and *mens rea* (guilty mind), and although his *body* bludgeoned Barbara, did his *mind*? Parks claims that the answer is no, maintaining that he was unaware of these unlawful acts because he was sleepwalking. Your likely reaction is just the opposite: "Yes! He is guilty!" How could someone possibly sleep through a twenty-minute drive and a subsequent murder?

The police thought they had an open-and-shut case of financially motivated murder, but expert witnesses testified otherwise. After measuring Parks's sleeping brain activity with EEG, five sleep specialists—all of whom had also approached the case with extreme skepticism—confirmed Parks's account. They testified that Parks could indeed have been asleep through the entire grisly murder. The judge agreed. Parks was found not guilty and walked out of the courtroom a free man, on the condition that he take a special regime of sleep medication. Since that tragic day in May, Parks has never so much as raised a finger against anyone, suggesting that his murdered mother-in-law might have been right—perhaps Parks really was a "gentle giant."

The story of Kenneth Parks probably makes you uneasy. It's possible that a man escaped justice, which stymies the process of dyadic completion—the compulsion to blame suffering on an intentional agent. Also unnerving is the possibility of sleepwalking murderers, because you never know when your son-in-law or wife or neighbor could murder *you*. But perhaps most unsettling is the possibility that *you* might be like Parks.

What would happen if you suddenly woke up and found yourself covered in a loved one's blood? It would be tragic enough to lose a family member, never mind spending your life in prison for a crime for which you had neither motivation nor memory. You might think that this could never happen to you, but don't be too smug, as there are many who, like Parks, do heinous deeds while asleep.[1] Deep down in your unconscious, you too could be a murderer. You think not? But how well do you know your own mind?

Out of all the minds in the world, our own seems special. It's the only mind that unambiguously belongs in the mind club. We are certain that we possess both agency and experience because we experience our minds from the *inside*. Our dualistic friend seventeenth-century philosopher René Descartes imagined the possibility of an omnipotent demon bent on deceiving him. This demon could give him visual, auditory, and even tactile hallucinations and make the world appear very different from how it was in reality. In the grip of such a demon, Descartes wondered what—if anything—he could know about the world with certainty.[2] After much thought, he finally concluded that the only thing that was unquestionably true was that *he* existed, because he was thinking. "*Je pense, donc je suis,*" he affirmed, or, in English, "I think, therefore

I am."*³ In other words, the only thing any of us can be sure about is our own minds.

Although we can be certain of the *existence* of our own mind, it is unclear how well we *understand* it. People are also reasonably certain of the existence of the sun, but it was only relatively recently that it came to be understood to be a giant ball of hydrogen powered by nuclear fusion millions of miles away through the void of space. For millennia people believed the sun to be a mystical deity (Ra in Egypt, Helios in Greece, and Surya in Hinduism) and dedicated an entire day of the week to this god: Sunday.⁴ It seems incredible that something so familiar and important could be misunderstood for so long—and perhaps it is the same with our minds. Perhaps your understanding of your thoughts and feelings is like the Egyptians' understanding of the sun.

You may bristle at this analogy, because there is one big difference between the sun and our minds: we are minds and not suns. If we all were (conscious) suns, we would presumably know about the importance of nuclear fusion. As we are minds, we should presumably know instead about our minds' inner workings. What's more, our own minds also seem relatively easy to learn about. To understand nuclear fusion, you need things like telescopes or particle accelerators, but to understand your thoughts and feelings, you need only a quiet moment and the capacity for introspection. Like centuries of philosophers, you can simply sit in an armchair and observe what it's like to have sensations, beliefs, and desires.

The sticking point, however, is whether we truly have the capacity for introspection. Part of the inspiration behind the science of

....

* If you are pretentious, or just into brevity, you might prefer the Latin: *Cogito ergo sum.*

psychology is the realization that our knowledge of the world may be biased, and this knowledge may be *most* distorted when it concerns the self. As proof, simply ask ten people whether they are above average in driving skill. The vast majority of people will say that they are indeed above average in looks,[5] and also in driving skill,[6] intelligence,[7] friendliness, and athletic ability.[8] Statistically speaking, this is impossible, as fully half the people in the world are below average in any ability.* If you want an accurate answer about someone's abilities, that person is actually the *worst* person to ask. Instead you should ask their friends or acquaintances, who are less motivated to exaggerate.[9]

It is especially difficult—or even impossible—to perceive *how* your mind works. As an example, please solve this math equation: $5 \times 8 = ?$ If you answered 40, congratulations—but the real question is how you figured it out. It is unlikely that you got five apples and then counted them eight times over. Instead you likely accessed some mathematical machinery that churned unconsciously and then spit out an answer into your conscious mind. At no point did you ever observe how this was working.

For an even simpler example of the inaccessibility of your mental mechanisms, take a look at the sky. How do you see it as blue? There is no *real* color out there but instead a specific wavelength of light that our cones, retinas, and visual cortex tag as "blue." You have no idea how that happens and could not intervene even if you wanted to. You cannot by force of will make the sky look red. And while we're talking about the force of will—what is the *will*, really? How is it that your body translates thoughts (e.g., "I should get out

....

* Yes, that means that there is a fifty-fifty chance that you are below average in lovemaking ability.

297

of bed") to actions (e.g., getting out of bed)?[10] These questions are enough to make anyone dizzy.

In the Temple of Apollo at Delphi, the ancient Greeks inscribed the motto "γνῶθι σεαυτόν," telling people, "Know thyself," perhaps because knowing oneself is a fundamental step to understanding others. As other minds are a matter of perception, it is important to understand the person doing the perceiving—you. When you observe the world, are you clear-eyed and farsighted, or is the world bent through the thick prescription lenses of self-deception?

Instead of asking about the agency and experience of other minds, this chapter investigates how we know our own agency and experience. We will see how the most basic assumptions about our minds, such as free will or the existence of the self, may be illusory. We have been judging whether other cryptominds belong in the mind club, but do *you* really belong with all the other minds? Not only are you unaware of the deepest truths about yourself, but you likely can't even explain why you buy some consumer goods instead of others. Take panty hose, for example.

In 1977 famed psychologists Richard Nisbett and Tim Wilson presented female participants with four pairs of panty hose and asked them to pick the one they liked most. After carefully evaluating each pair, the women typically chose the one on the right, and when asked why, they would often reference the silkiness or smoothness or durability of that specific pair. The only hitch was that each pair was identical, with the exact same silkiness, smoothness, and durability. Why did they choose the pair on the right? Likely because most people are right-handed and it's convenient to reach to the right. Importantly, when they were asked if the order of the pantyhose might have influenced their decision, participants insisted that such a small detail could hardly have been an influence, firmly believing in their fallacious reasoning.[11]

This lack of self-insight can sometimes become apparent in the dating lives of friends. Among a string of boyfriends, someone might explain that she loved number one because he was handsome and well dressed, number two because he was kind and had warm eyes, and number three because he was extraverted and funny. However, if you ran a statistical analysis, you might find that the majority of the variance is accounted for by income (she likes rich men). If you told her this, she might completely disavow your utilitarian account and argue that money doesn't matter to her. It may be true that she doesn't *think* money matters, but kisses speak louder than words.

Consider online dating, where people search for that quirky special someone who completes them. How do people decide whom to message? Do they look at their witty profiles? Their astrological signs? Online daters may convince themselves that these things matter, but most of the variance is accounted for by whether women are young, attractive, and extraverted and whether men are tall, muscular, and wealthy.[12] We invent the other reasons to feel less shallow.

A compelling demonstration of our lack of self-insight comes from Swedish researchers Lars Hall and Petter Johansson, who repeatedly presented participants with two pictures, each of a different woman. In each trial participants would select the woman they found more attractive, and then were asked to explain their choice: *Why* was she prettier? Explanations would typically include "She's radiant" or "A nice shape of the face" or "She looks very hot!" Nothing remarkable so far, but in one key trial, the experimenter would perform a small sleight of hand and switch the pictures after participants made their selection.

In other words, in one trial, participants were asked to explain why they had selected the person they *hadn't* selected. For example, if you were presented with Kate Moss and Kate Upton (two very different models) and selected Upton, the experimenter would then show you Moss and ask why you chose her (even though you didn't). Despite the fact that people had selected the other model just seconds ago, more than 70 percent of them didn't notice the switch. Even more striking, people were more than happy to provide reasons for why they preferred the face that they didn't prefer, commenting again on facial structure, stunning smiles, and twinkling eyes.[13]

More than the panty hose study, this study on "choice blindness" seriously undermines the accuracy of self-knowledge. With

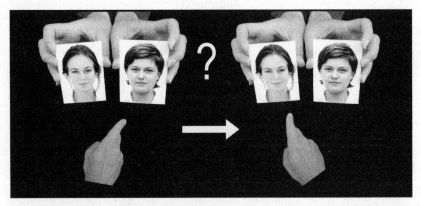

Figure 48: Choice Blindness
Participants demonstrate choice blindness when they describe why they liked the face they didn't actually prefer.

P. JOHANSSON, L. HALL, B. TÄRNING, S. SIKSTRÖM, AND N. CHATER, "CHOICE BLINDNESS AND PREFERENCE CHANGE: YOU WILL LIKE THIS PAPER BETTER IF YOU (BELIEVE YOU) CHOSE TO READ IT," *JOURNAL OF BEHAVIORAL DECISION MAKING* 27 (2014): 281–89.

the panty hose, people could have actually thought that the pair on the right was silkier and chosen it because of this perception. This would suggest that people are wrong about some unimportant perceptions about the world (e.g., silkiness) but not about themselves. On the other hand, the picture study suggests that people are wrong about *themselves* because they don't even realize their own (extremely recent) choices.

You could argue that judgments of attractiveness are special, but Hall and Johansson have also replicated this study with taste. In a supermarket they approached shoppers for a taste test between two jams and asked them to indicate their preference. Participants easily chose a preference between the two, such as cinnamon-apple over grapefruit, and the experimenter would record their preference. Participants were then asked to taste their favorite jam again and describe why they liked it. As in the picture study, the experimenters swapped the jams, so the fan of cinnamon-apple tasted grapefruit instead. Even with a dramatic difference in flavor profiles, fewer than 30 percent of participants detected the switch; the rest happily told the researchers about their love of citrus-flavored sweets.

Rather than giving true explanations for their behavior or choices, it seems that people simply provide after-the-fact justifications, just as you might when watching someone else's behavior. Neuroscientist Michael Gazzaniga has suggested that our conscious self is just an "interpreter" that spins plausible stories for our behavior after the fact.[14] Many times these stories are right. The reason we ordered the chocolate cake instead of the fruit flan is because we love chocolate. But that's not a *special* reason that only you can know. A stranger can infer the exact same reason when observing your behavior, suggesting that we may know little more about ourselves than an educated outsider. This logic turns mind perception on its head. We've always discussed how *other* minds are ultimately inaccessible and a matter of perception, but our own minds may be almost as inaccessible and perceived.

What is most striking about our lack of self-insight is not necessarily that we make up explanations but our total confidence in their correctness. We seldom pause to consider that we might be mistaken about our reasons for acting—or anything else. Instead we consistently try to confirm what (we think) we already know, a tendency called the *confirmation* bias. More technically, the confirmation bias is the systematic distortion in the search, interpretation, and recall of information in order to support preexisting theories[15]—and there are zillions of examples.[16] You are falling prey to confirmation bias when you selectively recount the driving accidents of Asian Americans (theory: Asian people are bad drivers)[17] or selectively seek out stories of violence perpetrated by African Americans (theory: black people are violent)[18] or selectively find anecdotes in which handguns shoot burglars rather than schoolchildren (theory: handguns save lives).[19]

We can do a remarkably effective example of the confirmation bias right here, between us. Take this sequence of three numbers: 2, 4, 8. Your job is to come up with the rule that governs the number progression. Your first guess is likely that we multiply the previous number by two (i.e., $x_n = 2 \times x_{n-1}$), making the next number 16. Nope. Perhaps the trick is to add an extra 2 in each step, giving us the next number of 14 (i.e., 2 + 2 = 4 + 4 = 8, 8 + 6 = 14). Nope. Or maybe there is some mysterious link to the Fibonacci sequence? Nope. The rule is simple: each number has to be bigger than the last one.

You might now complain that all your other suggestions also fit this pattern, but these other suggestions were too specific and missed the broader point. Theories like $x_n = 2 \times x_{n-1}$ are the equivalent of saying that only Asian people are bad drivers when in fact *everyone* is a bad driver. The reason that people almost always miss this rule is that they ask questions trying to confirm their hypotheses rather than *disconfirm* them. People always ask, "Is the next number 16?" and never ask, "Is the next number −100?"

The confirmation bias both consistently leads us astray and imbues us with confidence, undermining the process of discovery. This is why scientists typically try to *dis*confirm their hypotheses, or at least the hypotheses of their rivals. This can lead them to be quite skeptical of the established wisdom of anything, whether it involves the flatness of the Earth (actually round!), the unimportance of sanitation with respect to disease (cholera is actually caused by poop!), or the firmness of matter (actually mostly empty space!). Social psychology really began as a skeptical reaction to intuitive accounts of human behavior, with the most classic example being a study first reported in 1963 by Stanley Milgram.

In the aftermath of the World War II, people all over the world grappled with how average Germans could have been complicit—or worse—in the wholesale slaughter of innocent Jews. The prevailing theory at the time was that Germans were an especially tractable people, but Milgram had other ideas. He believed that even God-fearing Americans could be persuaded to kill others through only polite insistence, and he designed a paradigm to test this hypothesis. In this famous paradigm participants were asked to teach another person a list of words and—in order to help them learn—to shock the "learner" for every mistake. On each trial the shock level increased; Milgram wanted to know how many everyday Americans would continue with the experiment all the way to the end, administering the maximum—and ostensibly lethal—voltage of 450 volts.

Most experts believed that only 1 percent to 4 percent of people would go all the way (i.e., a few sadists), but as you may already know, 65 percent of people obeyed to the deadly end. Of course, participants weren't happy about it. Writes Milgram, "At one point, [the participant] pushed his fist into his forehead and muttered: 'Oh God, let's stop it.' And yet he continued to respond to every word of the experiment and obeyed to the end."[20] Neither participants nor observers had imagined the scale of this obedience to authority. This study powerfully demonstrates that we too can do terrible things: the path of least resistance sinks us imperceptibly into moral turpitude.

Of course, people typically chafe at this "social psychological" explanation, believing that there is one fundamental, metaphysical truth that does give us ultimate choice over our moral actions—the existence of free will. Perhaps because of the Christian roots of Western society, we feel that there is a human faculty that allows True Choice—unfettered by situations and others—that can justify an eternity in heaven or hell. Our entire legal system is predicated on the idea that we are the ultimate deciders of our own actions. How can we sentence someone to death if they did not ultimately deserve it? How can we keep someone in the soul-crushing isolation of solitary confinement if they didn't freely choose their acts?

This sense of ultimate free will accords not only with the legal system but also with our experiences. We feel like we choose our college, our spouse, and our jobs, and we feel like we freely select which fridge, car, and toothbrush to buy. Even more fundamentally, we seem to choose to move our hands and feet, turn our heads, stretch our backs, and move our mouths to talk. This basic kind of free will may seem obviously true, but scientists doubt its existence, thanks to the work of Benjamin Libet.

Libet's study was simple from the perspective of participants, who watched a quickly rotating clock (imagine a second hand moving at triple speed) and lifted their finger whenever they got the conscious urge. While participants flexed their free will with this simple motor movement, they also mentally noted the position of the clock. Importantly, this wasn't the time at which the participants actually moved their finger but instead the time that they *chose* to move. We'll call this time "W" for "will."

Libet also collected EEG data from electrodes on each participant's scalp, particularly from the supplementary motor cortex, a small strip of brain near the crown of the head. This brain region is integral to movement. It begins the process of movement (by releasing electrical energy), which triggers other brain regions (the motor cortex), which in turn triggers the nerves that cause the actual muscle movement. We'll label the activation of the supplementary motor cortex time "B" for "brain." Finally, Libet measured the time at which the finger moved—"M" for "movement."

We now have three times that we are concerned about: W, the time of will; B, the time of brain activation; and M, the time of movement. Through the hundreds of trials Libet could accurately determine the order of these events and, by doing so, test the concept of free will. Integral to the study is a single undisputable logical fact: causes must come *before* events. If there is free will, then time W (the conscious decision to move) must come before time B (when the brain starts preparing to move your finger).

Unfortunately for ultimate human freedom, W most definitely

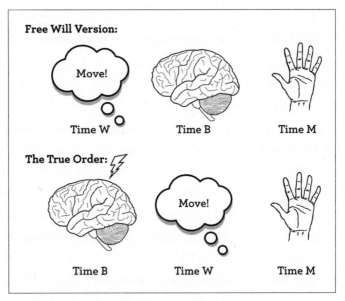

Figure 49: Two Possibilities for the Timing Of Movement
Free will suggests that conscious choice precedes brain
activation, but it instead follows it.

follows B: the conscious decision to move comes 350 milliseconds
after the supplementary motor area starts firing. In plain language,
Libet revealed that you decide to move your finger only after your
brain has already started moving it.[21] As brain activation precedes
your decision to move, it's not really a decision at all. Instead, it's
like "choosing" to go skydiving after someone has already thrown
you out of a plane. In the plainest language possible, Libet revealed
that free will is an illusion.

When this information is revealed, people have the experience of falling through darkness, grasping for any possible free-will
handhold. Maybe the equipment was faulty? No, people have replicated this study many times with different equipment. Maybe there
was a lag time before people noticed the stopwatch? No, the exper-

imenters calculated and compensated for potential lag for each individual participant. Maybe supplementary motor cortex activity was actually the brain activity of free will? But this suggests that it is your brain that has free will, and it just tells your conscious self afterward. When Libet's article was first published in 1985, the journal invited commentaries from twenty-six scientists, who mostly tried to debunk the study. Unfortunately, none of their criticisms stuck and even thirty years later we are left with the sobering finding: free will is a feeling we get only *after* our unconscious brain has already decided our movements.

In another demonstration of the illusory nature of free will, researchers used a procedure called transcranial magnetic stimulation (TMS), which involves placing giant doughnut-shaped electromagnets next to participants' heads and then pulsing them on and off. Because magnetism interacts with electricity, and neurons run on electricity, these pulses can activate different brain regions. Researchers told participants to move either their left or their right hand while activating the participants' motor cortex. Importantly, the choice of which hand to move was entirely up to the participants—but they nevertheless "freely chose" the hand corresponding to the nature of the TMS stimulation. Pulsing a clockwise current through the magnets made participants choose to move their right hand, and pulsing a counterclockwise current made participants choose to move their left hand.[22] Strikingly, despite being marionettes of the magnet-wielding researchers, these participants still felt completely free when selecting which hand to move.

These two studies converge on the idea that every movement and decision you make arises not from some independent source of free will but from the roiling, preconscious electrical activity of the brain. This does not sit well with many people, including Benjamin

Libet. Realizing the soul-destroying conclusions of his original study, he redirected his career to disprove himself and save ultimate human freedom. After a number of studies, Libet believed that he had succeeded, having discovered that although we lack free will, we have *free won't*. He claimed that the small amount of time (one hundred to two hundred milliseconds) between the initial activation of the supplementary motor cortex (time B) and the actual movement (time M) was enough for the conscious mind to intervene and arrest the movement. Essentially, he argued for a conscious executive veto power. Unfortunately, studies show that free won't is *also* preceded by unconscious neural activity.[23] It is your brain—not conscious "you"—that decides to move your finger, and it is your brain—not conscious "you"—that also decides to stop moving your finger.

These results caused much hand-wringing among scientists, theologians, and legal scholars, but one philosopher was unfazed. In a book titled *Elbow Room: The Varieties of Free Will Worth Wanting*, Daniel Dennett argues that the conclusions aren't so dire.[24] He asks us to imagine what kind of free will we really want. Do we want a free will that is totally unconnected to any previous behaviors or events in the world, like a completely random quantum coin flip? Unlikely. Instead, we all want a free will that makes the best kind of decisions for us, given our desires, intentions, and past experiences. It generally seems that we have this kind of free will, even if it does come from unconscious brain processes: we choose cars, spouses, and jobs we generally like, and that's better than choosing at random just to exert some metaphysical independence.

Unfortunately, this kind of free will, while being functional for everyday life, may not be strong enough to support ultimate moral responsibility—the idea that people freely choose to do good and evil and therefore deserve harsh punishments for crimes (including death). Neuroscientists—who see firsthand how brains cause behavior—suggest that there is no such thing as just deserts.[25] There are good reasons to punish others for wrongdoing, such as deterrence (making bad deeds costly)[26] and separation (keeping the bad people out of society),[27] but slaking our thirst for retribution is not one of them. The lack of free will suggests that heaven and hell are populated not by sinful souls but by people whose souls happened to have bad brains.

Although it may undermine justifications for executions and cruel and unusual forms of punishment, it is not clear that we should broadcast the fact that humans lack "ultimate" free will. Imagine what might happen if you splashed the headline YOU ARE NOT RESPONSIBLE FOR YOUR ACTIONS across the *New York Times*. A study by psychologists Jonathan Schooler and Kathleen Vohs suggests that such a headline would likely cause an immediate crime spree and license people to succumb to their basest desires. In their study participants read an essay either affirming or denying free will; those who read arguments against free will were more likely to cheat on a math test and to claim a larger sum of money than they deserved.[28] Free will may be an illusion, but it's a useful one, because it makes people—or at least their brains—feel more accountable and act more prosocially.

These findings raise a quandary for psychologists, who typically go into science for two broad reasons: (1) revealing the truth about human experience and (2) improving the human condition. In the case of free will, these aims are in direct contradiction, because revealing the truth leads to hopelessness and immorality. This dilemma is reminiscent of a scene from the movie *The Matrix* in which the protagonist is presented with a choice between two pills:

a red pill revealing the cold, ugly truth of the world and a blue pill allowing the blissful ignorance of a beautiful illusion. Psychologists—and now you—are also faced with this choice. Do you tell your coworkers that they lack ultimate responsibility and risk having them eat your lunch from the fridge, or do you let them keep their erroneous belief that they are the ultimate authors of every decision?

Not only is ultimate self-control an illusion, but everyday self-control—a facet of agency—also seems illusive. People want to believe that they can resist temptation, but high rates of obesity, alcoholism, and infidelity suggest otherwise. People chronically overestimate their discipline in staying on task and chronically underestimate (typically by half) how long they will take to finish work.[29] If people underestimate their likelihood of shocking another person to death, perhaps it isn't surprising that they also underestimate the duration (and budgets) of projects and how much chocolate they'll eat.

Of course, simply learning that we are bad at self-control doesn't provide a clear way of improving it. Psychology is often relatively better at pointing out problems than at solving them and can sometimes seem like a reverse Midas touch, draining the color from everything. The magic of love? The mystery of God? The experience of free will? All tricks of the brain. However, self-control is one domain where psychology actually does offer some pretty good tips on how to increase agency. The general tip is to *never rely on self-control.*

This answer may seem evasive, but it is consistent with the social-psychological concept that people are typically at the mercy of their environment, which influences them via cues they seldom detect. The best way to exert self-control is to never put yourself in situations where you have to exert it, and instead to focus on structuring your environment such that succumbing to temptation is impossible. For example, the best way to avoid eating fatty snacks at home is to never purchase them at the grocery store. No matter how strong your midnight cravings at home, you simply cannot yield. At the very least, you would have to expend extensive energy to drive to the all-night convenience store, during which time your cravings could subside.

This is the principle behind computer programs such as Stay-Focused, which lock you out of Facebook and Reddit so you can get writing done. These programs work mainly in two ways. The first is to calculate—and draw your attention to—your time off task, because frittering away minutes on Tumblr is less likely when you are faced with how those minutes add up to hours. The second way is to provide strict limits on how long you can access those sites, by locking you out once you hit your self-imposed quota.

These gimmicks are called "commitment devices" because they force your commitment to self-control. The drug Antabuse is a commitment device for alcoholism. Normally your body breaks down alcohol into acetaldehyde, which is then quickly converted into acetic acid. A hangover is essentially the effects of acetaldehyde in your system, and Antabuse works by blocking the conversation of acetaldehyde into harmless acetic acid. In other words, it loads your system up on acetaldehyde, giving you the world's worst hang-over, starting only five to ten minutes after your first drink. A less extreme commitment device is simply asking another person to help you exert self-control, for instance by taking your keys and not giving them back if you are drunk.

Commitment devices are used to great effect in books and movies. In *Fight Club* the protagonist tells other members to castrate him if he ever disobeys the leader of the Fight Club. In Stephen King's "Quitters, Inc." a man's desire to quit smoking leads him to the eponymous company, which claims a 98 percent success rate.[30] The method is simple: the company spies on you around the clock, and if you sneak a cigarette, they abduct a family member and torture him or her. Even the 2 percent who fail the program also never smoke again, because after the tenth mistake, the company executes you.

Beyond preemptive drugs, enforcer friends, or familial torture there is one especially powerful method to increase self-control: *implementation intentions*. They are surprisingly simple and effective. In the first test of their power, NYU psychologist Peter Gollwitzer recruited participants and assigned them to write and then mail an essay over Christmas break—a pretty onerous task for college students. Half the participants were simply reminded to make sure they wrote it, whereas the other half were asked to make a plan for when and where they were going to write it, such as "After opening gifts, I will go up to my desk, turn on my computer, and write the essay." Gollwitzer found that the simple act of picking a time and place in advance increased the rate of essay completion from 32 percent to 71 percent.[31] That's a huge effect, especially given how minimal the intervention.

More generally, implementation intentions take the form of "if/when *X*, then *Y*." For the Christmas essay the *X* is "after opening gifts" and the *Y* "go upstairs and turn on the computer." For weight loss the implementation intention might be "When I get hungry, I will open the fridge and take out vegetables, not cake." For quitting smoking it might be "When I crave a cigarette, I will unwrap a piece of Nicorette and then do ten push-ups." For quitting drinking it might be "If friends call inviting me out to the bar, I will suggest that we go to a movie." Implementation intentions have been found to work in all these domains[32] and others, including performing breast exams and reducing feelings of anxiety.[33]

You may believe that implementation intentions are too simplistic to work, and you wouldn't be alone. When he first heard of the Christmas essay study, our University of North Carolina colleague Paschal Sheeran was incredulous and reran the study, expecting to find nothing. Instead he replicated the effect and became an instant convert, and he now uses implementation intentions to increase patients' adherence to cancer-fighting regimens. In one study Sheeran increased attendance at cervical cancer screenings from 69 percent to 92 percent with simple implementation intentions.[34]

The reason implementation intentions work so well is because they export self-control, but this time to the unconscious self. As the Libet study revealed (and Freud long emphasized), our conscious self often plays second fiddle to our unconscious self, and implementation intentions create a simple program for your unconscious mind to control itself. By treating the self more like a robot than a person—if X, then Y, beep—implementation intentions allow you to achieve your goal without ever having to wrestle with the demons of temptation. Not all demons are so easily banished, however, and there is one domain of self-control where not even implementation intentions hold much sway: the control of thoughts.

At this point in the chapter, we would like you to do a simple task: *do not think of a white bear.*

Seriously. Put the book down, and for a few seconds try not to think of a white bear.

People can frequently do this task for a small amount of time, but then the white bear starts slipping back into consciousness. In fact, the more you try *not* to think of it, the more frequently and ferociously it appears. This inability to banish thoughts from our minds was addressed by a young Dostoyevsky, who wrote, "Try not to think of a polar bear, and you will see that the cursed thing will come to mind every minute."[35] A century later, one of us (Dan) rediscovered this phenomenon and charted the surprising territory of thought suppression, documenting how the mind struggles to control itself.

In Dan's classic study, he followed Dostoyevsky and simply instructed people not to think of a white bear. After five minutes of "thought suppression," he told them they could think of whatever they wanted. During the entire study, participants recorded how many times a white bear came to mind, and the data revealed an intriguing pattern. People could initially somewhat suppress their thoughts, but after they were freed from mental control, thoughts of white bears powerfully rebounded; white bears were all they could think about. Incredibly, after suppression people thought about the forbidden thought even more than those who were never asked to suppress. This illustrates the ironic effects of mental con-trol:[36] attempting to control the mind led it instead to become more unruly. Trying to stop the mind from thinking about something is like trying to stop a three-year-old from playing with a shiny new toy. When you tell it not to do something, it wants to do that thing even more.

These ironic processes can lead to a variety of striking effects, most of them involving doing exactly the wrong thing at the wrong time. Studies find that ironic mental processes cause golfers to miss putts the harder they try to make them,[37] cause people to dream more about people they try not to think about,[38] and make the heartbroken talk more about their exes.[39] These ironic effects also help explain the terrible persistence of obsessions, whether in everyday life or in extreme cases like obsessive-compulsive disorder. Consider people who are obsessed with cleanliness. The harder they try not to think about the germs swirling around them, the filth colonizing doorknobs and other people's hands, the more vivid these concerns become and the more powerful their need to disinfect.

Although people suppress thoughts relatively often, we even more frequently strive for the opposite—concentration—trying to hold thoughts *in* consciousness and stay focused on work, lovemaking, or our child's Christmas pageant. Just as we are poor at suppression, we are poor at concentration. If you've ever read entire pages of a book only to realize minutes later that you have no idea what you've been reading, you know what we're talking about.

In fact, as you've read this very chapter, there were likely times when your eyes were mechanically reading while your mind drifted away to something else, such as weekend plans or the uncomfortable burbling in your stomach. Although this mind wandering is a common human experience, it is relatively difficult to study because your conscious self is often not aware of it—otherwise it would stop wandering and refocus. This is what makes it so psychologically interesting from a self-knowledge perspective: you can ponder (distracting) thoughts without knowing that you're thinking them.

Every challenge has a solution, however, and psychologists Jonathan Schooler and Jonathan Smallwood found a way to study mind wandering in the lab. In their study people read *War and Peace* (typically regarded as a very boring book) and were told to press a button every time they caught themselves zoning out. Occasionally a prompt would also pop up and ask them if they were paying attention. As it turns out, participants' minds were wandering 13.2 percent of the time that the prompt popped up. Considering that they received this pop-up prompt only six times during the study, it's altogether likely that the correct percentage was actually significantly higher.[40]

Not only does mind wandering undermine reading comprehension and productivity, but it also makes us unhappy. In a large-scale study led by Matthew Killingsworth, thousands of participants downloaded an iPhone app called Track Your Happiness, which probed people randomly throughout the day, asking them to report what they were currently doing, what they were currently thinking of, and their level of happiness. Unsurprisingly, the researchers found a relationship between the activities people were doing and their happiness: people were happier when hanging out with friends or having sex than they were when taking care of their children or commuting.

More striking was the high correlation between mind wandering and unhappiness. People who had their mind in the "here and now," who were thinking about their current activity, were happier than those who were letting their attention wander, even if that "here and now" activity was unpleasant. This suggests that you shouldn't distract yourself while doing menial tasks but instead focus your attention upon them, perhaps observing how the suds fluff off dinner plates while doing the dishes or marveling at the strength of the smell as you change your daughter's diaper.[41]

The state of being when the mind is fully engaged with a task has been called "flow" by psychologist Mihaly Csikszentmihalyi* and is typically experienced when the demands of a task are perfectly matched by your capacities.[42] If you have ever felt the minutes slip away while driving winding mountain roads or cooking elaborate

....

* Pronounced "Mee-hy Cheek-sent-mə-hy-ee."

meals or painting a fresh canvas, you have experienced flow. Flow is the one time that our restless minds are quiet, when the self disappears and you stop worrying about your work or your weight and focus only on the present. This kind of state sounds blissful—and it is—and so it seems the path to happiness involves making the self disappear. But this presumes that we even know how to define the "self," that elusive quality that makes you "you."

One answer to this question can be arrived at by asking people around you. If you asked your best friend what makes you special, he or she might point to your limitless generosity or your macabre sense of humor or your incredible self-restraint. It seems that there could be as many essences of the self as there are people, each with unique interests and personality, but researchers Nina Strohminger and Shaun Nichols thought there might be something that is *most* essential. In a series of studies they asked people to envision a scenario in which a man named Jim receives a brain transplant. There were a number of variations on the story: the surgery might have gone perfectly well, or perhaps Jim lost his ability to recognize objects, or perhaps he lost his memory or his motivation.

The more abilities Jim lost, the more distressing these scenarios were to participants and the more they judged that Jim was someone different. But there was one version of the story in which Jim was judged as *most* changed, and that was when he lost his sense of morality. Without the ability to know right from wrong, participants judged that Jim was truly transformed into someone else. Someone could forget everything and could lose the ability to walk and talk, but if they still had their same kind (or cruel) heart, they would be perceived to be fundamentally the same person.[43]

From the perspective of others, the self seems fundamentally bound to morality, but is the same true of your own perspective?

Philosophers have long sought the essence of the self from the inside, asking how you know that you are the same "you" this morning that you were last night. How do you know that you're not a completely different person from day to day or from year to year? This question is not as crazy as it seems, as you likely have very little in common with seven-year-old you, and yet you cannot help feeling that there is a thread connecting you to him or her. Some candidates for qualities that anchor our identity are our looks (snub-nosed, bushy eyebrows), our personalities (quick to anger or to laugh), our preferences (an insatiable sweet tooth), and our interests (hang gliding or gardening), each of which likely persist over time. One philosopher, Derek Parfit, suggested an even better definition of the self.

Parfit is a philosopher who was trained and now teaches at Oxford and lives a monastic existence. Most of Parfit's time is spent alone in thought, and each day he dons the same outfit: a white shirt and black trousers. Interestingly, Parfit has a complete inability to create mental images, so he cannot picture his house or his wife unless they are right in front of him. It is perhaps this difficulty that makes Parfit so uniquely gifted at thinking in the abstract and that is the reason he thinks the central facet of identity is memory.[44]

According to Parfit, you know that you are the same person from day to day because your memories remain constant and connect to one another in an orderly chain. Even though you are far older now, you still remember your first waterslide, your first kiss, your first heartbreak, and your first car accident. Even as you accrue more memories, these earlier memories stick around, connecting your future self to your past self.

To emphasize the importance of memory, Parfit poses a number of thought experiments, many of which involve clones. For example, imagine a teleportation device that could transport you anywhere in the universe instantaneously. This device works by scanning all the matter of your body (and mind), destroying it, and then replicating it from the stored data in another location. Would this process be worth an instant trip to Paris? Would it even be *you* in Paris? Parfit argues that, yes, it's you in Paris, because that person/body/mind maintains psychological continuity through the same chain of memories.[45]

The centrality of memory in defining the self can make it tenuous, because any memories can potentially be forgotten. When people suffer from Alzheimer's, they slowly lose all their memories—and therefore themselves. As journalist David Shenk once wrote, "The fear of Alzheimer's is the fear of losing your identity while your healthy body walks on into oblivion. It is the fear of becoming a ghost."[46]

Beyond being lost, psychology suggests that memories can also be altered, with resulting fundamental changes to the self. In contrast to popular accounts of memories as indelible carvings in the stone tablets of our mind, they are more like theater productions—rough reenactments based on a loose script that changes over time. How many times have you recounted a memory over dinner only to have friends and family (or photos) show that you were mistaken?

A sense of self based upon something as fragile as memory seems troubling, but to Derek Parfit it is liberating. If the self is merely a chain of memories, then it should be relatively easy to dissolve these links and melt away the distance between ourselves and others. Expressing the exhilaration he felt from this insight, he writes, "My life seemed like a glass tunnel, through which I was moving faster every year, and at the end of which there was darkness. When I changed my view, the walls of my glass tunnel disappeared. I now live in the open air."[47]

To Parfit the self is simply a matter of perception. Just as we perceive the minds of others based upon their words and deeds, so too do we perceive our own minds based upon memories. This means that there is nothing special about ourselves compared with others: each of us is simply a collection of memories, and having one set of memories (your own) doesn't make you any better or worse than someone else with different memories. Indeed, if you had someone else's memories and they had yours, you would *be* them and they would *be* you. This arbitrariness of identity gave Parfit a profound sense of compassion for other people.

Parfit is not alone in viewing the self as an arbitrary construction rather than an enduring essence. Daniel Dennett makes an elegant analogy between the self and the center of gravity.[48] Any object with mass—whether a bowl, a piece of lumber, or even a brain—has a mathematical center, a precise location that would allow you to balance that object if you were to put it on a pointed stake. However, this center of gravity is not a "thing" that exists independently of all the stuff around it, and if you took apart the object, you would never find a separate little object that is the center of gravity. The self is a lot like that—it's just the theoretical point that lies at the center of all your mental experiences, memories, thoughts, feelings, sensations, goals, desires, and personal relationships. "You" is like a web without a spider, a collection of memories, thoughts, desires, and feelings that is fragile and tenuous and yet still glimmers in the sunshine of perception.

Or perhaps a better, if less elegant, analogy is that the self is like particleboard, that mainstay of affordable furniture. To all appearances particleboard is hard and very real, and like the self, it can—metaphorically—bear the weight of other people, break if struck too hard, and has sharp points that can hurt others. It is also fundamentally separate from other pieces of particleboard. However, upon closer inspection you would see that this material is merely a collection of little fibers pressed together and bound with glue. If you placed separate pieces of particleboard in a pool of water, the glue would slowly dissolve until all the fibers separated and floated together, completely intermingling.

In the case of your mind, the glue that binds together your memories—the fibers of your past experiences—is the fact that they happened to the same body, the same collection of cells that looks back at you in the mirror every morning. Despite the ultimate uncertainty surrounding the question of other minds, it is likely that everyone you know has the same powerful emotions and deep thoughts as you do. Unfortunately, your own collection of memories, thoughts, and feelings—your mind—prevents you from truly appreciating that fact. Being one mind prevents you from truly appreciating the minds of others. This is perhaps the deepest of paradoxes from the mind club.

Being trapped in our own minds prevents us from fundamentally connecting with others, and there is no way to escape our own minds. We are forever a point of view: even if we lose our memories, meditate away our desires, and quiet our constant quest for mental control, we are still a source of perception. But recognizing this fact provides the secret to transcending ourselves as much as we possibly can. By understanding that we *perceive* the world instead of understanding it directly, we can realize not only that the self is fragile and that free will is an illusion but also that other minds can be both more and less than they appear.

Through our odyssey of mysterious minds ranging from dogs to gods, we have seen that all the minds around us—and our very self—rest upon perception. Nevertheless, these perceptions have the psychological force of raw reality and are what compel us to love and to hate, to harm and to protect. The idea of the "mind club" could be interpreted as meaning that these perceptions of mind are not objectively real, but we suggest that they are the *only thing* that is real. We are perceivers, and from the perspective of perceivers, our perceptions are all we have, and that makes solid the ethereal. As the Buddha said, "Things are not as they are seen, nor are they otherwise."[49] We couldn't agree more.

Acknowledgments

There is no "I" in "book." Nor is there "we," or even "team," but there is "k" in both "book" and "thanks." And so we thank the many people who helped with this project along the way.

First, we thank our agent, Katinka Matson, whose wisdom and guidance helped turn a collection of strange minds into a book proposal. We thank our editor, Melanie Tortoroli, for her deft edits, big-picture vision, infectious excitement, and sage advice. We thank Georgia Bodnar and Hilary Roberts at Viking for overseeing the exacting process of making a manuscript into an actual—and better—book. We also thank the gifted illustrator Nicholas Blechman for making "the mind club" understandable at a glance through his cover design.

Deep gratitude goes to Kurt's two lab managers for their work on the manuscript. Peter Schmitt is a marvel at finding stories and studies about mind perception, at coaxing the Internet to reveal its riches, and at writing elegant summaries. Cameron Doyle has the nerves of a fighter pilot, the tenacity of a boxer, the mind of scholar, and a frightening attention to detail—all of which proved essential in finishing up the book.

Also essential were the illustrations of Jasmine Hromjak, Ryan Lantzy, Hanne Schrickx, and Aaron Scott, which brought zombies, God, animals, and the other cryptominds to life. Shawn Daley saved us with his rendition of sexist ads after we were denied permission by every ad agency in New York.

We thank the generous funding of NIMH and SSHRC for supporting the research discussed in the book, and are especially grateful to the John Templeton Foundation for seeing the science of mind perception—and other "big questions"—as worthy of funding. We also thank the students of our labs for their intellectual curiosity and hard work, including MPM-labbers Chelsea Schein, Jonathan Keeney, Neil Hester, and Amelia Goranson; Weg-labbers Heather Gray, Andrea Heberlein, Anna Jenkins, Carey Morewedge, Jesse Preston, and Adrian Ward; and the many amazing undergraduate research assistants from both labs.

For immensely helpful discussions, we thank our colleagues, including those at Harvard, Virginia, Maryland, and Carolina—especially Daniel Gilbert and Keith Payne. We also thank our friends, neighbors, and family, including Dan's daughters, Kelsey and Haley, and Kurt's parents, Ann and Phil, Mark and Louise, and in-laws, Sue, Steve, and Kim.

It almost goes without saying, but the support of our spouses was indispensable. Kristen Lindquist is an absolute saint for marrying me, and for dealing with that book-writing blend of obsession, mania, and neuroticism. As Dan always said before he passed away, he was the lucky one for getting to share his life with Toni Wegner.

Finally, we must extend our sincerest apologies to cats—including Kurt's cats, Chas and Cleo—for often maligning them in these pages. Nevertheless, we stand by our statements.

Notes

CHAPTER 1: WELCOME TO THE CLUB

1. S. Harnad, "Other Bodies, Other Minds: A Machine Incarnation of an Old Philosophical Problem," *Minds and Machines* 1 (1991): 43–54; I. Leudar and A. Costall, "On the Persistence of the 'Problem of Other Minds' in Psychology: Chomsky, Grice and Theory of Mind," *Theory & Psychology* 14 (2004): 601–21; H. Morick, *Wittgenstein and the Problem of Other Minds* (New York: McGraw-Hill, 1967).

2. D. C. Dennett, *Kinds of Minds: Toward an Understanding of Consciousness* (New York: Basic Books, 1996); D. R. Hofstadter, *I am a Strange Loop* (New York: Basic Books, 2007).

3. M. F. Washburn, *The Animal Mind: A Textbook of Comparative Psychology* (London: MacMillan, 1908).

4. A. M. Turing, "Computing Machinery and Intelligence," *Mind* 59 (1950): 433–60.

5. A. O. Lovejoy, *The Great Chain of Being: A Study of the History of an Idea* (Cambridge, MA: Harvard University Press, 1976).

6. D. C. Dennett, *Kinds of Minds*.

7. H. M. Gray, K. Gray, and D. M. Wegner, "Dimensions of Mind Perception," *Science* 315 (2007): 619.

8. K. Gray and D. M. Wegner, "Feeling Robots and Human Zombies: Mind Perception and the Uncanny Valley," *Cognition* 125 (2012): 125–30.

9. K. Gray, T. A. Knickman, and D. M. Wegner, "More Dead Than Dead: Perceptions of Persons in the Persistent Vegetative State," *Cognition* 121 (2011): 275–80.

10. K. Gray et al., "More Than a Body: Mind Perception and the Nature of Objectification," *Journal of Personality and Social Psychology* 101 (2011): 1207–20.

11. K. Gray and D. M. Wegner, "Torture and Judgments of Guilt," *Journal of Experimental Social Psychology* 46 (2010): 233–35.

12. K. Gray and D. M. Wegner, "Blaming God for Our Pain: Human Suffering and the Divine Mind," *Personality and Social Psychology Review* 14 (2010): 7–16.

13. Gray, Gray, and Wegner, "Dimensions of Mind Perception"; P. Robbins and A. I. Jack, "The Phenomenal Stance," *Philosophical Studies* 127 (2006): 59–85.

14. Confucius, *The Analects*, ed. Raymond Dawson (Oxford: Oxford University Press, 2008).

15. *I Ching: Book of Changes*, trans. James Legge (New York: Gramercy Books, 1996).

16. Laozi, *Tao Te Ching*, trans. Stephen Mitchell (New York: Harper Collins, 2000).

17. Aristotle, *Nicomachean Ethics*, trans. and ed. Roger Crisp (Cambridge: Cambridge University Press, 2014).

18. K. Gray, L. Young, and A. Waytz, "Mind Perception Is the Essence of Morality," *Psychological Inquiry* 23 (2012): 101–24.

19. H. L. A. Hart and T. Honoré, *Causation in the Law* (Oxford: Oxford University Press, 1985).

CHAPTER 2: THE ANIMAL

1. E. Fudge, *Perceiving Animals: Humans and Beasts in Early Modern English Culture* (Champaign, IL: University of Illinois Press, 2002).
2. J. D. Long, *Jainism: An Introduction* (London: I.B. Tauris, 2009).
3. D. Chamovitz, *What a Plant Knows: A Field Guide to the Senses* (New York: Scientific American/Farrar, Straus and Giroux, 2012).
4. R. Dahl, *The Collected Short Stories of Roald Dahl* (New Delhi: Penguin Books India, 1991).
5. M. Heil and R. Karban, "Explaining Evolution of Plant Communication by Airborne Signals," *Trends in Ecology & Evolution* 25 (2010): 137–44.
6. S. Allmann and I. Baldwin, "Insects Betray Themselves in Nature to Predators by Rapid Isomerization of Green Leaf Volatiles," *Science* 329 (2010): 1075–78.
7. A. Trewavas, "Aspects of Plant Intelligence," *Annals of Botany* 92 (2003): 1–20.
8. V. A. Shepherd, "At the Roots of Plant Neurobiology: A Brief History of the Biophysical Research of J. C. Bose," *Science and Culture* 78 (2012): 196–210.
9. C. Backster, "Evidence of a Primary Perception in Plant Life," *International Journal of Parapsychology* 10 (1968): 329–48.
10. "Deadly Straw," *MythBusters*, Discovery Channel, original air date September 6, 2006.
11. P. R. Sanberg, "'Neural Capacity' in *Mimosa pudica*: A Review," *Behavioral Biology* 17 (1976): 435–52.
12. A. G. Volkov et al., "Kinetics and Mechanism of *Dionaea muscipula* Trap Closing," *Plant Physiology* 146 (2007): 694–702.
13. D. C. Dennett, *Kinds of Minds: Toward an Understanding of Consciousness* (New York: Basic Books, 1996).

14. C. K. Morewedge, J. Preston, and D. M. Wegner, "Timescale Bias in the Attribution of Mind," *Journal of Personality and Social Psychology* 93 (2007): 1–11.

15. R. W. Mitchell, N. S. Thompson, and H. L. Miles, *Anthropomorphism, Anecdotes, and Animals* (Albany, NY: State University of New York Press, 1997).

16. J. Aronoff, A. M. Barclay, and L. A. Stevenson, "The Recognition of Threatening Facial Stimuli," *Journal of Personality and Social Psychology* 54 (1988): 647–55.

17. S. Baron-Cohen, S. Wheelwright, and T. Jolliffe, "Is There a 'Language of the Eyes'? Evidence from Normal Adults, and Adults with Autism or Asperger Syndrome," *Visual Cognition* 4 (1997): 311–31.

18. N. J. Emery, "The Eyes Have It: The Neuroethology, Function and Evolution of Social Gaze," *Neuroscience & Biobehavioral Reviews* 24 (2000): 581–604.

19. J. E. Opfer, "Identifying Living and Sentient Kinds from Dynamic Information: The Case of Goal-Directed Versus Aimless Autonomous Movement in Conceptual Change," *Cognition* 86 (2002): 97–122.

20. F. Heider and M. Simmel, "An Experimental Study of Apparent Behavior," *American Journal of Psychology* 57 (1944): 243–59.

21. A. S. Heberlein and R. Adolphs, "Impaired Spontaneous Anthropomorphizing Despite Intact Perception and Social Knowledge," *Proceedings of the National Academy of Sciences* 101 (2004): 7487–91.

22. C. Sanz, D. Morgan, and S. Gulick, "New Insights into Chimpanzees, Tools, and Termites from the Congo Basin," *American Naturalist* 164 (2004): 567–81.

23. A. C. Hannah and W. C. McGrew, "Chimpanzees Using Stones to Crack Open Oil Palm Nuts in Liberia," *Primates* 28 (1987): 31–46.

24. "Animal News: Spear-Wielding Chimps Studied," *National Geographic Mission Programs*, April 11, 2008, http://video.nationalgeographic.com/video/news/animals-news/chimp-spear-wcvin/.

25. G. R. Hunt and R. D. Gray, "The Crafting of Hook Tools by Wild New Caledonian Crows," *Proceedings of the Royal Society of London B* 271 (2004): S88–S90.

26. A. A. S. Weir, J. Chappell, and A. Kacelnik, "Shaping of Hooks in New Caledonian Crows," *Science* 297 (2002): 981.

27. "The Crow and the Pitcher," *Aesop's Fables,* www.aesopfables.com/cgi/aesop1.cgi?sel&TheCrowandthePitcher2.

28. A. H. Taylor et al., "New Caledonian Crows Learn the Functional Properties of Novel Tool Types," *PLOS ONE* 6 (2011): e26887.

29. D. J. Povinelli, A. B. Rulf, and D. T. Bierschwale, "Absence of Knowledge Attribution and Self-Recognition in Young Chimpanzees (*Pan troglodytes*)," *Journal of Comparative Psychology* 108 (1994): 74.

30. B. Hare et al., "Chimpanzees Know What Conspecifics Do and Do Not See," *Animal Behaviour* 59 (2000): 771–85.

31. N. S. Clayton, J. M. Dally, and N. J. Emery, "Social Cognition by Food-Caching Corvids: The Western Scrub-Jay as a Natural Psychologist," *Philosophical Transactions of the Royal Society of London B* 362 (2007): 507–22.

32. A. A. Pack and L. M. Herman, "Bottlenosed Dolphins (*Tursiops truncatus*) Comprehend the Referent of Both Static and Dynamic Human Gazing and Pointing in an Object-Choice Task," *Journal of Comparative Psychology* 118 (2004): 160–71.

33. G. Wang et al., "The Genomics of Selection in Dogs and the Parallel Evolution Between Dogs and Humans," *Nature Communications* 4 (2013): 1860.

34. B. Hare and M. Tomasello, "Domestic Dogs (*Canis familiaris*) Use Human and Conspecific Social Cues to Locate Hidden Food," *Journal of Comparative Psychology* 113 (1999): 173.

35. D. O. Hebb, "Emotion in Man and Animal: An Analysis of the Intuitive Processes of Recognition," *Psychological Review* 53 (1946): 88.

36. M. Lewis and J. Brooks-Gunn, *Social Cognition and the Acquisition of Self* (New York: Plenum Press, 1979), http://jpepsy.oxfordjournals.org/content/6/4/463.full.pdf.

37. G. G. Gallup, "Chimpanzees: Self-Recognition," *Science* 167 (1970): 86–87; D. Reiss and L. Marino, "Mirror Self-Recognition in the Bottlenose Dolphin: A Case of Cognitive Convergence," *Proceedings of the National Academy of Sciences* 98 (2001): 5937–42; J. M. Plotnik, F. B. De Waal, and D. Reiss, "Self-Recognition in an Asian Elephant," *Proceedings of the National Academy of Sciences* 103 (2006): 17053–57.

38. M. Rowlands, "The Kindness of Beasts: Dogs Rescue Their Friends and Elephants Care for Injured Kin—Humans Have No Monopoly on Moral Behaviour," *Aeon Magazine*, October 24, 2012, http://aeon.co/magazine/being-human/mark-rowlands-animal-morality/; M. Bekoff and J. Pierce, *Wild Justice: The Moral Lives of Animals* (Chicago, IL: University of Chicago Press, 2009).

39. F. de Waal, "Moral Behavior in Animals," lecture, TEDxPeachtree, Atlanta, GA, November 2011, http://ted.com/talks/frans_de_waal_do_animals_have_morals.

40. S. Robson, "Body of Woman, 56, Who Collapsed and Died in Her Home Is Gnawed and Eaten by Her Own Cats on Her Kitchen Floor," *Daily Mail*, August 13, 2013, www.dailymail.co.uk/news/article-2391223/Janet-Veal-56-gnawed-eaten-CATS-kitchen-floor-died.html.

41. R. Schlesinger, "15 Years Ago Today: Gorilla Rescues Boy Who Fell in Ape Pit," CBS Chicago, August 16, 2011, http://chicago.cbslocal.com/2011/08/16/15-years-ago-today-gorilla-rescues-boy-who-fell-in-ape-pit/.

42. S. F. Brosnan and F. B. M. de Waal, "Monkeys Reject Unequal Pay," *Nature* 425 (2003): 297–99.

43. F. Aureli et al., "Kin-Oriented Redirection Among Japanese Macaques: An Expression of a Revenge System?," *Animal Behaviour* 44 (1992): 283–91.

44. K. Alvarez and E. van Leeuwen, "Paying It Forward: How Helping Others Can Reduce the Psychological Threat of Receiving Help," *Journal of Applied Social Psychology* 45 (2015): 1–9, http://onlinelibrary.wiley.com/doi/10.1111/jasp.12270/abstract; K. Gray, A. F. Ward, and M. I. Norton, "Paying It Forward: Generalized Reciprocity and the Limits of Generosity," *Journal of Experimental Psychology: General* 143 (2014): 247–54.

45. K. L. Leimgruber et al., "Give What You Get: Capuchin Monkeys (*Cebus apella*) and 4-Year-Old Children Pay Forward Positive and Negative Outcomes to Conspecifics," *PLOS ONE* 9 (2014): e87035.

46. A. Öhman and S. Mineka, "Fears, Phobias, and Preparedness: Toward an Evolved Module of Fear and Fear Learning," *Psychological Review* 108 (2001): 483–522.

47. Canadian Press, "Swimming Sensation Momo the Cat Escapes Alberta Flood," CBC News Calgary, June 21, 2013, www.cbc.ca/news/canada/cal gary/swimming-sensation-momo-the-cat-escapes-alberta-flood-1.1370290.

48. "Animal Fighting Case Study: Michael Vick," Animal Legal Defense Fund, last revised January 2011, http://aldf.org/resources/laws-cases/animal -fighting-case-study-michael-vick/.

49. L. Corner, "Rain Phoenix's Unusual Childhood," *Guardian*, July 8, 2011, www.theguardian.com/lifeandstyle/2011/jul/09/rain-phoenix-river -joaquin-family.

50. Rich McCormick, "Judge Gives Chimpanzees Human Rights for the First Time," *The Verge*, April 21, 2015, http://www.theverge.com/2015/4/21/ 8460657/judge-gives-chimpanzees-human-rights-first-time.

51. L. Glendinning, "Spanish Parliament Approves 'Human Rights' for Apes," *Guardian*, June 26, 2008, www.guardian.co.uk/world/2008/jun/ 26/humanrights.animalwelfare; D. G. McNeil Jr., "When Human Rights Extend to Nonhumans," *New York Times*, July 13, 2008, www.nytimes .com/2008/07/13/weekinreview/13mcneil.html?pagewanted=all; L. Abend, "In Spain, Human Rights for Apes," *Time*, July 18, 2008, http://content .time.com/time/world/article/0,8599,1824206,00.html.

52. J. Bentham, *An Introduction to the Principles of Morals and Legislation* (Oxford: Clarendon Press, 1879).

53. R. Descartes, "Discourse on Method," in *Environmental Ethics: Divergence and Convergence*, eds. S. J. Armstrong and R. G. Botzler (New York: McGraw-Hill, 1993), 281–85, http://dhaydock.org/Philosophy/Unit% 202%20-%20Animal%20and%20Machine%20Minds/Descartes%20Ani mals%20as%20Machines.pdf.

54. D. M. Broom, H. Sena, and K. L. Moynihan, "Pigs Learn What a Mirror Image Represents and Use It to Obtain Information," *Animal Behaviour* 78 (2009): 1037–41.

55. S. Loughnan, N. Haslam, and B. Bastian, "The Role of Meat Consumption in the Denial of Moral Status and Mind to Meat Animals," *Appetite* 55 (2010): 156–59.

56. B. Bratanova, S. Loughnan, and B. Bastian, "The Effect of Categorization as Food on the Perceived Moral Standing of Animals," *Appetite* 57 (2011): 193–96.

57. J. S. Foer, *Eating Animals* (New York: Back Bay Books, 2010).

58. D. Moye, "Carlos Romero, Accused of Donkey Sex, Lambastes Florida's 'Backwards' Attitude Towards Animal Sex (NSFW)," *Huffington Post*, September 18, 2012, www.huffingtonpost.com/2012/09/18/carlos-romero -donkey-sex_n_1894146.html.

59. D. J. Bem, "Exotic Becomes Erotic: A Developmental Theory of Sexual Orientation," *Psychological Review* 103 (1996): 320.

60. J. G. Pfaus, T. E. Kippin, and S. Centeno, "Conditioning and Sexual Behavior: A Review," *Hormones and Behavior* 40 (2001): 291–321.

61. R. J. McNally and G. S. Steketee, "The Etiology and Maintenance of Severe Animal Phobias," *Behaviour Research and Therapy* 23 (1985): 431–35.

62. A. L. Podberscek and A. M. Beetz, *Bestiality and Zoophilia: Sexual Relations with Animals (Anthrozoos)* (New York: Bloomsbury Academic, 2009).

63. N. Humphrey, "Bugs and Beasts Before the Law," *Public Domain Review*, http://publicdomainreview.org/2011/03/27/bugs-and-beasts-before -the-law.

64. D. Nelles, "Wild Justice," *Maisonneuve*, September 6, 2012, http://mai sonneuve.org/article/2012/09/6/wild-justice/.

65. E. V. Walter, "Nature on Trial: The Case of the Rooster That Laid the Egg," in *Methodology, Metaphysics and the History of Science*, eds. R. S. Cohn and M. W. Wartofsky (Dordrecht: D. Reidel, 1984), http://books.google .com/books?id=kGmB1f8svH0C&pg=PA295&lpg=PA295&dq=nature+

on+trial+rooster+that+laid+an+egg&source=bl&ots=idR3bm3Dea&
sig=_e4HOZ2TYzB6apLFD_nOsjzaDeI&hl=en&sa=X&ei=dZyKUM
HzA4O68wTZnIDoAg&ved=0CDQQ6AEwAg#v=onepage&q=nature%
20on%20trial%20rooster%20that%20laid%20an%20egg&f=false.

66. G. Archainbaud, "The Christmas Story," *Lassie*, CBS, December 21, 1958.

67. J. Old, "Bond Denied for Man Accused of Killing K-9 Deputy," wistv.com, December 16, 2011, www.wistv.com/story/16338890/k9-deputy-shot-dies.

68. "Pittsburgh K-9 Officer Rocco's Funeral Will Now Be Open to Public," wxpi.com, January 30, 2014, http://wpxi.com/news/news/k9-officer -stabbed-dies/nc7jG/.

CHAPTER 3: THE MACHINE

1. R. Schroeter, *Guys and Dolls* (documentary), BBC, 2002.

2. K. D. Williams, *Ostracism: The Power of Silence* (New York: Guilford Press, 2002).

3. R. F. Baumeister and M. R. Leary, "The Need to Belong: Desire for Interpersonal Attachments as a Fundamental Human Motivation," *Psychological Bulletin* 117 (1995): 497–529.

4. T. M. Vogt et al., "Social Networks as Predictors of Ischemic Heart Disease, Cancer, Stroke and Hypertension: Incidence, Survival and Mortality," *Journal of Clinical Epidemiology* 45 (1992): 659–66.

5. W. L. Gardner and M. L. Knowles, "Love Makes You Real: Favorite Television Characters Are Perceived as 'Real' in a Social Facilitation Paradigm," *Social Cognition* 26 (2008): 156–68.

6. N. Epley, A. Waytz, and J. T. Cacioppo, "On Seeing Human: A Three-Factor Theory of Anthropomorphism," *Psychological Review* 114 (2007): 864–86.

7. S. H. Valverde, "The Modern Sex-Doll Owner: A Descriptive Analysis," master's thesis, California State Polytechnic University, 2012, available at http://digitalcommons.calpoly.edu/theses/849/.

8. R. Schroeter, *Guys and Dolls.*

9. C. K. Morewedge, "Negativity Bias in Attribution of External Agency," *Journal of Experimental Psychology: General* 138 (2009): 535–45.

10. A. Waytz et al., "Making Sense by Making Sentient: Effectance Motivation Increases Anthropomorphism," *Journal of Personality and Social Psychology* 99 (2010): 410–35.

11. C. Nass, Y. Moon, and P. Carney, "Are People Polite to Computers? Responses to Computer-Based Interviewing Systems," *Journal of Applied Social Psychology* 29 (1999): 1093–1110.

12. A. De Angeli and R. Carpenter, "Stupid Computer! Abuse and Social Identities," paper presented at Abuse: the Darker Side of Human Computer Interaction, Rome, September 12, 2005, at www.agentabuse.org/deangeli.pdf.

13. N. Epley, A. Waytz, and J. T. Cacioppo, "On Seeing Human: A Three-Factor Theory of Anthropomorphism," *Psychological Review* 114 (2007): 864–86; I. Hallgren, "Seeing Agents When We Need To, Attributing Experience When We Feel Like It," *Review of Philosophy and Psychology* 3 (2012): 369–82; A. Waytz and L. Young, "Two Motivations for Two Dimensions of Mind," *Journal of Experimental Social Psychology* 55 (2014): 278–83, http://moralitylab.bc.edu/wp-content/uploads/2011/10/DualMotivationsMindJESP.pdf.

14. D. M. Wegner, R. Erber, and P. Raymond, "Transactive Memory in Close Relationships," *Journal of Personality and Social Psychology* 61 (1991): 923–29.

15. A. Clark, *Natural-Born Cyborgs: Minds, Technologies, and the Future of Human Intelligence* (Oxford: Oxford University Press, 2004).

16. B. Sparrow, J. Liu, and D. M. Wegner, "Google Effects on Memory: Cognitive Consequences of Having Information at Our Fingertips," *Science* 333 (2011): 776–78.

17. S. Ramirez et al., "Creating a False Memory in the Hippocampus," *Science* 341 (2013): 387–91; D. Armstrong and M. Ma, "Researcher Controls Colleague's Motions in 1st Human Brain-to-Brain Interface," *UW Today,*

August 27, 2013, www.washington.edu/news/2013/08/27/researcher -controls-colleagues-motions-in-1st-human-brain-to-brain-interface/.

18. *The Terminator*, directed by J. Cameron (Hemdale Films, 1984).

19. R. Kurzweil, *The Singularity Is Near: When Humans Transcend Biology* (New York: Penguin, 2006).

20. G. E. Moore, *Cramming More Components onto Integrated Circuits* (New York: McGraw-Hill, 1965).

21. G. Wood, *Edison's Eve: A Magical History of the Quest for Mechanical Life* (New York: Knopf, 2002).

22. J. Van den Berg et al., "Superhuman Performance of Surgical Tasks by Robots Using Iterative Learning from Human-Guided Demonstrations," paper presented at IEEE International Conference on Robotics and Automation, Anchorage, AK, May 2010, doi:10.1109/ROBOT.2010.5509621; R. Alterovitz and K. Goldberg, *Motion Planning in Medicine: Optimization and Simulation Algorithms for Image-Guided Procedures* (Berlin: Springer, 2008).

23. D. C. Dennett, "Consciousness in Human and Robot Minds," paper presented at IIAS Symposium on Cognition, Computation and Consciousness, Kyoto, Japan, September 1994, available at http://cogprints.org/429/ 1/concrobt.htm.

24. A. M. Turing, "Computing Machinery and Intelligence," *Mind* 59 (1950): 433–60.

25. W. Buckwalter and M. Phelan, "Does the S&M Robot Feel Guilty?," unpublished paper, City University of New York, 2011.

26. J. Weizenbaum, "ELIZA: A Computer Program for the Study of Natural Language Communication Between Man and Machine," *Communications of the ACM* 9 (1966): 36–45.

27. "Clever Bots," *Radiolab*, WNYC, www.radiolab.org/2011/may/31/clever -bots/?utm_source=sharedUrl&utm_media=metatag&utm_campaign= sharedUrl.

28. O. Alexander et al., "The Digital Emily Project: Achieving a Photoreal Digital Actor," USC Institute for Creative Technologies, http://gl.ict.usc .edu/Research/DigitalEmily/.

29. K. F. MacDorman et al., "Too Real for Comfort? Uncanny Responses to Computer Generated Faces," *Computers in Human Behavior* 25 (2009): 695–710; J. Seyama and R. S. Nagayama, "The Uncanny Valley: Effect of Realism on the Impression of Artificial Human Faces," *Presence: Teleoperators and Virtual Environments* 16 (2007): 337–51.

30. S. A. Steckenfinger and A. A. Ghazanfar, "Monkey Visual Behavior Falls into the Uncanny Valley," *Proceedings of the National Academy of Sciences* 106 (2009): 18362–66.

31. C. H. Ramey, "The Uncanny Valley of Similarities Concerning Abortion, Baldness, Heaps of Sand and Humanlike Robots," in *Proceedings of Views of the Uncanny Valley Workshop: IEEE-RAS International Conference on Humanoid Robots* (Tsukuba, Japan: December 5–7, 2005), 8–13.

32. E. Jentsch, "On the Psychology of the Uncanny," *Angelaki* 2 (1906): 7–16.

33. S. Freud, *The Uncanny* (London: Penguin Books, 1919).

34. K. Gray and D. M. Wegner, "Feeling Robots and Human Zombies: Mind Perception and the Uncanny Valley," *Cognition* 125 (2012): 125–30.

35. R. Adolphs et al., "A Mechanism for Impaired Fear Recognition After Amygdala Damage," *Nature* 433 (2005): 68–72.

36. Gray and Wegner, "Feeling Robots and Human Zombies."

37. J. Sytsma and E. Machery, "Two Conceptions of Subjective Experience," *Philosophical Studies* 151 (2009): 299–327.

38. Gray and Wegner, "Feeling Robots and Human Zombies."

39. D. J. Chalmers, "Consciousness and its Place in Nature," in *Blackwell Guide to Philosophy of Mind*, eds. S. Stich and F. Warfield (New York: Blackwell, 2003), 1–45.

40. Gray and Wegner, "Feeling Robots and Human Zombies."

41. W. Shakespeare, *The Tragedy of Hamlet, Prince of Denmark* (New York: Washington Square Press/Pocket Books, 1992).

42. G. Orwell, *1984* (New York: Signet Classics, 1950).

43. Gray and Wegner, "Feeling Robots and Human Zombies."

44. C. Breazeal, "Emotion and Sociable Humanoid Robots," *International Journal of Human-Computer Studies* 59 (2003): 119–55.

45. C. Breazeal, *Designing Sociable Robots* (Cambridge, MA: MIT Press, 2004).

46. T. Miedaner, "The Soul of the Mark III Beast," in *The Mind's I: Fantasies and Reflections on Self and Soul* (New York: Basic Books, 1981), 109–113.

47. C. Bartneck et al., "'Daisy, Daisy, Give Me Your Answer Do!' Switching Off a Robot," in *Proceedings of the 2nd ACM/IEEE International Conference on Human-Robot Interaction* (Washington, DC: March 9–11, 2007), 217–22, www.bartneck.de/publications/2007/daisy/.

48. M. Garber, "Funerals for Fallen Robots," *Atlantic*, September 20, 2013, www.theatlantic.com/technology/archive/2013/09/funerals-for-fallen -robots/279861/.

49. I. Asimov, *I, Robot* (New York: Signet Books, 1956).

CHAPTER 4: THE PATIENT

1. C. Siemaszko, "20 Years Ago: Lorena Bobbitt Cuts Off Penis of Then Husband John Wayne Bobbitt in Case That Horrified—and Fascinated— the Nation," *New York Daily News*, June 23, 2013, available at www.nydaily news.com/news/crime/20-years-today-lorena-bobbitt-cuts-husband -penis-case-horrified-fascinated-nation-article-1.1379112.

2. E. Scarry, *The Body in Pain: The Making and Unmaking of the World* (New York: Oxford University Press, 1985), available at http://books.google .com/books?hl=en&lr=&id=uFluGXva-ZkC&oi=fnd&pg=PA3&dq=lan guage+pain+expression+scarry&ots=FeZxX6UVE_&sig=wEaB23T79a KAr9MYdXxGw2R9nlc#v=onepage&q=language%20pain%20expres sion%20scarry&f=false.

3. D. Purves et al., "Central Pain Pathways: The Spinothalamic Tract," in *Neuroscience* (Sunderland, MA: Sinauer Associates, 2001), at www.ncbi .nlm.nih.gov/books/NBK10967/.

4. American Chronic Pain Association, "Neuropathic Pain," www.theacpa
.org/condition/neuropathic-pain.

5. Leprosy Mission International, "What Is Leprosy?," www.leprosymission
.org/what-is-leprosy.html.

6. V. S. Ramachandran and D. Rogers-Ramachandran, "Synaesthesia in Phantom Limbs Induced with Mirrors," *Proceedings of the Royal Society of London B: Biological Sciences* 263 (1996): 377–86.

7. J. L. Straus and S. von Ammon Cavanaugh, "Placebo Effects: Issues for Clinical Practice in Psychiatry and Medicine," *Psychosomatics* 37 (1996): 315–26; T. Koyama et al., "The Subjective Experience of Pain: Where Expectations Become Reality," *Proceedings of the National Academy of Sciences of the United States of America* 102 (2005): 12950–55.

8. C. M. Williams et al., "Efficacy of Paracetamol for Acute Low-Back Pain: A Double-Blind, Randomised Controlled Trial," *Lancet* 384 (2014): 1586–96.

9. I. Kirsch et al., "Initial Severity and Antidepressant Benefits: A Meta-analysis of Data Submitted to the Food and Drug Administration," *PLOS Medicine* 5 (2008): e45.

10. I. Kirsch, "Challenging Received Wisdom: Antidepressants and the Placebo Effect," *McGill Journal of Medicine* 11 (2008): 219–22; J. R. Davidson et al., "Fluoxetine, Comprehensive Cognitive Behavioral Therapy, and Placebo in Generalized Social Phobia," *Archives of General Psychiatry* 61 (2004): 1005.

11. A. Catlin and R. L. Taylor-Ford, "Investigation of Standard Care Versus Sham Reiki Placebo Versus Actual Reiki Therapy to Enhance Comfort and Well-Being in a Chemotherapy Infusion Center," *Oncology Nursing Forum* 38 (2011): E212–20; N. Assefi et al., "Reiki for the Treatment of Fibromyalgia: A Randomized Controlled Trial," *Journal of Alternative and Complementary Medicine* 14 (2008): 1115–22.

12. T. Brygge et al., "Reflexology and Bronchial Asthma," *Respiratory Medicine* 95 (2001): 173–79; J. Jones et al., "Reflexology Has No Immediate

Haemodynamic Effect in Patients with Chronic Heart Failure: A Double Blind Randomised Controlled Trial," *Complementary Therapies in Clinical Practice* 19 (2013): 133–38.

13. M. Frith, "Urine: The Body's Own Health Drink?" *Independent*, February 21, 2006, www.independent.co.uk/life-style/health-and-families/health-news/urine-the-bodys-own-health-drink-467303.html.

14. H. Gurnee, *The Late Show with David Letterman*, original air date March 31, 1994.

15. J. Caple, "Pee Is Only a Wee Bit Gross," *Page 2*, ESPN, http://sports.espn.go.com/espn/page2/story?page=caple/040511.

16. American Cancer Society, "Placebo Effect" (last revised April 10, 2015), www.cancer.org/treatment/treatmentsandsideeffects/complementaryandalternativemedicine/placebo-effect.

17. A. Schweiger and A. Parducci, "Nocebo: The Psychologic Induction of Pain," *Pavlovian Journal of Biological Science* 16 (1981): 140–43.

18. A. Arntz and L. Claassens, "The Meaning of Pain Influences Its Experienced Intensity," *Pain* 109 (2004): 20–25.

19. A. D. Craig and M. C. Bushnell, "The Thermal Grill Illusion: Unmasking the Burn of Cold Pain," *Science* 265 (1994): 252–55.

20. R. Melzack, "The McGill Pain Questionnaire: From Description to Measurement," *Anesthesiology* 103 (2005): 199–202; R. Melzack and P. D. Wall, "Pain Mechanisms: A New Theory," *Science* 150 (1965): 971–79.

21. R. C. Kupers et al., "Morphine Differentially Affects the Sensory and Effective Pain Ratings in Neurogenic and Idiopathic Forms of Pain," *Pain* 47 (1991): 5–12.

22. Kemi, "Hit by Car, Hit by Morphine," *Erowid Experience Vaults*, March 4, 2011, www.erowid.org/experiences/exp.php?ID=28149.

23. A. Gopnik and J. W. Astington, "Children's Understanding of Representational Change and Its Relation to the Understanding of False Belief and the Appearance-Reality Distinction," *Child Development* 59 (1988): 26–37.

24. N. Epley, C. K. Morewedge, and B. Keysar, "Perspective Taking in Children and Adults: Equivalent Egocentrism but Differential Correction," *Journal of Experimental Social Psychology* 40 (2004): 760–68; J. Rawls, *A Theory of Justice* (Cambridge, MA: Harvard University Press, 1971).

25. D. Hume, *Essays, Moral, Political, and Literary* (Indianapolis, IN: Library of Economics and Liberty, 1987), www.econlib.org/library/LFBooks/Hume/hmMPL1.html.

26. A. Smith, *The Theory of Moral Sentiments* (Indianapolis, IN: Liberty Fund, 1759).

27. Epley, Morewedge, and Keysar, "Perspective Taking in Children and Adults."

28. R. Gordon, "Folk Psychology as Simulation," *Mind & Language* 2 (1986): 158–71, 571–80; T. Singer et al., "Empathy for Pain Involves the Affective but Not Sensory Components of Pain," *Science* 303 (2004): 1157–62.

29. B. Pascal, "On the Means of Belief," in *Pensées* (1669), www.bartleby.com/48/1/4.html.

30. C. D. Burt and K. Strongman, "Use of Images in Charity Advertising: Improving Donations and Compliance Rates," *International Journal of Organisational Behaviour* 8 (2005): 571–80.

31. Singer, "Empathy for Pain Involves the Affective but Not Sensory Components of Pain."

32. D. M. Wegner, B. Sparrow, and L. Winerman, "Vicarious Agency: Experiencing Control Over the Movements of Others," *Journal of Personality and Social Psychology* 86 (2004): 838–48.

33. P. Singer, "The Drowning Child and the Expanding Circle," *New Internationalist*, April 1997, www.utilitarian.net/singer/by/199704--.htm.

34. B. Cialdini et al., "Reinterpreting the Empathy-Altruism Relationship: When One Into One Equals Oneness," *Journal of Personality and Social Psychology*, 73 (1997): 481–94.

35. K. Gray and D. M. Wegner, "Feeling Robots and Human Zombies: Mind Perception and the Uncanny Valley," *Cognition* 125 (2012): 125–30; A. J. M.

Dijker, "Perceived Vulnerability as a Common Basis of Moral Emotions," *British Journal of Social Psychology* 49 (2010): 415–23.

36. Dijker, "Perceived Vulnerability as a Common Basis of Moral Emotions."

37. B. Hutchinson, "Raging Rivers? Fur Sure! Park Ave. Attack on Sable Coat," *New York Daily News*, December 17, 1997, www.nydailynews .com/archives/news/raging-rivers-fur-park-ave-attack-sable-coat-article-1.783036.

38. S. Russel, "When Extreme Animal Rights Activists Attack," *Pacific Standard*, March 16, 2012, www.psmag.com/legal-affairs/when-extreme -animal-rights-activists-attack-40430; J. Doward, "Kill Scientists, Says Animal Rights Chief," *Guardian*, July 25, 2004, www.theguardian.com/ society/2004/jul/25/health.animalrights.

39. M. S. James, "Prison Is 'Living Hell' for Pedophiles," ABC News, August 26, 2003, http://abcnews.go.com/US/story?id=90004.

40. Dijker, "Perceived Vulnerability as a Common Basis of Moral Emotions."

41. C. D. Cameron and B. K. Payne, "Escaping Affect: How Motivated Emotion Regulation Creates Insensitivity to Mass Suffering," *Journal of Personality and Social Psychology* 100 (2011): 1–15.

42. L. Logan, "The Problem with How We Treat Bipolar Disorder," *New York Times*, April 26, 2013, http://mobile.nytimes.com/2013/04/28/magazine/ the-problem-with-how-we-treat-bipolar-disorder.html?from=science.

43. D. R. Rhodes et al., "Speaking and Interruptions During Primary Care Office Visits," *Family Medicine* 33 (2001): 528–32.

44. J. Halpern, "What Is Clinical Empathy?," *Journal of General Internal Medicine* 18 (2003): 670–74; O. S. Haque and A. Waytz, "Dehumanization in Medicine: Causes, Solutions, and Functions," *Perspectives on Psychological Science* 7 (2012): 176–86.

45. D. Schulman-Green, "Coping Mechanisms of Physicians Who Routinely Work with Dying Patients," *OMEGA: Journal of Death Dying* 47 (2003): 253–64.

46. T. Szasz, *The Second Sin* (Garden City, NY: Anchor Press, 1973).

47. H. H. Strupp and S. W. Hadley, "Specific vs. Nonspecific Factors in Psychotherapy: A Controlled Study of Outcome," *Archives of General Psychiatry* 36 (1979): 1125–36.

48. T. Furmark et al., "Common Changes in Cerebral Blood Flow in Patients with Social Phobia Treated with Citalopram or Cognitive-Behavioral Therapy," *Archives of General Psychiatry* 59 (2002): 425–33; L. R. Baxter, J. M. Schwartz, and K. S. Bergman, "Caudate Glucose Metabolic Rate Changes with Both Drug and Behavior Therapy for Obsessive-Compulsive Disorder," *Archives of General Psychiatry* 49 (1992): 681–89; P. Porto et al., "Does Cognitive Behavioral Therapy Change the Brain? A Systematic Review of Neuroimaging in Anxiety Disorders," *Journal of Neuropsychiatry and Clinical Neurosciences* 21 (2009): 114–25.

49. A. Nadler and J. D. Fisher, "The Role of Threat to Self-Esteem and Perceived Control in Recipient Reaction to Help: Theory Development and Empirical Validation," in *Advances in Experimental Social Psychology*, ed. L. Berkowitz (Orlando, FL: Academic Press, 1986), 19, 81–116.

50. S. L. Brown et al., "Caregiving Behavior Is Associated with Decreased Mortality Risk," *Psychological Science* 20 (2009): 488–94.

51. E. I. Langer and J. Rodin, "The Effects of Choice and Enhanced Personal Responsibility for the Aged: A Field Experiment in an Institutional Setting," *Journal of Personality and Social Psychology* 34 (1976): 191–98.

52. D. Breese, "Son Lifts Car Off Father's Chest," *Alaska Star*, May 29, 2008, http://classic.alaskastar.com/stories/052908/new_20080529003.shtml.

53. K. Gray, "Moral Transformation: Good and Evil Turn the Weak into the Mighty," *Social Psychology and Personality Science* 1 (2010): 253–58.

54. M. K. Gandhi, *Autobiography: The Story of My Experiments with Truth*, trans. M. Desai (New York: Dover, 1983).

55. A. Grant, *Give and Take* (New York: Viking, 2013).

56. K. Gray and D. M. Wegner, "Moral Typecasting: Divergent Perceptions of Moral Agents and Moral Patients," *Journal of Personality and Social Psychology* 96 (2009): 505–20.

57. Gray and Wegner, "Moral Typecasting."

58. G. Spence, *Win Your Case: How to Present, Persuade, and Prevail—Every Place, Every Time* (New York: St. Martin's Press, 2006).

59. *Daily Mail* reporter, "'Affluenza' Teen Ethan Couch Reaches Undisclosed Settlement with Victims' Families," *Daily Mail Online*, March 18, 2014, available at www.dailymail.co.uk/news/article-2583768/Affluenza-teen -avoided-jail-fatal-drunk-driving-accident-reaches-undisclosed -settlement-two-three-families-victims.html.

60. K. Gray and D. M. Wegner, "To Escape Blame, Don't Be a Hero—Be a Victim," *Journal of Experimental Social Psychology* 47 (2011): 516–19.

61. L. A. Zebrowitz and S. M. McDonald, "The Impact of Litigants' Baby-facedness and Attractiveness on Adjudications in Small Claims Courts," *Law and Human Behavior* 15 (1991): 603–23.

62. "1993: Two Boys Charged with Toddler's Murder," BBC: On This Day, http://news.bbc.co.uk/onthisday/hi/dates/stories/february/20/newsid _2552000/2552185.stm.

63. C. Alexander, "Parting Glances: Oranges & Lemons Sliced," *PrideSource*, February 2, 2006, www.pridesource.com/article.html?article=17348.

64. J. Leclaire, "Satan's End-Time Strategy to Outlaw Traditional Marriage in Full Swing," *Charisma News*, June 26, 2013, www.charismanews.com/ opinion/watchman-on-the-wall/40034-satan-s-end-time-strategy -to-outlaw-traditional-marriage-in-full-swing.

65. P. DeScioli, S. Gilbert, and R. Kurzban, "Indelible Victims and Persistent Punishers in Moral Cognition," *Psychological Inquiry* 23 (2012): 143–49.

66. K. Gray, C. Schein, and A. F. Ward, "The Myth of Harmless Wrongs in Moral Cognition: Automatic Dyadic Completion from Sin to Suffering," *Journal of Experimental Psychology: General* 143 (2014): 1600–15.

67. J. Haidt, *The Righteous Mind: Why Good People Are Divided by Politics and Religion* (New York: Pantheon Books, 2012).

68. J. Graham, J. Haidt, and B. A. Nosek, "Liberals and Conservatives Rely on Different Sets of Moral Foundations," *Journal of Personality and Social Psychology* 96 (2009): 1029–46.

CHAPTER 5: THE ENEMY

1. L. Siems, "Mohamedou Ould Slahi's Guantánamo Memoirs: How the United States Kept a Gitmo Detainee Silent for More Than a Decade," *Slate*, April 30, 2013, www.slate.com/articles/news_and_politics/for eigners/2013/04/mohamedou_ould_slahi_s_guant_namo_memoirs _how_the_united_states_kept_a_gitmo.html.

2. C. D. Leonnig and D. Priest, "Detainees Accuse Female Interrogators," *Washington Post*, February 10, 2005, A01.

3. Ina and Lacy Pauley family, "Hatfield-McCoy Feud Timeline," http://dpauley.us/Feud_Timeline.pdf.

4. Y. Dunham, A. S. Baron, and S. Carey, "Consequences of 'Minimal' Group Affiliations in Children," *Child Development* 82 (2011): 793–811.

5. M. Billig and H. Tajfel, "Social Categorization and Similarity in Intergroup Behaviour," *European Journal of Social Psychology* 3 (1973): 27–52.

6. Ibid.

7. Ibid.

8. S. Bloom, "Lesson of a Lifetime," *Smithsonian*, September 2005, www .smithsonianmag.com/history-archaeology/lesson_lifetime.html.

9. M. Sherif, *Intergroup Conflict and Cooperation: The Robbers Cave Experiment* (Norman, OK: University Book Exchange, 1961).

10. J. C. Mitani, D. P. Watts, and S. J. Amsler, "Lethal Intergroup Aggression Leads to Territorial Expansion in Wild Chimpanzees," *Current Biology* 20 (2010): 507–8.

11. F. de Waal, "The Brutal Elimination of a Rival Among Captive Male Chimpanzees," *Ethology and Sociobiology* 7 (1986): 237–51.

12. J. Goodall, "Infant Killing and Cannibalism in Free-Living Chimpanzees," *Folia Primatologica* 28 (1977): 259–89.

13. "Chimpanzee Attack Leaves Man in Intensive Care in South Africa," *Guardian*, June 29, 2012, www.theguardian.com/world/2012/jun/29/ chimpanzee-attacks-researcher-south-africa.

14. D. Quammen, "The Left Bank Ape: An Exclusive Look at Bonobos," *National Geographic*, March 2013, http://ngm.nationalgeographic.com/ 2013/03/125-bonobos/quammen-text.

15. A. R. Krosch and D. M. Amodio, "Economic Scarcity Alters the Perception of Race," *Proceedings of the National Academy of Sciences* 111 (2014): 9079–84.

16. N. Haslam, "Dehumanization: An Integrative Review," *Personality and Social Psychology Review* 10 (2006): 252–64.

17. L. Back and J. Solomos, *Theories of Race and Racism* (New York: Routledge, 2000).

18. D. Hopkins, *Down, Up, and Over: Slave Religion and Black Theology* (Minneapolis, MN: Fortress Press, 2000), 28.

19. P. A. Goff et al., "Not Yet Human: Implicit Knowledge, Historical Dehumanization, and Contemporary Consequences," *Journal of Personality and Social Psychology* 94 (2008): 292–306.

20. P. G. Devine, "Stereotypes and Prejudice: Their Automatic and Controlled Components," *Journal of Personality and Social Psychology* 56 (1989): 5–18.

21. R. Shapiro and J. Mirkinson, "Republican Attendees Threw Nuts at Black CNN Camerawoman, Called Her an 'Animal,'" *Huffington Post*, August 28, 2012, www.huffingtonpost.com/2012/08/28/republican-cnn-attack -animal-peanuts-racist_n_1838249.html.

22. M. Luther, *Table Talk*, ed. W. Hazlitt (Grand Rapids, MI: Christian Classics Ethereal Library, 2004), 227, http://ntslibrary.com/PDF%20Books/ Luther%20Table%20Talk.pdf.

23. A. Chua, *Battle Hymn of the Tiger Mother* (New York: Penguin Press, 2011), 26.

24. C. Geronimi, *Education for Death* (Walt Disney Pictures, 1943), www .youtube.com/watch?v=eU1LHeim_hA.

25. I. Kant, *The Metaphysical Elements of Ethics* (Echo Library, 1780): 163.

26. M. C. Nussbaum, "Objectification," *Philosophy and Public Affairs* 24 (1995): 249–91.

27. T. Saguy et al., "Interacting Like a Body," *Psychological Science* 21 (2010): 178–82.

28. D. Archer et al., "Face-ism: Five Studies of Sex Differences in Facial Prominence," *Journal of Personality and Social Psychology* 45 (1983): 725–35.

29. Ibid.

30. N. Schwarz and E. Kurz, "What's in a Picture? The Impact of Face-ism on Trait Attribution," *European Journal of Social Psychology* 19 (1989): 311–16.

31. K. Gray et al., "More Than a Body: Mind Perception and the Nature of Objectification," *Journal of Personality and Social Psychology* 101 (2011): 1207–20.

32. N. A. Heflick et al., "From Women to Objects: Appearance Focus, Target Gender, and Perceptions of Warmth, Morality and Competence," *Journal of Experimental Social Psychology* 47 (2011): 572–81.

33. M. Cikara, J. L. Eberhardt, and S. T. Fiske, "From Agents to Objects: Sexist Attitudes and Neural Responses to Sexualized Targets," *Journal of Cognitive Neuroscience* 23 (2010): 540–51.

34. Centers for Disease Control and Prevention, "Autism Spectrum Disorder (ASDs)," 2013, www.cdc.gov/ncbddd/autism/data.html.

35. S. Baron-Cohen, *Mindblindness: An Essay on Autism and Theory of Mind* (Cambridge, MA: MIT Press, 1995); P. Carruthers, "Autism as Mind-Blindness: An Elaboration and Partial Defence," in *Theories of Theories of Mind*, eds. P. Carruthers and P. K. Smith (Cambridge: Cambridge University Press, 1996), 257–73.

36. L. M. Oberman and V. S. Ramachandran, "The Simulating Social Mind: The Role of the Mirror Neuron System and Simulation in the Social and Communicative Deficits of Autism Spectrum Disorders," *Psychological Bulletin* 133 (2007): 310–27.

37. S. Baron-Cohen, A. M. Leslie, and U. Frith, "Does the Autistic Child Have a 'Theory of Mind'?," *Cognition* 21 (1985): 37–46.

38. L. Kanner, "Autistic Disturbances of Affective Contact," *Nervous Child* 2 (1943): 217–50.

39. Ibid.

40. K. Gray et al., "Distortions of Mind Perception in Psychopathology," *Proceedings of the National Academy of Sciences* 108 (2011): 477–79.

41. L. Surian and A. M. Leslie, "Competence and Performance in False Belief Understanding: A Comparison of Autistic and Normal 3-Year-Old Children," *British Journal of Developmental Psychology* 17 (1999): 141–55.

42. Gray et al., "Distortions of Mind Perception in Psychopathology"; J. M. Moran et al., "Impaired Theory of Mind for Moral Judgment in High-Functioning Autism," *Proceedings of the National Academy of Sciences* 108 (2011): 2688–92.

43. NPR staff, "'Best Practices': Learning to Live with Asperger's," *All Things Considered*, NPR, February 3, 2012, www.kqed.org/news/story/2012/02/03/83577/best_practices_learning_to_live_with_aspergers.

44. H. M. Cleckley, *The Mask of Sanity: An Attempt to Clarify Some Issues About the So-called Psychopathic Personality* (Maryland Heights, MO: Mosby, 1955).

45. B. B. Lahey et al., "Predicting Future Antisocial Personality Disorder in Males from a Clinical Assessment in Childhood," *Journal of Consulting and Clinical Psychology* 73 (2005): 389–99.

46. G. Fairchild et al., "Facial Expression Recognition, Fear Conditioning, and Startle Modulation in Female Subjects with Conduct Disorder," *Biological Psychiatry* 68 (2010): 272–79.

47. P. Babiak, C. S. Neumann, and R. D. Hare, "Corporate Psychopathy: Talking the Walk," *Behavioral Sciences & the Law* 28 (2010): 174–93.

48. M. Koenigs et al., "Damage to the Prefrontal Cortex Increases Utilitarian Moral Judgments," *Nature* 446 (2007): 908–11.

49. R. J. R. Blair, "The Amygdala and Ventromedial Prefrontal Cortex in Morality and Psychopathy," *Trends in Cognitive Sciences* 11 (2007): 387-92.

50. L. G. Aspinwall, T. R. Brown, and J. Tabery, "The Double-Edged Sword: Does Biomechanism Increase or Decrease Judges' Sentencing of Psychopaths?," *Science* 337 (2012): 846–49.

51. D. A. Davis, *The Jeffrey Dahmer Story: An American Nightmare* (New York: St. Martin's Paperbacks, 1991).

52. Z. Rubin and A. Peplau, "Belief in a Just World and Reactions to Another's Lot: A Study of Participants in the National Draft Lottery," *Journal of Social Issues* 29 (1973): 73–93.

53. M. Lerner, *The Belief in a Just World: A Fundamental Delusion* (New York: Springer, 1980).

54. A. Elliott, "Complications Grow for Muslims Serving in U.S.," *New York Times*, November 8, 2009, A1.

55. J. Stephens and J. Jouvenal, "Muslim Cabdriver Alleges Assault by Passenger Who Cited Boston Bombing," *Washington Post*, April 30, 2013, available at www.washingtonpost.com/local/muslim-cabdriver-alleges-assault-by-passenger-who-cited-boston-bombings/2013/04/30/9fa45a7c-b0d2-11e2-bbf2-a6f9e9d79e19_story.html.

56. "Rwanda: How the Genocide Happened," BBC News, May 17, 2011, at www.bbc.co.uk/news/world-africa-13431486.

57. E. L. Paluck, "Reducing Intergroup Prejudice and Conflict Using the Media: A Field Experiment in Rwanda," *Journal of Personality and Social Psychology* 96 (2009): 574–87.

58. M. Eksteins, *Rites of Spring: The Great War and the Birth of the Modern Age* (New York: Mariner Books, 2000).

CHAPTER 6: THE SILENT

1. M. Roach, *Stiff: The Curious Lives of Human Cadavers* (New York: W. W. Norton & Company, 2003), discussed at http://en.wikipedia.org/wiki/Stiff:_The_Curious_Lives_of_Human_Cadavers.

2. E. A. Poe, "The Tell-Tale Heart," *The Pioneer* 1 (1843).

3. S. Spielberg, *Indiana Jones and the Temple of Doom* (Paramount Pictures, 1984); R. Hughart and B. Haaland, "War Is the H-Word," *Futurama*, November 26, 2000; V. Salva, *Jeepers Creepers* (Metro-Goldwyn-Mayer, 2001); T. Maylam, *Split Second* (Astro Distribution, 1992).

4. A. M. Capron and L. R. Kass, "A Statutory Definition of the Standards for Determining Human Death: An Appraisal and a Proposal," *University of Pennsylvania Law Review* 121 (1972): 87–118.

5. "'My Lobotomy': Howard Dully's Journey," *All Things Considered*, NPR, November 16, 2005, www.npr.org/2005/11/16/5014080/my-lobotomy -howard-dullys-journey.

6. "Prefrontal Lobotomy," *Journal of the American Medical Association* 123 (1943): 418–20.

7. W. L. Laurence, "Lobotomy Banned in Soviet as Cruel," *New York Times*, August 22, 1953, 13.

8. J. R. Thogmartin, "Report of Autopsy," Medical Examiner District Six, Pasco & Pinellas Counties, June 13, 2005, www.blogsforterri.com/archives/ 5050439_autopsy%20report%20and%20supporting%20documents.pdf.

9. D. S. Weisberg et al., "The Seductive Allure of Neuroscience Explanations," *Journal of Cognitive Neuroscience* 20 (2011): 470–77; A. Quart, "Neuroscience: Under Attack," *New York Times*, November 23, 2012, available at www.nytimes.com/2012/11/25/opinion/sunday/neuroscience -under-attack.html.

10. D. L. Ames et al., "Taking Another Person's Perspective Increases Self-Referential Neural Processing," *Psychological Science* 19 (2008): 642–44.

11. J. P. Mitchell, "Inferences About Mental States," *Philosophical Transactions of the Royal Society B: Biological Sciences* 364 (2009): 1309–16.

12. J. Hashmi et al., "Effect of Pulsing in Low-Level Light Therapy," *Lasers in Surgery and Medicine* 42 (2010): 450–66.

13. I. Feinberg, "Changing Concepts of the Function of Sleep: Discovery of Intense Brain Activity During Sleep Calls for Revision of Hypotheses as to Its Function," *Biological Psychiatry* 1 (1969): 331–48.

14. S. Herculano-Houzel, "Sleep It Out," *Science* 342 (2013): 316–17; J. M. Siegel, "Clues to the Functions of Mammalian Sleep," *Nature* 437 (2005): 1264–71; J. M. Siegel, "Why We Sleep," *Scientific American* 289 (2003): 92–97.

15. Siegel, "Clues to the Functions of Mammalian Sleep."

16. E. Kobylarz and N. Schiff, "Neurophysiological Correlates of Persistent Vegetative and Minimally Conscious States," *Neuropsychological Rehabilitation* 15 (2005): 323–32.

17. S. Laureys, A. M. Owen, and N. D. Schiff, "Brain Function in Coma, Vegetative State, and Related Disorders," *Lancet Neurology* 3 (2004): 537–46.

18. E. Landsness et al., "Electrophysiological Correlates of Behavioural Changes in Vigilance in Vegetative State and Minimally Conscious State," *Brain* 134 (2011): 2222–32.

19. F. Perrin et al., "Brain Response to One's Own Name in Vegetative State, Minimally Conscious State, and Locked-In Syndrome," *Archives of Neurology* 63 (2006): 562–69.

20. The Multi-Society Task Force on PVS, "Medical Aspects of the Persistent Vegetative State," *New England Journal of Medicine* 330 (1994): 1499–1508, http://nejm.org/doi/pdf/10.1056/NEJM199405263302107.

21. O. Pfungst, *Clever Hans (The Horse of Mr. Von Osten): A Contribution to Experimental Animal and Human Psychology* (Project Gutenberg, 1911), www.gutenberg.org/files/33936/33936-h/33936-h.htm#CHAPTER_II.

22. H. Sharon et al., "Emotional Processing of Personally Familiar Faces in the Vegetative State," *PLOS ONE* 8 (2013): e74711.

23. L. Gómez-Gómez, "Plant Perception Systems for Pathogen Recognition and Defence," *Molecular Immunology* 41 (2004): 1055–62; E. E. Farmer and C. A. Ryan, "Interplant Communication: Airborne Methyl Jasmonate Induces Synthesis of Proteinase Inhibitors in Plant Leaves," *Proceedings of the National Academy of Sciences* 87 (1990): 7713–16; D. F. Rhoades, "Responses of Alder and Willow to Attack by Tent Caterpillars and Webworms: Evidence for Pheromonal Sensitivity of Willows," in *Plant*

Resistance to Insects, ed. P. A. Hedin, (Washington, DC: American Chemical Society, 1983), 55–68.

24. A. M. Owen and M. R. Coleman, "Detecting Awareness in the Vegetative State," *Annals of the New York Academy of Sciences* 1129 (2008): 130–38.

25. T. Judt, "Night," *New York Review of Books*, January 14, 2010, available at www.nybooks.com/articles/archives/2010/jan/14/night/.

26. R. Christopher deCharms et al., "Control Over Brain Activation and Pain Learned by Using Real-Time Functional MRI," *Proceedings of the National Academy of Sciences of the United States of America* 102 (2005): 18626–31.

27. I. Parker, "Reading Minds: If a Person Cannot Move, Talk, or Even Blink, Is It Possible to Communicate with His Brain?," *New Yorker*, January 20, 2003, 52.

28. J. Foer, "The Unspeakable Odyssey of the Motionless Boy," *Esquire*, October 2, 2008, available at www.esquire.com/features/unspeakable-odyssey -motionless-boy-1008.

29. *Times* staff writer, "Julia Tavalaro, 68; Poet and Author Noted for Defying Severe Paralysis," *Los Angeles Times*, December 21, 2003, http://articles .latimes.com/2003/dec/21/local/me-tavalaro21.

30. *Nicklinson v. Ministry of Justice*, High Court of Justice, Queen's Bench Division, Administrative Court, August 16, 2012, https://judiciary.gov .uk/wp-content/uploads/JCO/Documents/Judgments/nicklinson -judgment-16082012.pdf.

31. Transcript of conversation between Armin Meiwes and Bernd-Jürgen Brandes, 2001, http://pastebin.com/9z2ZxVX3.

32. "German Cannibal Gets Eight-and-a-Half Years," *Guardian*, January 30, 2004, www.theguardian.com/uk/2004/jan/30/germany.world.

33. *Nicklinson v. Ministry of Justice.*

34. J. F. Burns, "Tony Nicklinson, Who Fought for Assisted Suicide, Dies at 58," *New York Times*, August 22, 2012, A9.

35. P. Brickman, D. Coates, and R. Janoff-Bulman, "Lottery Winners and Accident Victims: Is Happiness Relative?," *Journal of Personality and Social Psychology* 36 (1978): 917–27.

36. M. Murrell, "With Help from Friends, Paraplegic Returns to Hunting," *Topeka Capital-Journal*, May 18, 2013, http://cjonline.com/sports/2013-05-18/marc-murrell-help-friends-paraplegic-returns-hunting; M. Rubenstein, "Pasco Paraplegic Finds Himself in Faith and Family," *Tampa Bay Times*, June 24, 2011, www.tampabay.com/news/humaninterest/pasco-paraplegic-finds-himself-in-faith-and-family/1177251.

37. P. W. Chen, "Making Your Wishes Known at the End of Life," *New York Times*, April 15, 2010, www.nytimes.com/2010/04/16/health/15chen.html?ref=health.

38. T. Lewin, "Ignoring 'Right to Die' Directives, Medical Community is Being Sued," *New York Times*, June 2, 1996, www.nytimes.com/1996/06/02/us/ignoring-right-to-die-directives-medical-community-is-being-sued.html; E. Lavandera, J. Rubin, and G. Botelho, "Texas Judge: Remove Brain-Dead Woman from Ventilator," CNN, January 24, 2014, www.cnn.com/2014/01/24/health/pregnant-brain-dead-woman-texas/index.html?hpt=hp_t1.

39. K. Gray, T. A. Knickman, and D. M. Wegner, "More Dead Than Dead: Perceptions of Persons in the Persistent Vegetative State," *Cognition* 121 (2011): 275–80.

40. B. K. Waltke, "Old Testament Texts Bearing on the Problem of the Control of Human Reproduction," in *Birth Control and the Christian*, eds. W. O. Spitzer and C. L. Saylor (Carol Stream, IL: Tyndale House, 1969), 5–23.

41. C. Stipe et al., "A Protestant Affirmation on the Control of Human Reproduction," *Journal of the American Scientific Affiliation* 22 (1970): 46–47.

42. W. Blackstone, *Commentaries on the Laws of England* (Chicago: University of Chicago Press, 1765), http://press-pubs.uchicago.edu/founders/documents/amendIXs1.html.

43. A. Smith, *A Complete History of the Lives and Robberies of the Most Notorious Highwaymen, Footpads, Shoplifts, & Cheats of Both Sexes* (1714; London: George Routledge & Sons, Ltd, 1926).

44. S. J. Lee et al., "Fetal Pain: A Systematic Multidisciplinary Review of the Evidence," *Journal of the American Medical Association* 294 (2005): 947–54.

45. "New Law Requires Women to Name Baby, Paint Nursery Before Getting Abortion," *Onion*, January 14, 2010, www.theonion.com/video/new-law-requires-women-to-name-baby-paint-nursery,14393/.

46. J. S. Bard, "The Diagnosis Is Anencephaly and the Parents Ask About Organ Donation: Now What? A Guide for Hospital Counsel and Ethics Committees," *Western New England Law Review* 21 (1999): 49–95.

47. V. Starnes et al., "Cardiac Transplantation in Children and Adolescents," *Circulation* 76 (1987): V43–47; J. J. Malatack et al., "Choosing a Pediatric Recipient for Orthotopic Liver Transplantation," *Journal of Pediatrics* 111 (1987): 479–89; B. J. Zitelli et al., "Evaluation of the Pediatric Patient for Liver Transplantation," *Journal of Pediatrics* 78 (1986): 559–65.

48. J. Palfreman, "Prisoners of Silence," *Frontline*, PBS, October 19, 1993.

49. D. L. Wheeler et al., "An Experimental Assessment of Facilitated Communication," *Mental Retardation* 31 (1993): 49–59.

CHAPTER 7: THE GROUP

1. L. Spinney, "Karma of the Crowd," *National Geographic*, February 2014, http://ngm.nationalgeographic.com/2014/02/kumbh-mela/spinney-text.

2. G. Humphrey, "The Psychology of the Gestalt," *Journal of Educational Psychology* 15 (1924): 401–12.

3. R. Wageman, "Interdependence and Group Effectiveness," *Administrative Science Quarterly* 40 (1995): 145–80.

4. A. J. Morton and L. Avanzo, "Executive Decision-Making in the Domestic Sheep," *PLOS ONE* 6 (2011): e15752.

5. A. Waytz and L. Young, "The Group-Member Mind Tradeoff: Attributing Mind to Groups Versus Group Members," *Psychological Science* 23 (2012): 77–85.

6. C. K. Morewedge et al., "Lost in the Crowd: Entitative Group Membership Reduces Mind Attribution," *Consciousness and Cognition* 22 (2013): 1195–205.

7. Waytz and Young, "The Group-Member Mind Tradeoff."

8. J. Knobe and J. Prinz, "Intuitions About Consciousness: Experimental Studies," *Phenomenology and the Cognitive Sciences* 7 (2008): 67–83.

9. S. Neville, "Baby Jessica Turns 25 and Unlocks the $800,000 Trust Fund Well-Wishers Donated After Her Horrific Ordeal Stuck in a Well," *Daily Mail*, March 26, 2011, www.dailymail.co.uk/news/article-1370116/Baby -Jessica-turns-25-unlocks-800-000-trust-fund-wishers-donated -horrific-ordeal-stuck-well.html.

10. World Hunger Education Service, "2015 World Hunger and Poverty Facts and Statistics," WorldHunger.org, updated March 24, 2015, www .worldhunger.org/articles/Learn/world%20hunger%20facts%202002 .htm.

11. D. A. Small and G. Loewenstein, "Helping a Victim or Helping the Victim: Altruism and Identifiability," *Journal of Risk and Uncertainty* 26 (2003): 5–16.

12. T. S. Rai, "Corporations Are Cyborgs: Organizations That Can Think But Cannot Feel Elicit Anger as Villains But Fail to Elicit Sympathy as Victims," *Organizational Behavior and Human Decision Processes* 126 (January 2015): 18–26.

13. P. Rucker, "Mitt Romney Says 'Corporations Are People,'" *Washington Post*, August 11, 2011, www.washingtonpost.com/politics/mitt-romney -says-corporations-are-people/2011/08/11/gIQABwZ38I_story.html.

14. *Citizens United v. Federal Election Commission*, 130 S. Ct. 876, 2010, www.supremecourt.gov/opinions/09pdf/08-205.pdf.

15. "Attack in B Minor for Strings," *The Colbert Report*, Comedy Central, January 16, 2012.

16. C. Smythe, "HSBC Judge Approves $1.9B Drug-Money Laundering Accord," *Bloomberg*, July 3, 2013, www.bloomberg.com/news/2013-07-02/ hsbc-judge-approves-1-9b-drug-money-laundering-accord.html.

17. "Questions About the 9/11 Attacks? 9/11 Truth Movement?," *911Truth .org*, www.911truth.org/.

18. K. Adachi, "Vaccine Dangers," *Educate-Yourself*, http://educate-yourself .org/vcd/.

19. J. Knobe, "Intentional Action and Side Effects in Ordinary Language," *Analysis* 63 (2003): 190–93.

20. "Deputies: At Least 5 Teens Beat Homeless Man," News 4 JAX, October 14, 2011, www.news4jax.com/news/Deputies-At-Least-5-Teens-Beat -Homeless-Man/1915874.

21. S. S. Wiltermuth and C. Heath, "Synchrony and Cooperation," *Psychological Science* 20 (2009): 1–5.

22. S. Wiltermuth, "Synchrony and Destructive Obedience," *Social Influence* 7 (2012): 78–89.

23. M. Lea, R. Spears, and D. de Groot, "Knowing Me, Knowing You: Anonymity Effects on Social Identity Processes Within Groups," *Personality and Social Psychology Bulletin* 27 (2001): 526–37.

24. P. A. Ellison et al., "Anonymity and Aggressive Driving Behavior: A Field Study," *Journal of Social Behavior & Personality* 10 (1995): 265–72.

25. G. Charness and U. Gneezy, "What's in a Name? Anonymity and Social Distance in Dictator and Ultimatum Games," *Journal of Economic Behavior & Organization* 68 (2008): 29–35.

26. E. Donnerstein et al., "Variables in Interracial Aggression: Anonymity, Expected Retaliation, and a Riot," *Journal of Personality and Social Psychology* 22 (1972): 236–45.

27. A. Silke, "Deindividuation, Anonymity, and Violence: Findings from Northern Ireland," *Journal of Social Psychology* 143 (2003): 493–99.

28. Kaipotainment, "X-Men Origins: Wolverine Cat," YouTube, February 14, 2014, www.youtube.com/watch?v=3d4XMUYj-9k#aid=P-t9eoF1XJ8.

29. "Rafael Morelos, Gay Washington Teen, Commits Suicide After Reportedly Enduring Anti-Gay Bullying, Cyberbullying," *Huffington Post*, February 6, 2012, www.huffingtonpost.com/2012/02/06/rafael-morelos-gay -washington-suicide_n_1258471.html.

30. A. D. Santana, "Virtuous or Vitriolic: The Effect of Anonymity on Civility in Online Newspaper Reader Comment Boards," *Journalism Practice* 8 (2014): 18–33.

31. P. McGuire, "A Jailbait Loving Perv Destroyed Amanda Todd's Life," *Vice*, October 15, 2012, www.vice.com/read/a-jailbait-loving-perv-destroyed-amanda-todds-life; C. Sieczkowski, "Amanda Todd's Alleged Bully Named by Anonymous After Teen's Tragic Suicide," *Huffington Post* October 16, 2012, www.huffingtonpost.com/2012/10/16/amanda-todd-bully-anonymous-suicide_n_1969792.html.

32. D. Stanglin, "Student Wrongly Tied to Boston Bombings Found Dead," *USA Today*, April 25, 2013, www.usatoday.com/story/news/2013/04/25/boston-bombing-social-media-student-brown-university-reddit/2112309/.

33. M. Gladwell, *The Tipping Point: How Little Things Can Make a Big Difference* (New York: Hachette Digital, 2000).

34. J. L. Freedman and S. C. Fraser, "Compliance Without Pressure: The Foot-in-the-Door Technique," *Journal of Personality and Social Psychology* 4 (1966): 195–202.

35. G. Stanton, "Why Save Darfur Hasn't Saved Darfur: United to End Genocide is Making All the Same Mistakes," *Genocide Watch*, March 11, 2012, www.genocidewatch.org/images/Sudan_12_03_11_Why_Save_Darfur_Didn_t_Save_Darfur.doc.

36. K. Lewis, K. Gray, and J. Meierhenrich, "The Structure of Online Activism," *Sociological Science*, February 2014.

37. "Nonprofits Outspent For-Profits on Prospecting," *NonProfit Times*, June 26, 2012, www.thenonprofittimes.com/news-articles/nonprofits-outspent-for-profits-on-prospecting/.

38. K. Kristofferson, K. White, and J. Peloza, "The Nature of Slacktivism: How the Social Observability of an Initial Act of Token Support Affects Subsequent Prosocial Action," *Journal of Consumer Research* 40 (2014): 1149–66.

39. M. Ringelmann, "Recherches sur les moteurs animes travail de l'homme," *Annales de l'Institut national agronomique* 12 (1913): 1–40.

40. B. Latane, K. Williams, and S. Harkins, "Many Hands Make Light the Work: The Causes and Consequences of Social Loafing," *Journal of Personality and Social Psychology* 37 (1979): 822.

41. C. Bergin, "Remembering the Mistakes of Challenger," *NASA Spaceflight*, January 28, 2007, www.nasaspaceflight.com/2007/01/remembering-the-mistakes-of-challenger/; Rogers Commission, *Report of the Presidential Commission on the Space Shuttle Challenger Accident*, June 6, 1986, http://history.nasa.gov/rogersrep/v1ch6.htm.

42. J. Seabrook, "Crush Point," *New Yorker*, February 7, 2011, www.newyorker.com/reporting/2011/02/07/110207fa_fact_seabrook.

43. L. Null and J. Lobur, *The Essentials of Computer Organization and Architecture* (Burlington, MA: Jones & Bartlett Learning, 2010), http://electro.fisica.unlp.edu.ar/arq/downloads/Bibliografia/Linda%20Null%20-%20Essentials%20of%20Computer%20Organization%20and%20Architecture%202003.pdf.

44. I. Scharf, T. Pamminger, and S. Foitzik, "Differential Response of Ant Colonies to Intruders: Attack Strategies Correlate with Potential Threat," *Ethology* 117 (2011): 731–39.

45. J. L. Deneubourg et al., "The Self-Organizing Exploratory Pattern of the Argentine Ant," *Journal of Insect Behavior* 3 (1990): 159–68.

46. W. M. Wheeler, "The Ant-Colony as an Organism," *Journal of Morphology* 22 (1911): 307–25.

47. N. R. Franks et al., "Reconnaissance and Latent Learning in Ants," *Proceedings of the Royal Society B: Biological Sciences* 274 (2007): 1505–9.

48. Wheeler, "Ant-Colony as an Organism."

49. F. Galton, "Vox Populi," *Nature* 75 (1907): 450–51.

50. M. Horowitz, "Good Judgment in Forecasting International Affairs (and an Invitation for Season 3)," *Washington Post*, November 26, 2013, www.washingtonpost.com/blogs/monkey-cage/wp/2013/11/26/good

-judgment-in-forecasting-international-affairs-and-an-invitation
-for-season-3/.

51. P. E. Tetlock, B. A. Mellers, and D. Moore, "The Good Judgment Project,"
www.goodjudgmentproject.com/index.html; A. Spiegel, "So You Think
You're Smarter Than a CIA Agent," *Morning Edition*, NPR, April 2, 2014,
www.npr.org/blogs/parallels/2014/04/02/297839429/-so-you-think
-youre-smarter-than-a-cia-agent.

CHAPTER 8: THE DEAD

1. Social Security Administration, "Top Names Over the Last 100 Years,"
2014, www.ssa.gov/oact/babynames/decades/century.html.

2. D. L. Hoyert et al., "Deaths: Preliminary Data for 2011," *National Vital
Statistics Reports* 61 (2012): 1–51.

3. J. M. Bering, "The Folk Psychology of Souls," *Behavioral and Brain Sci-
ences* 29 (2006): 453–62; J. Bering, *The Belief Instinct: The Psychology of
Souls, Destiny, and the Meaning of Life* (New York: W. W. Norton, 2012);
J. M. Bering and D. F. Bjorklund, "The Natural Emergence of Reasoning
About the Afterlife as a Developmental Regularity," *Developmental Psy-
chology* 40 (2004): 217–33.

4. P. Bloom, *Descartes' Baby: How the Science of Child Development Explains
What Makes Us Human* (New York: Basic Books, 2004).

5. V. A. Kuhlmeier, P. Bloom, and K. Wynn, "Do 5-Month-Old Infants See
Humans as Material Objects?," *Cognition* 94 (2004): 95–103.

6. J. Pike, "STAR GATE [Controlled Remote Viewing]," FAS.org, 2005,
www.fas.org/irp/program/collect/stargate.htm.

7. J. McMoneagle, *Memoirs of a Psychic Spy: The Remarkable Life of U.S.
Government Remote Viewer 001* (Newburyport, MA: Hampton Roads,
2006).

8. "TBS's 1989 '$1,000 Challenge' Test of Local 'Psychic' Joan Morin,"
Tampa Bay Skeptics Report, Fall 1989, www.tampabayskeptics.org/
Morin.html.

9. J. M. Bering, C. H. Blasi, and D. F. Bjorklund, "The Development of After-life Beliefs in Religiously and Secularly Schooled Children," *British Journal of Developmental Psychology* 23 (2005): 587–607.

10. Bering and Bjorklund, "Natural Emergence of Reasoning About the Afterlife."

11. K. Gray, T. A. Knickman, and D. M. Wegner, "More Dead Than Dead: Perceptions of Persons in the Persistent Vegetative State," *Cognition* 121 (2011): 275–80.

12. B. Brier, *Valley of the Kings*, in *The New Book of Knowledge* (New York: Scholastic, 2005), http://scholastic.com/browse/article.jsp?id=3753817.

13. D. Harrison and K. Svensson, *Vikingaliv* (Stockholm: Natur och Kultur, 2007).

14. G. McEntyre, "Man Buried Upright on Harley-Davidson," KSDK.com, January 31, 2014, http://ksdk.com/story/news/local/2014/01/31/bill-standley-buried-on-harley-davidson/5095369/.

15. S. Nichols, "Imagination and Immortality: Thinking of Me," *Synthese* 159 (2007): 215–33.

16. B. B. Hagerty, "Decoding the Mystery of Near-Death Experiences," *All Things Considered*, NPR, May 22, 2009, www.npr.org/templates/story/story.php?storyId=104397005; K. Broome, "The Day I Died," BBC documentary, 2002.

17. T. Burpo, *Heaven Is for Real* (Nashville, TN: Thomas Nelson, 2010); "Heaven Is for Real," *Fox & Friends*, November 15, 2010, http://video.foxnews.com/v/4419243/heaven-is-for-real/#sp=show-clips.

18. D. Mobbs and C. Watt, "There Is Nothing Paranormal About Near-Death Experiences: How Neuroscience Can Explain Seeing Bright Lights, Meeting the Dead, or Being Convinced You Are One of Them," *Trends in Cognitive Sciences* 15 (2011): 447–49.

19. N. A. Tassell-Matamua, "Near-Death Experiences and the Psychology of Death," *OMEGA: Journal of Death and Dying* 68 (2013): 259–77.

20. D. MacDougall, "21 Grams: Hypothesis Concerning Soul Substance Together with Experimental Evidence of the Existence of Such

Substance," *Journal of the American Society for Psychical Research* 1 (1907): 237–62.

21. E. Becker, *The Denial of Death* (New York: Free Press, 1997).

22. "Salmon: Running the Gauntlet," *Nature*, PBS, May 1, 2011, www.pbs .org/wnet/nature/lessons/the-lifecycle-of-salmon/enhanced-video -resource/7395/.

23. K. D. Roeder, "An Experimental Analysis of the Sexual Behavior of the Praying Mantis (*Mantis religiosa L.*)," *Biological Bulletin* 69 (1935): 203–20.

24. S. Freud, "Our Attitude Towards Death," in *Reflections on War and Death*, trans. A. A. Brill and A. B. Kuttner (New York: Moffat, Yard & Co., 1918), www.bartleby.com/282/2.html.

25. J. Greenberg et al., "Evidence for Terror Management Theory II: The Effects of Mortality Salience on Reactions to Those Who Threaten or Bolster the Cultural Worldview," *Journal of Personality and Social Psychology* 58 (1990): 308–18.

26. E. A. W. Budge, *The History of Alexander the Great, Being the Syriac Version, Edited from Five Manuscripts of the Pseudo-Callistehenes with an English Translation* (Cambridge: Cambridge University Press, 1889).

27. J. L. Barger et al., "A Low Dose of Dietary Resveratrol Partially Mimics Caloric Restriction and Retards Aging Parameters in Mice," *PLOS ONE* 3 (2008): e2264.

28. J. Liu and A. Mori, "Stress, Aging, and Brain Oxidative Damage," *Neurochemical Research* 24 (1999): 1479–97.

29. C.-K. Lee et al., "Gene Expression Profile of Aging and Its Retardation by Caloric Restriction," *Science* 285 (1999): 1390–93.

30. B. W. Penninx et al., "Effects of Social Support and Personal Coping Resources on Mortality in Older Age: The Longitudinal Aging Study Amsterdam," *American Journal of Epidemiology* 146, no. 6 (1997): 510–19.

31. D. Buettner, "The Island Where People Forget to Die," *New York Times*, October 24, 2012, MM36.

32. N. A. Heflick and J. L. Goldenberg, "No Atheists in Foxholes: Arguments for (But Not Against) Afterlife Belief Buffers Mortality Salience Effects for Atheists: Atheism and Mortality Salience," *British Journal of Social Psychology* 51 (2012): 385–92.

33. J. Cohen, et al., "Influence of Physicians' Life Stances on Attitudes to End-of-Life Decisions and Actual End-of-Life Decision-Making in Six Countries," *Journal of Medical Ethics* 34 (2008): 247–53.

34. S. Sharp, D. Carr, and C. Macdonald, "Religion and End-of-Life Treatment Preferences: Assessing the Effects of Religious Denomination and Beliefs," *Social Forces* 91 (2012): 275–98.

35. A. Norenzayan and I. G. Hansen, "Belief in Supernatural Agents in the Face of Death," *Personality and Social Psychology Bulletin* 32 (2006): 174–87.

36. T. Pyszczynski et al., "Whistling in the Dark: Exaggerated Consensus Estimates in Response to Incidental Reminders of Mortality," *Psychological Science* 7 (1996): 332–36.

37. "Clip: Flag Desecration Amendment Debate," C-SPAN, June 28, 1995, www.c-span.org/video/?c3879314/clip-flag-desecration-amendment-debate.

38. J. Greenberg et al., "Sympathy for the Devil: Evidence that Reminding Whites of Their Mortality Promotes More Favorable Reactions to White Racists," *Motivation and Emotion* 25 (2001): 113–33.

39. J. Arndt et al., "To Belong or Not to Belong, That is the Question: Terror Management and Identification with Gender and Ethnicity," *Journal of Personality and Social Psychology* 83 (2002): 26–43.

40. A. Rosenblatt et al., "Evidence for Terror Management Theory: I. The Effects of Mortality Salience on Reactions to Those who Violate or Uphold Cultural Values," *Journal of Personality and Social Psychology* 57 (1989): 681–90.

41. J. T. Jost et al., "Political Conservatism as Motivated Social Cognition," *Psychological Bulletin* 129 (2003): 339–75.

42. K. R. Truett, "Age Differences in Conservatism," *Personality and Individual Differences* 14 (1993): 405–11.

43. D. Eylon and S. T. Allison, "The 'Frozen in Time' Effect in Evaluations of the Dead," *Personality and Social Psychology Bulletin* 31 (2005): 1708–17.

44. S. T. Allison et al., "The Demise of Leadership: Positivity and Negativity Biases in Evaluations of Dead Leaders," *Leadership Quarterly* 20 (2009): 115–29.

CHAPTER 9: GOD

1. B. Pascal, "Of the Means of Belief," in *Pensées* (1669; Harvard Classics, 1909–14), www.bartleby.com/48/1/4.html.

2. J. Rée, "*In Our Time*'s Greatest Philosopher Vote," *BBC Radio*, www.bbc .co.uk/radio4/history/inourtime/greatest_philosopher_soren_kierkeg aard.shtml.

3. Pascal, "Of the Means of Belief."

4. H. M. Gray, K. Gray, and D. M. Wegner, "Dimensions of Mind Perception," *Science* 315 (2007): 619.

5. J. L. Barrett and A. H. Johnson, "The Role of Control in Attributing Intentional Agency to Inanimate Objects," *Journal of Cognition and Culture* 3 (2003): 208–17; J. L. Barrett, "Exploring the Natural Foundations of Religion," *Trends in Cognitive Sciences* 4 (2000): 29–34; K. Barnes and N. J. S. Gibson, "Supernatural Agency: Individual Difference Predictors and Situational Correlates," *International Journal for the Psychology of Religion* 23 (2012): 42–62.

6. L. Hearn, "Jikininki," in *Kwaidan: Ghost Stories and Strange Tales of Old Japan* (Dover Publications, 1932), 176, available at www.sacred-texts .com/shi/kwaidan/kwai08.htm.

7. "Keres," *Theoi Greek Mythology*, www.theoi.com/Daimon/Keres.html.

8. S. E. Guthrie, *Faces in the Clouds: A New Theory of Religion* (Oxford: Oxford University Press, 1995).

9. S. Nasar, "The Lost Years of a Nobel Laureate," *New York Times*, November 13, 1994, available at www.nytimes.com/1994/11/13/business/the-lost-years-of-a-nobel-laureate.html?pagewanted=print&src=pm.

10. W. Smith, "Haruspices," in *A Dictionary of Greek and Roman Antiquities* (London: John Murray, 1875), available at http://penelope.uchicago.edu/Thayer/E/Roman/Texts/secondary/SMIGRA*/Haruspices.html.

11. L. G. Healy, "Jesus Cheese Toast," *GoUpstate.com*, April 22, 2009, www.goupstate.com/article/20090422/ARTICLES/904221068.

12. KENS 5 staff, "'Blessing from God': Texas Man Finds Jesus on Breakfast Taco," *KENS5 Eyewitness News San Antonio*, August 8, 2012, www.kens5.com/news/Beeville-man-finds-Jesus-in-breakfast-taco-165198506.html.

13. A. Knutson, "22 People Who Found Jesus in Their Food," *BuzzFeed Life*, March 29, 2013, www.buzzfeed.com/arielknutson/people-who-found-jesus-in-their-food.

14. R. Boyd and P. J. Richerson, "Culture and the Evolution of Human Cooperation," *Philosophical Transactions of the Royal Society B: Biological Sciences* 364 (2009): 3281–88.

15. D. Abel, "In Canada, Cod Remain Scarce Despite Ban," *Boston Globe*, March 4, 2012, available at www.boston.com/news/local/massachusetts/articles/2012/03/04/in_canada_cod_remain_scarce_despite_ban/; A. M. Spooner, *Environmental Science for Dummies* (Hoboken, NJ: For Dummies, 2012); M. Bergman, *Tax Evasion and the Rule of Law in Latin America: The Political Culture of Cheating and Compliance in Argentina and Chile* (University Park, PA.: Penn State University Press, 2011).

16. K. D. Williams, *Ostracism: The Power of Silence* (New York: Guilford Press, 2002).

17. R. Dunbar, *Grooming, Gossip, and the Evolution of Language* (Cambridge, MA: Harvard University Press, 1998).

18. A. F. Shariff and A. Norenzayan, "God Is Watching You: Priming God Concepts Increases Prosocial Behavior in an Anonymous Economic Game," *Psychological Science* 18 (2007): 803–9.

19. A. F. Shariff, A. Norenzayan, and J. Henrich, "The Birth of High Gods: How the Cultural Evolution of Supernatural Policing Influenced the Emergence of Complex, Cooperative Human Societies, Paving the Way for Civilization," in *Evolution, Culture, and the Human Mind*, ed. M. Schaller et al. (New York: Psychology Press, 2009), 119–36, www.psy press.com/evolution-culture-and-the-human-mind-9780805859119.

20. Ibid.

21. W. M. Gervais and A. Norenzayan, "Like a Camera in the Sky? Thinking About God Increases Public Self-Awareness and Socially Desirable Responding," *Journal of Experimental Social Psychology* 48 (2012): 298–302.

22. N. Forsyth, *The Old Enemy* (Princeton, NJ: Princeton University Press, 1989).

23. A. F. Shariff and M. Rhemtulla, "Divergent Effects of Beliefs in Heaven and Hell on National Crime Rates," *PLOS ONE* 7 (2012): e39048.

24. L. Saad, "In U.S., 22% Are Hesitant to Support a Mormon in 2012," *Gal lup.com*, June 20, 2011, www.gallup.com/poll/148100/Hesitant-Support -Mormon-2012.aspx.

25. W. M. Gervais, A. F. Shariff, and A. Norenzayan, "Do You Believe in Atheists? Distrust Is Central to Anti-Atheist Prejudice," *Journal of Personality and Social Psychology* 101 (2011): 1189–206; P. Edgell, J. Gerteis, and D. Hartmann, "Atheists as 'Other': Moral Boundaries and Cultural Membership in American Society," *American Sociological Review* 71 (2006): 211–34.

26. Gervais, Shariff, and Norenzayan, "Do You Believe in Atheists?"

27. "Atheism and Morality," *Conservapedia*, www.conservapedia.com/Athe ism_and_morality.

28. J. L. Preston and R. S. Ritter, "Different Effects of Religion and God on Prosociality with the Ingroup and Outgroup," *Personality and Social Psychology Bulletin* 39 (2013): 1471–83.

29. Z. K. Rothschild, A. Abdollahi, and T. Pyszczynski, "Does Peace Have a Prayer? The Effect of Mortality Salience, Compassionate Values, and Religious Fundamentalism on Hostility Toward Out-Groups," *Journal of Experimental Social Psychology* 45 (2009): 816–27.

30. L. B. Whitbeck and V. Gecas, "Value Attributions and Value Transmission Between Parents and Children," *Journal of Marriage and Family* 50 (1988): 829–40.

31. H. Yin Wong and B. Merrilees, "The Performance Benefits of Being Brand-Orientated," *Journal of Product & Brand Management* 17 (2008): 372–83.

32. P. F. Stack, "Mormonism Leading Way in U.S. Religious Growth," *Salt Lake Trubune,* May 2, 2012, http://sltrib.com/sltrib/news/54026798-78/lds-religious-church-largest.html.csp.

33. Ibid.

34. R. W. Walker, R. E. Turley, and G. M. Leonard, *Massacre at Mountain Meadows* (New York: Oxford University Press, 2011).

35. N. F. Cott, "Young Women in the Second Great Awakening in New England," *Feminist Studies* 3 (1975): 15–29.

36. T. Smith, *General Social Survey,* 2012, www.marketplace.org/topics/wealth-poverty/income-upshot/behind-data-belief-god-and-income.

37. K. Laurin, A. Kay, and D. A. Moscovitch, "On the Belief in God: Towards an Understanding of the Emotional Substrates of Compensatory Control," *Journal of Experimental Social Psychology* 44 (2008): 1559–62.

38. J. M. Bering and B. D. Parker, "Children's Attributions of Intentions to an Invisible Agent," *Developmental Psychology* 42 (2006): 253–62.

39. D. Kelemen, "Why Are Rocks Pointy? Children's Preference for Teleological Explanations of the Natural World," *Developmental Psychology* 35 (1999): 1440–52.

40. F. Newport, "In U.S., 46% Hold Creationist View of Human Origin," *Gallup Politics,* June 1, 2012, www.gallup.com/poll/155003/Hold-Creationist-View-Human-Origins.aspx.

41. Hastings, H. L., *Was Moses mistaken: Or, creation and evolution.* (Boston, MA: Scriptural Tract Repository, 1893).

42. B. Murphy, "Tsunami Survivors Cling Tightly to Faith Across Ravaged Region," *Baylor Media Communications*, 2005, www.baylor.edu/media communications/index.php?id=25982.

43. D. Montanaro, "Robertson on Haiti: 'Pact to the Devil,'" *NBC News*, January 13, 2010, http://firstread.nbcnews.com/_news/2010/01/13/4436174 -robertson-on-haiti-pact-to-the-devil?lite.

44. Murphy, "Tsunami Survivors Cling Tightly to Faith Across Ravaged Region."

45. P. Rozin and E. B. Royzman, "Negativity Bias, Negativity Dominance, and Contagion," *Personality and Social Psychology Review* 5 (2011): 296–320; J. Kiley Hamlin, K. Wynn, and P. Bloom, "Three-Month-Olds Show a Negativity Bias in Their Social Evaluations: Social Evaluation by 3-Month-Old Infants," *Developmental Science* 13 (2010): 923–29; J. J. Skowronski and D. E. Carlston, "Negativity and Extremity Biases in Impression Formation: A Review of Explanations," *Psychological Bulletin* 105 (1989): 131–42; A. Vaish, T. Grossmann, and A. Woodward, "Not All Emotions Are Created Equal: The Negativity Bias in Social-Emotional Development," *Psychological Bulletin* 134 (2008): 383–403; C. K. Morewedge, "Negativity Bias in Attribution of External Agency," *Journal of Experimental Psychology: General* 138 (2009): 535–45.

46. A. C. Kay et al., "God and the Government: Testing a Compensatory Control Mechanism for the Support of External Systems," *Journal of Personality and Social Psychology* 95 (2008): 18–35.

47. S. Harrison, "Proverbs 3.5–6, Sort Of," *Google Prayers*, www.thechur chofgoogle.org/Scripture/google_prayers.html.

48. J. L. Barrett and F. C. Keil, "Conceptualizing a Nonnatural Entity: Anthropomorphism in God Concepts," *Cognitive Psychology* 31 (1996): 219–47.

49. Westboro Baptist Church, "God Hates Fags," 2014, www.godhates fags.com/.

50. Javon, "If You're a Gay Christian, Does God Still Love You?" *GayChristian101*, www.gaychristian101.com/if-youre-a-gay-christian-does-god-still-love-you.html.

51. L. Ross, D. Greene, and P. House, "The 'False Consensus Effect': An Egocentric Bias in Social Perception and Attribution Processes," *Journal of Experimental Social Psychology* 13 (1977): 279–301.

52. N. Epley et al., "Believers' Estimates of God's Beliefs Are More Egocentric Than Estimates of Other People's Beliefs," *PNAS* 106 (2009): 21533–38.

53. J. Weiss, "Fathering and Fatherhood," *Encyclopedia of Children and Childhood in History and Society*, 2008, www.faqs.org/childhood/Fa-Gr/Fathering-and-Fatherhood.html.

54. G. Owens et al., "The Prototype Hypothesis and the Origins of Attachment Working Models: Adult Relationships with Parents and Romantic Partners," *Monographs of the Society for Research in Child Development* 60 (1995): 216–33.

55. A. McDonald et al., "Attachment to God and Parents: Testing the Correspondence vs. Compensation Hypotheses," *Journal of Psychology & Christianity* 24 (2005): 21–28; L. A. Kirkpatrick, "God as a Substitute Attachment Figure: A Longitudinal Study of Adult Attachment Style and Religious Change in College Students," *Personality and Social Psychology Bulletin* 24 (1998): 961–73.

56. A. McDonald et al., "Attachment to God and Parents."

57. D. Baillie, "Is There a Creator?" in *Through the Wormhole, with Morgan Freeman*, producer Geoffrey Sharp, Science (2010).

58. N. Gross and S. Simmons, "The Religiosity of American College and University Professors," *Sociology of Religion* 70 (2009): 101–29.

59. S. J. Gould, "Nonoverlapping Magisteria," *Natural History* 106, (1997): 16–22.

CHAPTER 10: THE SELF

1. L. Lyon, "7 Criminal Cases That Invoked the 'Sleepwalking Defense,'" *U.S. News & World Report*, May 8, 2009, http://health.usnews.com/health-news/family-health/sleep/articles/2009/05/08/7-criminal-cases -that-invoked-the-sleepwalking-defense; J. E. Brody, "When Can Killers Claim Sleepwalking as a Legal Defense?" *New York Times*, January 16, 1996, C1.

2. R. Descartes, A *Discourse on Method. Meditations on First Philosophy. Principles of Philosophy* (London: Dent, 1981).

3. Ibid., 27.

4. R. K. Barnhart, *Barnhart Concise Dictionary of Etymology* (New York: HarperCollins, 1995).

5. N. Epley and E. Whitchurch, "Mirror, Mirror on the Wall: Enhancement in Self-Recognition," *Personality and Social Psychology Bulletin* 34 (2008): 1159–70.

6. O. Svenson, "Are We All Less Risky and More Skillful Than Our Fellow Drivers?" *Acta Psychologica (Amsterdam)* 47 (1981): 143–48.

7. J. Kruger and D. Dunning, "Unskilled and Unaware of It: How Difficulties in Recognizing One's Own Incompetence Lead to Inflated Self-Assessments," *Journal of Personality and Social Psychology* 77 (1999): 1121–34.

8. J. Krueger, "Enhancement Bias in Descriptions of Self and Others," *Personality and Social Psychology Bulletin* 24 (1998): 505–16; M. D. Alicke and O. Govorun, "The Better-Than-Average Effect," in *The Self in Social Judgment*, eds. M. D. Alicke, D. A. Dunning, and J. Krueger (New York: Psychology Press, 2005), 304.

9. O. P. John and R. W. Robins, "Accuracy and Bias in Self-Perception: Individual Differences in Self-Enhancement and the Role of Narcissism," *Journal of Personality and Social Psychology* 66 (1994): 206.

10. W. James, *The Principles of Psychology* (Cambridge, MA: Harvard University Press, 1890).

11. T. Wilson and R. E. Nisbett, "The Accuracy of Verbal Reports About the Effects of Stimuli on Evaluations and Behavior," *Social Psychology* 41 (1978): 118.

12. A. Bryan, G. Webster, and A. Mahaffey, "The Big, the Rich, and the Powerful: Physical, Financial, and Social Dimensions of Dominance in Mating and Attraction," *Personality and Social Psychology Bulletin* 37 (2011): 365–82.

13. P. Johansson, "Failure to Detect Mismatches Between Intention and Outcome in a Simple Decision Task," *Science* 310 (2005): 116–19.

14. M. S. Gazzaniga, *The Mind's Past* (Berkeley, CA: University of California Press, 1998).

15. R. S. Nickerson, "Confirmation Bias: A Ubiquitous Phenomenon in Many Guises," *Review of General Psychology* 2 (1998): 175–220.

16. E. Jonas et al., "Confirmation Bias in Sequential Information Search After Preliminary Decisions: An Expansion of Dissonance Theoretical Research on Selective Exposure to Information," *Journal of Personality and Social Psychology* 80 (2001): 557–71; M. Jones and R. Sugden, "Positive Confirmation Bias in the Acquisition of Information," *Theory and Decision* 50 (2001): 59–99; J. Klayman, "Varieties of Confirmation Bias," *Psychology of Learning and Motivation* 32 (1995): 385–418.

17. K. Chow, "Dueling Stereotypes: Bad Asian Drivers, Good at Everything," *Code Switch*, July 11, 2013, http://npr.org/blogs/codeswitch/2013/07/09/200500744/dueling-stereotypes-bad-asian-drivers-good-at-everything-asiana.

18. V. Jones, "Are Blacks a Criminal Race? Surprising Statistics," *Huffington Post*, October 5, 2005, http://huffingtonpost.com/van-jones/are-blacks-a-criminal-rac_b_8398.html.

19. "The Myth of the Almighty Gun," Final Call News, April 23, 2013, http://finalcall.com/artman/publish/Perspectives_1/article_9781.shtml.

20. S. Milgram, "Behavioral Study of Obedience," *Journal of Abnormal and Social Psychology* 67 (1963): 317–78.

21. B. Libet, "Unconscious Cerebral Initiative and the Role of Conscious Will in Voluntary Action," in *Behavioral and Brain Sciences*, vol. 8 (New York: Springer, 1985), 529–66.

22. K. Ammon and S. C. Gandevia, "Transcranial Magnetic Stimulation Can Influence the Selection of Motor Programmes," *Journal of Neurology, Neurosurgery & Psychiatry* 53 (1990): 705–7.

23. E. Filevich, S. Kühn, and P. Haggard, "There Is No Free Won't: Antecedent Brain Activity Predicts Decisions to Inhibit," *PLOS ONE* 8 (2013): e53053.

24. D. C. Dennett, *Elbow Room: The Varieties of Free Will Worth Wanting* (Cambridge, MA: MIT Press, 1984).

25. J. D. Greene and J. Cohen, "For the Law, Neuroscience Changes Nothing and Everything," *Philosophical Transactions of the Royal Society B: Biological Sciences* 359 (2004): 1775–85.

26. J. Andenaes, *Punishment and Deterrence* (Ann Arbor, MI: University of Michigan Press, 1974).

27. Sentencing Council, "Indeterminate Prison Sentences," http://sentenc ingcouncil.judiciary.gov.uk/sentencing/indeterminate-prison-sentences .htm.

28. K. D. Vohs and J. W. Schooler, "The Value of Believing in Free Will: Encouraging a Belief in Determinism Increases Cheating," *Psychological Science* 19 (2008): 49–54.

29. D. Kahneman and A. Tversky, *Intuitive Prediction: Biases and Corrective Procedures* (DTIC document, June 1977), available at http://oai.dtic.mil/ oai/oai?verb=getRecord&metadataPrefix=html&identifier=ADA047747.

30. S. King, "Quitters, Inc.," in *Night Shift* (Garden City, NY: Doubleday, 1978).

31. P. M. Gollwitzer and V. Brandstätter, "Implementation Intentions and Effective Goal Pursuit," *Journal of Personality and Social Psychology* 73 (1997): 186–99.

32. M. Hagger et al., "An Intervention to Reduce Alcohol Consumption in Undergraduate Students Using Implementation Intentions and Mental

Simulations: A Cross-National Study," *International Journal of Behavioral Medicine* 19 (2012): 82–96.

33. P. M. Gollwitzer and G. Oettingen, "The Emergence and Implementation of Health Goals," *Psychological Health* 13 (1998): 687–715.

34. P. Sheeran and S. Orbell, "Using Implementation Intentions to Increase Attendance for Cervical Cancer Screening," *Health Psychology* 19 (2000): 283–89.

35. F. Dostoyevsky, "An Essay Concerning the Bourgeois," in *Winter Notes on Summer Impressions*, trans. D. Patterson (Evanston, IL: Northwestern University Press, 1997), 49.

36. D. M. Wegner, "Ironic Processes of Mental Control," *Psychological Review* 101 (1994): 34–52.

37. D. M. Wegner, M. Ansfield, and D. Pilloff, "The Putt and the Pendulum: Ironic Effects of the Mental Control of Action," *Psychological Science* 9 (1998): 196–99.

38. D. M. Wegner, R. M. Wenzlaff, and M. Kozak, "Dream Rebound: The Return of Suppressed Thoughts in Dreams," *Psychological Science* 15 (2004): 232–36.

39. D. M. Wegner and D. B. Gold, "Fanning Old Flames: Emotional and Cognitive Effects of Suppressing Thoughts of a Past Relationship," *Journal of Personality and Social Psychology* 68 (1995): 782–92.

40. J. W. Schooler, E. D. Reichle, and D. V. Halpern, "Zoning Out While Reading: Evidence for Dissociations Between Experience and Metaconsciousness," in *Thinking and Seeing: Visual Metacognition in Adults and Children* (Cambridge, MA: MIT Press, 2004), 203–26.

41. M. Killingsworth, "Want to Be Happier? Stay in the Moment" (lecture, TEDxCambridge, Cambridge, MA, November 2011).

42. M. Csikszentmihalyi, *Flow: The Psychology of Optimal Experience* (New York: Harper & Row, 1990).

43. N. Strohminger and S. Nichols, "The Essential Moral Self," *Cognition* 131 (2014): 159–71.

44. L. MacFarquhar, "How to Be Good," *New Yorker*, September 5, 2011, 43–53.

45. D. Parfit, *Reasons and Persons* (Oxford: Oxford University Press, 1986).

46. D. Shenk, *The Forgetting: Alzheimer's: Portrait of an Epidemic* (New York: Doubleday, 2001).

47. D. Parfit, *Reasons and Persons*.

48. D. C. Dennett, "The Self as a Center of Narrative Gravity," in *Self and Consciousness: Multiple Perspectives*, ed. F. Kessel, P. Cole, and D. Johnson (Hillsdale, NJ: Erlbaum, 1992), available at http://cogprints.org/266/.

49. D. T. Suzuki, trans., *The Lankavatara Sutra: A Mahayana Text* (London: Routledge & K. Paul, 1973).

Index